1830's-1990's
American

Sterling Silver

Flatware

A Collector's Identification & Value Guide
by Maryanne Dolan

BOOKS AMERICANA
INC.

ISBN 0-89689-095-3

TABLE OF CONTENTS

Dedicated to MY THREE SONS,
STERLING CHARACTERS ALL.

Acknowledgements:

To those who contributed to the making of this book, my deepest gratitude:

Mr. Edmund P. Hogan, of International, the first gentleman of American Silver for his cooperation, hospitality and long memory;

Sinclair Weeks, Jr., of Reed and Barton, ever gracious and helpful;

Denham C. Lunt, Jr., who carries on the Lunt tradition with grace and insightful knowledge.

Marianne Hickman of Oneida Silversmiths for her patience and sense of company history;

Mrs. Denise Stroham of Manchester Silver whose assistance was invaluable and whose love of silver is inspiring;

Mrs. Virginia G. Pugh of Kirk Steiff for her thorough research and willingness to share material;

Nora Valery Simiola of Wallace Silversmiths for her kindness, empathy and very practical help;

John H. Wiseman of Walter Drake Silver Exchange for his generous offer of the use of company facilities which I was unable to accept but which I appreciate.

All photographs of International Silver Patterns by: Rich Croteau Associates of Waterbury, Connecticut

INTRODUCTION

Silver collecting has usually focused on spectacular holloware, coin silver, souvenir spoons and eye-catching serving pieces. It follows then that the real value lies in sterling flatware, a neglected area, still underappreciated and tremendously undervalued.

The new concept of amassing a series of place settings in different patterns for interest at the table has lent impetus to a new thrust in collecting silver which gives hope that the older patterns will be more diligently sought after and once again put to use to dazzle your dinner guests and build a whole new generation of those who appreciate the wonderful old silver. For value and conversation starters nothing beats the old patterns. Try a few place settings of RADIANT or PALM or ORLEANS and see what consternation you have wrought.

The earliest of the factory-made silver is relatively plain and so blends in with any table setting. The Victorian is ornate, often beautiful but almost always showy. The Art Deco, Art Nouveau and Arts and Crafts are all represented.

Regardless of style or time period American silver is well made, well designed and of good quality metal. It was so well attuned to the differing public taste at time of manufacture that most of it will accommodate to any fashion in vogue today. In fact much American silver rivals or surpasses any silver flatware made anywhere in the world. As this world of American sterling silver flatware becomes less truly American and the silver factories piloted by the old type American entrepreneurial silver men become a thing of our industrial past, it behooves us, the American collectors to preserve this silver not only for its utility but for its beauty and historic interest. Much of our silver is trickling out of the country; pattern by pattern it is going elsewhere. It is one of life's greatest ironies that brides are choosing stainless and silverplate over sterling flatware, on the secondary market one of the greatest values in history. Intrinsically the value will always maintain itself, and if given minimal care, 100 years from now it will be centuries old and still useful and attractive.

Sterling has character, it lends a feeling of solidity and elegance to any table and a sense of luxury to the owner. There is really nothing like it and never will be again.

A little time, not too much money and a desire to own some pure Americana, a great love of silver and you will have a stunning legacy to leave your grandchildren.

Prices are entirely variable in this field, depending not only upon region but on individual dealers; these variations are enormous. When prices stabilize and the hobby of collecting older silver flatware becomes more popular, silver pieces will become more costly and scarcity will become even more of a factor.

Think sterling silver flatware; it is still available, it is underpriced, it is valuable in itself, it is useful, it is often quite lovely, it can be bizarre which in itself fascinates, it is fun.

Every man (or woman) may not have been born with a silver spoon in his mouth as Cervantes noted, but given today's opportunities and prices it would be very easy to insure that all your descendants have access to one from your collection.

138 Belle Avenue
Pleasant Hill, CA 94523

iv

AMERICAN STERLING SILVER FLATWARE

The American silver story is not limited to that beautiful, valuable metal. It is also the story of people; apprentices, skilled craftsmen, peddlers turned entrepreneurs. Most of all it is the story of the long love affair Americans have had with this lustrous beauty - born in the roots of the old world, adapted to life in the new, and changing often to meet the needs and demands of the future. Silver is and always has been unique, a utilitarian status symbol and as life in America has altered and informality has become the watchword, sterling silver has maintained a life of its own; it holds a special place in the American psyche.

Gold and silver attraction seem burled in the human genes. While gold remains unobtainable to all but the few, silver has, in effect, become the chosen substitute. At birth babies are often gifted with silver cups or spoons, sterling follows us through life. On all great occasions silver gifts are considered desirable and eagerly welcomed. Aside from its intrinsic value which can fluctuate wildly, what makes silver so precious to us? It is beautiful, it is useful, true; what we cannot explain in any definitive way is the feeling the owning of sterling silver flatware engenders - it is all symbolism - silver makes a statement about you its owner, but it also embodies some of the American dream. Sterling silver represents the level above the mundane, it is a higher plateau.

To the intelligent collector it is the Holy Grail at the end of a treasure hunt. Soon, sooner than we Americans like to think, our old silver will be scarce and very expensive. The old patterns speak of a way of life we think of as halcyon but may very well have been the bad good old days. Those days were indeed different - they were fascinating. The silver almost talks to us of the 18th and 19th century adaptations of the English, of the opulence of Victorian, of the elegance and softness of the Edwardian, the no nonsense Arts and Crafts, the angular Deco. Silver has seen us through depressions and wars, upheavals and periods of quiet. Silver has been there and much of it is still here to interpret those times for us. Our old silver is really a national resource, neglected, but alive and well. To follow the trail of American silver is to trod the paths of history. In the United States silver has had three identities.

Silverware has been made in America since its beginning and in its first phase all of it was "coin" which actually used coins then in circulation which were melted down and made into silver items. Some of this is marked by the maker and some is not. In the 19th century silver in this country had three personalities:

1. From about 1830 to 1850 silver in America was often marked C.D.: Coin, Dollar or Pure Coin. Any of these marks guaranteed that the piece of silver was the same quality as the silver coins produced by the United States Mint, i.e. 900 parts pure silver out of 1000 parts metal, it is generally referred to as "coin silver". It does not mean that coins were actually melted down to make it as had occurred earlier.

2. The word "sterling" which came into use about 1860 and more widely after the Civil War and is still the terminology used means that a piece of silver is 925 parts pure silver out of 1000 parts metal. This is mandated by the U.S. Government.

3. The third type became available during the 19th century and is called SILVERPLATE. This is simply a process of covering a base metal with coats of pure silver by means of electroplating. It was introduced into this country in a very big way by Rogers Bros. Silversmiths in 1847 and is an easily remembered date because of the popularity of Rogers Bros. 1847 patterns. Most silverplate was issued in 4 grades depending on the amount of silver added to the base metal.

These designations are important ones to the collector and to lovers of American silver generally. It is also important to know the historical background of our collectibles.

Visualize the typical customer of the 18th century American silversmith. His knee breeches, waistcoat and tricorn hat were specially tailored for him and he was no doubt a man of influence. His good wife wanted a new tea set perhaps, or a set of spoons; he would describe it and the shop owner, the smith, would draw a design or show the customer a similar piece. The customer would pay in silver coins which would be weighed and costs would be computed or sometimes there would be an exchange which would entail more coins, or old silver pieces to be turned in and weighed toward the cost of the new, more modern pieces. The shop itself would be fairly small and filled with the tools of the trade. The smith himself would own it and might have an apprentice or two.

This silversmith, also often called a goldsmith, was usually a man of substance and importance in the colonies. He was an urban man, independent and the equal of all in a land where no aristocracy was supposed to exist and each thought himself as good as the next. He was a man of integrity. He often took the place of a bank for in many places there were no banks until the late 18th century. He was independent and his silver showed his individuality. Even when he may have been transplanted from his native England or France he remembered the old designs, but he adapted them, modified them, simplified them, until early American silver could compete with and often surpassed English silver of the same period. He was a man of great skill and taste and the quality of his silver testifies to his craftsmanship and discernment. He was one of many - there were over 400 silversmiths in the colonies - but to a man, he was proud. Proud of his work and proud of this new land and more often than not took an active role in politics and the life of the community. He certainly had a sense of future but not even he could have envisioned life in the United States in the 1990s.

In 1981 at a local auction three pieces of silver, almost unrecognizable as such beneath the tarnish were sold for $20. Two were recent plate, the 3rd an authentic argyle, an American "cann" with its flat topped coin silver cover, c.1790.

Unmarked but thoroughly authenticated - how did such a piece appear here, who had owned it, who made it? It is incredible to think such a treasure fell so easily into the hands of a relatively casual buyer. It is a lesson in the rewards of some knowledge and persistence since the owner is an inverterate auction previewer, even if rarely a buyer. The typical flat top shows the tool markings of the original silversmith and the fit is so exact we know immediately he was a man of dexterity and skill and from its style probably a New Englander.

The collector should never stop searching, great antiques are where you find them. Silver is often one of the all time great 'sleepers'.

Silver was considered a kind of portable currency by these settlers from the old world. It endowed status, could easily be melted down (as has been done widely in our own time) or used as barter by those who had brought it with them both for security and aesthetics. In the light of the need to use silver for other than table purposes, the silversmith became a necessity in the colonies. They were the new entrepreneurs, they were pleased with themselves, anxious to advance the nation's cause, proud of their trade. Like all achievers, the silversmith has left his mark, he founded a dynasty of which, even those who came long after and made silver in a different way, carried on many of the same traditions and for many generations had basically the same attitudes.

The Rise of the Manufacturers

The day of exchanging coins for new shapes in silver passed and with it the personal touch. The small shop where the smith did everything passed too and with the rise of the Industrial revolution vast changes took place in the silver industry. It was many years, however, before flatware was made almost entirely by machine and for some time it was still formed and decorated partially by hand. But as surely as pewter gave way to brittania, and brittania gave way to silverplate, they all gave way to sterling.

The population of the United States was growing, the middle class was becoming more affluent and even though silverplate resembles sterling so closely this middle class wanted the real thing. Although the sterling mark has been required by the United States government only since 1907, there is evidence that a group of Irish silversmiths working in Baltimore in the late 18th century used the term. The Gorham Company was one of the first of the large firms to use the sterling mark consistently beginning in the early 1860s but one by one the other manufacturers followed and by the 1890s such marking was commonplace.

In the development of almost any product many minds and hands are involved but the final achievement is usually credited to one man (often the most important person) and in the case of machines for making silver undoubtedly tinkerers had been busy for years before the stamping machine for making spoons from a solid sheet was attributed to William Gale. This machine, while a major step forward, was still not a nearly perfect way to speed up the process and although it was promoted in the 1820s it was not until much later that really practical machines were introduced. As a contemporary 19th century writer has it "all this time the industry has been emerging from a condition represented by the word 'shop' to the height and amplitude indicated by the word 'manufactory' ''. While writers of the time exalted in the "uniformity of perfection" in these factories, the loss of the individual craftsman was not yet keenly felt."

It was the advent of an efficient steam engine (which took more than 10 years to perfect) stamping out spoons which paved the way for all other machines to come. These early models were accurately described as "ponderous". The machines which pounded out the salvers and other large objects were huge and the pounding arm itself could weigh one and one half tons. The various stages of making silver demanded separate rooms in the large factories. The chasers in their own domain working on silver filled with hardened pitch to facilitate its ornamentation; these were true artists and in the early days mostly of European background. The polishing rooms were literally awhirl, the process involved soft wheels which revolved with amazing speed. The polishing was done in a series of changing wheels each heightening the luster. Other rooms would hold the Modelers, the Moulders, the die-cutters, embossers, engravers, pattern makers, the burnishers. There was even a separate place where all the sweepings from the factory would be treated to recover the particles of silver. Making silver was a complicated, sensitive process which called for meticulous care.

As the lone artisan working in his little shop receded from the scene and machines did most of the work, silver found a greater audience. But is was largely due to the Centennial Exposition of 1876 in Philadelphia that the beginnings of a great awakening to our beautiful silver was stirring. About 1906 an exhibition was held in the Boston Museum of Fine Arts and to that exhibition we owe the foundations of many great collections, one started after Judge Clearwater saw the silver display in Philadelphia now reposes in the Metropolitan Museum of Art in New York. Judge Clearwater was collecting our already older silver dating from the late 1600s to 1830. 1830 is a highly significant date - it denotes the major thrust of the Industrial Revolution which forever diminished the role of the individual artisan. By 1830 the big factories were becoming the established way. Almost all writers of the time were over-awed - "It is a literal truth," they gloated, "that 4,000 men working in scattered shops by ancient methods could not accomplish as much as 400 men who work under one roof and one direction aided by modern machinery." The statement is worth keen analysis. The machines gave us magnificent silver, true, but men such as Samuel Kirk and Horace Wilcox would probably not have fit in. The production of silver in the United States is an accurate, even precise, record of the history of our country.

As collectors, really conservators, of American silver, bear in mind that every hallmark does not guarantee excellence but the field is so wide open that your own taste need be your only guide. While rarity can influence price, it does not necessarily denote beauty and it is interesting that some patterns of American silver are so rare many people have never actually seen them.

Today as stainless for everyday use becomes more widespread, and as fewer American companies produce less silverware, there is less sterling flatware on the market and the antique value of your old tableware increases without pause. People often equate the value of antique silver with the day to day selling price of silver on the money market. Indeed in 1980 even at the very largest and most prestigious antique shows buyers were seen carrying their small weighing scales, buying by the ounce completely negating the imaginative design work and the skill involved in the original making and the hours it might have taken to fashion a particular piece. When in that year, 1980, silver reached nearly $50 an ounce there were many with little thought of all that, the main concern was the price of the silver itself. Many rushed to sell their pieces, even heirlooms, for melt down prices. The loss was incalculable and we may never know what was forfeit to the collectors, the museums, and to those yet to come. The fact that so much was lost has increased the antique value of the silver which has remained. It is clearly evident that silver collecting is becoming vastly popular once again and in such a market it behooves the collector to buy what you need or desire when you see it. The silver world seems populated with particularly knowledgeable dealers and highly sophistocated collectors. The beginner should be grateful for this, talking with such people can be a tremendous learning experience.

When sterling silver is discussed the value of the metal itself seems to dominate but the flatware is above and beyond that. It has an aura which gives the knife or fork added value which is not easily defined. It is a feeling of pride. Not only because of the beauty but because everyone has always known that sterling silver is not just tableware. It is an investment and a love affair. It is an heirloom the moment you buy it and no matter how much you use it, it never loses its allure. The tiny scratches from frequent use seem only to add to the soft look which most old silver possesses, this patina not only does not detract from the value, it is an added fillip when the silver is passed on. No one buys sterling silver to use for a time and then to discard it, sterling goes on forever. The Victorians with their mad passion for clutter, gave us so many unique and interesting, often amusing, pieces, we should be ever grateful. A Saratoga chip server? A cracker spoon? An almond scoop? It is a wonderful world of the beautifully bizarre. We should preserve it. Today it is often these odd serving pieces and the more ornate flatware sets we are all searching for.

As the early American silversmith worked his magic in simple, classic styles, technology continued to advance until the all important die which impressed the design on silver was refined to the point where designs could be formed on both sides of the piece. It is this period silver, from about 1875 to the early 1900s which is most widely sought after today. Many of the patterns, magnificent and truly impressive are now obsolete but turn up in most unlikely places. The search to fill out one of the patterns for which the dies have been destroyed is an adventure and will take the collector from dealer to dealer, to auctions, to flea markets, to house sales to newspaper ads. Your life will become one long exciting search and when you have found your heart's desire you will own a great treasure. Many very active silver dealers, long in the business, profess never to having seen some of the early patterns. It is not always possible to have handled even a representative sampling of the early patterns of some companies. Often the companies themselves do not own examples. Great companies such as International did have a sample of each pattern ever produced but such is not always the case.

All fashion is cyclical. The old, ornate patterns of the late 19th century are now leading most want lists while for too many years they were in complete disfavor, interest almost non-existent. Silver is a wonderful indicator of public taste. Much of it reflects the architecture, the way of life, the fashions, the attitudes - imagine a backyard barbecue set with Louis XV by Whiting. So we know that as the Victorians set a table with so many pieces of silver at one time the table must have been a sturdy one and the general way of life a fussy one.

As interest rises in this type silverware, canny collectors should be seeking the pieces of the 1930s, 40s and 50s. The 1920s are already gaining a following, but all of these periods are highly stylized and typical and should be kept in mind. Wise collectors always collect on the rising curve.

Silver does not require the constant care some critics suggest. I own a set of service for 12 which I use fairly often but not daily, it is kept happily in its mahogany chest, washed immediately and carefully after use in non abrasive liquid detergent and warm water, dried immediately with a linen cloth and put away. It has never shown tarnish. Silver is resistant to most acids and corrosion but never let food stay on your sterling. Silver outlasts most of the things you own today, certainly it will outlast your paper money and in the long run silver may buy you anything you want. It won't rust, it is saleable. Is it any wonder the Egyptians called it white gold?

American silver has been at all times a thing to be coveted and now as we move into the era of fewer American makers, manufacturing fewer pieces of silver in this country those pieces of true Americana become artifacts to be treasured. Sterling silver flatware can be considered an art form - as with all art it is often a visual delight. It can be admired if not always for sheer beauty certainly for its craftsmanship, it can be displayed as any art might but it has the added dimension of being useful, it is intrinsically valuable although the antique value of old silver is never in question, its ownership gives one a feeling of elegance, even magnificence and the hunt is exciting. There are probably many still undocumented patterns.

It is part magic, this sterling flatware, some deep conviction that the 1890s fork you hold in your hand or admire on your table is more than just a piece of pretty metal formed by some long gone skilled craftsman. It is history and you own it. Such joy!

THE ALVIN CORPORATION

ALVIN STERLING
[TRADE MARK]

The Alvin Silver Company, once a vital and profitable American enterprise, is a typical example of creativity and initiative becoming lost in the huge corporate conglamerate structure. In its beginnings it exhibited all the energy and hope that made American industry so influential. In its heyday, Alvin, was above all, a company on the go.

Incorporated in August 1886 (some ads as late as 1966 list 1885 or 1886) it had Edwin F. Hyatt as its President, William H. Jamouneau as its Secretary and Henry L. Leibe as Treasurer. Two of these officers had been connected previously with Thomas G. Brown & Sons for long periods of time.

Although Jamouneau is usually considered the first president of Alvin, he did not actually assume the principal office until May of 1889 when Edwin Hyatt withdrew because of ill health. Early reports speak of all these stockholders as "young and enterprising men."

They were certainly willing to branch out. One of their first successes, aesthetically as well as commercially, was a process for depositing pure silver on both metallic and non-metallic bodies such as cane and umbrella handles. Although the process was patented on January 5, 1886, imitators sprang up everywhere and Alvin took out large advertisements warning about patent infringement. In an 1890's ad the Alvin Manufacturing Company of 24 Boudinot Street, Newark, New Jersey, thundered that "any infringements will be vigorously prosecuted". Dealers were warned that they incurred "personal liability be exposing or offering for sale goods that infringe on the stated patent unless it is offered by the company's accredited agent." Almost palpable is the indignation behind such a threatening advertisement, but after such outrage the manners of the time surfaced in the polite closing, "Very truly yours, Alvin Manufacturing Co."

The strong language points up one of the real and ongoing problems of the silver manufacturers of that period. As soon as a new design was perfected, or even before, if the competitor's spy system was operating well, it would be copied in whole or in part or with slight variations, and rushed into production by other companies. It was a fact of silver life, and with slight differences and with a new name a pattern could be produced by rival companies without much fear of retaliation. This widespread piracy explains why so many older patterns look so much alike.

Alvin, in spite of, or because of this problem, and given the nature of its leaders, was not loath to try other, innovative avenues. One of its lines included glass goods with silver deposit which became instantly popular and was referred to as the "Alvin Ornamentation". It was big money maker. The catalogues listing these pieces were things of beauty in themselves and even in an age of outstanding lithography, the Alvin catalogues were considered exceptional. These are rare, and expensive but worth seeking. The fact that this aspect of the business was done in such a careful, superior way was a general hallmark of the company.

Company leadership was so vigorous and its early patterns so popular that within two years of its founding the company had expanded its floor capacity and manufacturing facilities to meet demand. Henry Leibe, although now just a name in company annals, was the factory superintendent and he pursued excellence of design and increased production with the greatest verve. He was considered a whirlwind. Contemporary reports speak of Leibe and the other stockholders as "forward looking". The rapid expansion of the company proves that analysis.

Through the years and a series of moves, the company name has always been retained. For a time it operated as an adjunct of Joseph Fahys & Co., who were watch case manufacturers located in Sag Harbor, New York. Into the early 1920's the Alvin address was still Sag Harbor.

According to old sources, Simons Brothers sterling silver dies as well as Peter Krider Company patterns and dies were sold to the Alvin Manufacturing Company in 1908 and about the same time Alvin began making electroplated flatware.

In 1928 Gorham purchased Alvin and by the 1930's the Alvin Company had branch offices in New York City and Chicago and made not only sterling flatware but holloware, toiletware, silverplated flatware and novelties, including handbag fittings.

Although it maintained the Alvin name, the company became in reality simply a part of Gorham, which itself was a division of Textron, Inc. When Alvin became a Gorham satellite most of the original dies were included in the deal, although a great number of early patterns are now absolete. Alvin remained a separate entity and promoted a program which offered certain obsolete and inactive patterns made to special order. In addition, the company said it was "willing to make to order any pattern, all items and sizes and weights if the dies and tools for those items are still in existence." An old-time obliging American company indeed, Alvin after all those years was still more than willing to do a bit extra for its customers and proved that "obsolete" is not always obsolete.

For this service of course the company assessed charges, but since old Alvin patterns are not easily found this was a boon to those trying to fill out a service. To collectors it made a difference, but the program was never extremely popular so the impact was small.

Several years ago when silverplated flatware achieved renewed popularity, Gorham took advantage of the trend, and issued a line of silverplated flatware apparently using original designs based on Alvin company sterling. This is a tribute to the minds which engineered the long success of Alvin and proves again that good taste is timeless whatever the genre.

None of the patterns issued by Alvin seems to have been among the most consistently preferred in recent years by

ALVIN

buyers or collectors. Nevertheless some of the designs were quite popular and the patterns range a broad spectrum from utterly simple to rather subdued ornate, and more than with many companies, Alvin designs seem more easily recognizable as to period of production. Some of the more decorative patterns seem to be making a strong comeback among collectors which would excite those original executives who were movers and shakers in a basically conservative industry.

In 1985 it was recorded in doomsday language that the ALVIN SILVERCOMPANY ''is out of production..'' Thus Alvin, as part of Gorham, passed into the hands of Dansk, Ltd., and that company promised that ''WE OFFER ALVIN FLATWARE PATTERNS UNDER OUR ANNUAL MADE-TO-ORDER PROGRAM.''

Raphael, one of the most intricate and beautiful patterns ever made by any silver company, would alone account for continuing interest in the silver of the Alvin Company. The pattern is now being recast and even in its new guise is popular. Bridal Rose, Viking and Fleur de Lis, as well as Old Orange Blossom are marvelously detailed and striking in concept and are a tribute to the company's designers. It is rewarding to know that the company's claim that it always marked its silver will keep the name Alvin alive for future collectors.

ALVIN PRICES

NOTE: Prices reflect secondary markets. Some more recent patterns can still be purchased as retail.

Pattern	Date of Issue	Dinner fork	Dessert knife	Dessert fork	Tea-spoon	Pattern	Date of Issue	Dinner fork	Dessert knife	Dessert fork	Tea-spoon
Antique	c.1907	$20	$19	$23	$18	Cellini	1929	$30	$24	$35	$24

Antique

Cellini

Antique No. 8	c.1909	22	20	25	20	Chapel Bells	1939	33	28	32	27

Antique No. 8

Chapel Bells

Apollo	c.1905	30	22	32	24	Chased Romantique	1936	30	26	32	25

Apollo

Chased Romantique

Avilla	1969	32	26	32	25	Chateau Rose	1940	36	30	38	28

Avilla

Chateau Rose

Bridal Bouquet (Designed by Alex H. Staf of Providence, RI)	1932	35	27	35	28	Chippendale, Old	c.1899	40	30	45	30

Bridal Bouquet

Chippendale (Old)

Bridal Rose	1903	55	50	52	35	Chippendale	1921	26	23	27	19

Bridal Rose

Chippendale 1921

Pattern	Date of Issue	Dinner fork	Dessert knife	Dessert fork	Tea-spoon
Deleware	c.1910	$24	$22	$28	$21

Deleware

Pattern	Date of Issue	Dinner fork	Dessert knife	Dessert fork	Tea-spoon
Della Robbia	1922	35	28	35	26

Della Robbia

| Duquesne | 1921 | 22 | 20 | 25 | 20 |

Duquesne

| English Rose | c.1936 | 38 | 32 | 38 | 26 |

English Rose

| Eternal Rose | 1963 | 30 | 25 | 38 | 23 |

Eternal Rose

| Evangeline | 1907 | 25 | 22 | 26 | 20 |

Evangeline

| Evangeline No. 7 | c.1908 | 26 | 24 | 28 | 21 |

Evangeline No. 7

| Flanders, Old | c.1905 | 35 | 28 | 38 | 26 |

Flanders Old

Pattern	Date of Issue	Dinner fork	Dessert knife	Dessert fork	Tea-spoon
Flanders, new	c.1925	$28	$25	$30	$24

Flanders (new)

| Fleur De Lis | 1907 | 55 | 40 | 60 | 35 |

Fleur De Lis

| Florence Nightingale | 1919 | 28 | 21 | 30 | 22 |

Florence Nightingale

| Francis I | 1913 | 30 | 25 | 30 | 26 |

designed by Charles W. Harman for Joseph Fahys & Co.

Francis I

| French Scroll | 1953 | 30 | 25 | 32 | 24 |

French Scroll

| Gainsborough | c.1925 | 25 | 22 | 24 | 20 |

Gainsborough

| Hamilton | c.1913 | 25 | 22 | 25 | |

Hamilton

| Hampton | c.1911 | 28 | 24 | 30 | 22 |

Hampton

ALVIN

Pattern	Date of Issue	Dinner fork	Dessert knife	Dessert fork	Tea-spoon
Josephine	1910	$28	$24	$30	$24

Josephine 1910

Pattern	Date of Issue	Dinner fork	Dessert knife	Dessert fork	Tea-spoon
Kenmore	c.1920	23	20	25	20

Kenmore c.1920

Lady Beatrice	c.1912	27	24	28	21

Lady Beatrice

Lorna Doone	1925	24	20	25	18

designed by Peter J. Gordon for Joseph Fahys & Co.

Lorna Doone

Lorraine	1904	36	30	38	28

Lorraine

Majestic	1900	48	42	45	30

Majestic

Marie Antoinette	before 1915	37	30	35	25

Marie Antoinette

Pattern	Date of Issue	Dinner fork	Dessert knife	Dessert fork	Tea-spoon
Maryland	c.1910	$38	$27	$32	$25

Maryland

1923 Prices

		Per Doz.
Tea Spoons,	trade	$15.75
	medium	16.75
	heavy	20.00
Dessert Spoons,	medium	32.00
	heavy	37.50
Table Spoons,	medium	42.00
	heavy	53.00
Soup Spoons,	medium	38.00
	heavy	45.00
Dessert Forks,	medium	32.00
	heavy	37.50
Desert Knives,		38.50
Dinner Forks,	medium	40.00
	heavy	50.00
Dinner Knives,		44.00

Maryland Hammered   same prices

Maryland Hammered

Mastercraft	1937	28	24	28	22

Mastercraft

Maytime	1936	25	22	26	20

Maytime

Miss Alvin	1931	25	23	25	19

Miss Alvin

Miss America	1932	25	23	25	19

Miss America

Pattern	Date of Issue	Dinner fork	Dessert knife	Dessert fork	Tea-spoon
Modern Colonial	c.1927	$28	$25	$26	$21

Modern Colonial

Pattern	Date of Issue	Dinner fork	Dessert knife	Dessert fork	Tea-spoon
Molly Stark	c.1915	30	26	32	22

Molly Stark

Pattern	Date of Issue	Dinner fork	Dessert knife	Dessert fork	Tea-spoon
Morning Glory	1909	45	38	38	32

Morning Glory

Pattern	Date of Issue	Dinner fork	Dessert knife	Dessert fork	Tea-spoon
Nuremberg	1903	45	35	42	28

The Nuremberg
Teaspoon
ea., $1.00 doz., $10.75
1.25   12.75
1.50   15.00

Dessert spoon
ea., 1.75 doz., 19.25

Dessert fork
ea., 1.75 doz., 19.25
Tablespoon
ea., 1.25 doz., 25.75
Table fork
ea., 2.25 doz., 25.75
Soup spoon
ea., 2.00 doz., 19.25
Dessert knife plated blade
doz., 20.00
Table knife plated blade
doz., 24.00

Pattern	Date of Issue	Dinner fork	Dessert knife	Dessert fork	Tea-spoon
Orange Blossom, Old	1905	55	47	60	28

Orange Blossom

Pattern	Date of Issue	Dinner fork	Dessert knife	Dessert fork	Tea-spoon
Orange Blossom	c.1920	30	26	38	24

Orange Blossom (new)

Pattern	Date of Issue	Dinner fork	Dessert knife	Dessert fork	Tea-spoon
Prouette	1961	40	35	42	28

Prouette

Pattern	Date of Issue	Dinner fork	Dessert knife	Dessert fork	Tea-spoon
Prince Eugene	1950	$48	$35	$48	$30

Prince Eugene

Pattern	Date of Issue	Dinner fork	Dessert knife	Dessert fork	Tea-spoon
Raleigh	c.1902	32	26	34	25

Pattern	Date of Issue	Dinner fork	Dessert knife	Dessert fork	Tea-spoon
Raphael (currently being recast)	c.1903	95	65	110	40

Raphael

Pattern	Date of Issue	Dinner fork	Dessert knife	Dessert fork	Tea-spoon
Regent	1932	28	24	28	22

Regent

Pattern	Date of Issue	Dinner fork	Dessert knife	Dessert fork	Tea-spoon
Richmond (designed by Peter J. Gordon for Joseph Fahys & Co., New York)	1921	28	24	28	23

Richmond

Pattern	Date of Issue	Dinner fork	Dessert knife	Dessert fork	Tea-spoon
Roanoke	c.1915	24	21	27	15

Roanoke

Pattern	Date of Issue	Dinner fork	Dessert knife	Dessert fork	Tea-spoon
Romantique (designed by James R. Price, Providence, RI)	1933	28	26	30	19

Romantique

Pattern	Date of Issue	Dinner fork	Dessert knife	Dessert fork	Tea-spoon
Rosecrest	1955	23	20	25	18

Rosecrest

ALVIN

Pattern	Date of Issue	Dinner fork	Dessert knife	Dessert fork	Tea-spoon
Shenandoah	c.1915	$26	$18	$25	$20

Shenandoah

Pattern	Date of Issue	Dinner fork	Dessert knife	Dessert fork	Tea-spoon
Southern Charm	1947	28	24	30	18

Southern Charm

Spring Bud	1956	23	20	25	15

Spring Bud

Star Blossom	1959	24	22	25	15

Star Blossom

Suffolk	1905	38	32	42	28

Suffolk

Virginia	c.1908	25	22	27	16

Virginia

Vivaldi	1966	48	35	50	30

Vivaldi

Pattern	Date of Issue	Dinner fork	Dessert knife	Dessert fork	Tea-spoon
William Penn	1907	$22	$19	$25	$16

William Penn

William Penn No. 7	1910	25	22	30	20

William Penn No. 7

Winchester	c.1915	30	25	35	24

Winchester

NOTE: Although little is known of the talented designers of silverware, several popular patterns were designed for Alvin in the 1930s & 1940s by James Russell Price of Cranston, Rhode Island.

BAKER-MANCHESTER
Manchester Silver Company, Inc.
Last Address: 400 Pavilion Avenue
Providence, Rhode Island

Trade Mark  Sterling

The Manchester Silver company survived for 98 years as a proud exponent of the American silversmith's craft. For almost a century the company had an unbroken record of production of its silver, but the year 1985 was a fateful one for Manchester. The company stopped all production and liquidated all its assets.

Manchester is one of only a few companies in this industry which survived as long as it did as an extended family enterprise. William Manchester founded the firm in 1887 as W.H. Manchester Co. and located his factory on Stewart Street in Providence, Rhode Island. Precise dates of early administrative changes are unknown, even in company records, but eventually his son succeeded him.

In 1920, when Frank Trumbull took over as President, Manchester Silver was located at 49 Pavilion Avenue in Providence. Company data is unclear as to when the move from Stewart Street to Pavilion Avenue was accomplished but as of 1985 the company was still located at that address. This stablility is evidence of the steady, even progress of a prosperous, rather low-key enterprise which until the fateful 1980's was not much affected in any spectacular way by the rise and fall of the general economy. It was essentially a ''backbone-of-the-industry'' company.

When Mr. Trumbull died in 1954, Edward L. McAlpine, his partner, became sole owner of Manchester. In 1975 at McAlpine's death, his daughter Mrs. Phebe McAlpine Shepard, assumed control of the company. In 1980 Mrs. Shepard's son, George Shepard, became owner and president. This interesting line of succession is a reflection of the cooperative ''family'' feeling which characterized the entire company. This smooth transition of executive power was reflected in the remarkably stable production of the factory.

No new patterns were issued by Manchester after the early 1950's but production continued steadily with the regular lines which are for the most part traditional in design and of good weight and quality. The fact that this very simplicity lent itself to easy coordination with almost all tableware is what probably made all the patterns popular and steady sellers.

Prices at retail were always kept as low as possible largely due to the standardized methods of manufacture. In all Manchester silver the bowls and tines of the pieces in all patterns are the same size and shape throughout the entire range. This effected considerable savings in die costs and labor which the company then conscientiously passed along to the customer. The master model of the die was cast in bronze but all remaining operations were done by machinery. This standardization was a great selling point. Another was the boast that no pattern was ever withdrawn, everything was open stock, although there is some evidence that in the early 1920's the Abraham Lincoln pattern was not being made.

Manchester silver was made in two weights, medium and heavy, and two knife and fork sizes were available in all patterns. For many years the Manchester line consisted of sterling holloware, flatware and specialty items, as well as karat gold on special orders. It always maintained its quality and its ability to compete. Even in the depressed 1930's the company continued to issue new patterns. Until its closing it had 24 active patterns, which if not reissued, will become scarce and valuable. J.C. Boardman & Co. of Wallingford, Connecticut which purchased all the tools and dies of Manchester are expected to fill special orders for Manchester patterns.

Manchester is an underrated company, probably because its manufacture was limited and advertising not a big budget item. If indeed Manchester had done nothing else, its Valenciennes pattern is so exquisitely beautiful it alone testifies to the company's excellence, and no doubt in time the older patterns will be increasingly sought after because of their scarcity and heavy weight.

Baker-Manchester existed only from 1914 to 1920 and the Manchester Silver Company always owned the tools and dies of Baker-Manchester but apparently never put them into production. The Baker-Manchester trademark of cross and crown is one of the most distinctive and memorable but its origin is obscure even to old time company members. It is not easy to find pieces with this mark, however, and since so few patterns were produced it would be a challenge to collect.

Those who made Baker-Manchester and the Manchester Silver Company such a dependable, vigorous part of the great American Silver picture have reason to be proud of their contribution. The company was a steady influence in the late years when the industry was changing so rapidly. It never sacrificed quality and if most of the patterns never moved, as with some bigger companies, into the realm of the esoteric. That may be the very factor which kept so much of it's silver selling so well for so long. Patterns such as Copenhagen and the Duke of Windsor, both issued in the 1930's, do show great foresight in design and certainly Valenciennes, Amaryllis and American Beauty are classic in their grace and elegance.

The story of Manchester, although lesser known than some of its bigger contemporaries, is really the story of American industry as it was - an energetic and resourceful founder, willing to work diligently and intelligently for himself, his family and his employees in a field which then held great promise. An ethic based on the principle ''to build up and hand down.'' The promise was fulfilled for many years and the company lived up to its commitment of fairness and loyalty to the customer. Even as the company prepared to close its doors forever a deep sense of poignancy and personal loss pervaded the process, and the chief concern of company personnel was the hope that the patterns would be again produced and someone would carry on the flatware line.

In November of 1985 all the flatware tools and dies of Manchester Silver Co., Inc., had been purchased by THE J.C. BOARDMAN & CO. of Wallingford, Connecticut. It is Boardman's intention to fill requests for Manchester Silver.

BAKER-MANCHESTER PRICES

Pattern	Date of Issue	Dinner fork	Dessert knife	Dessert fork	Tea-spoon
Bridal Wreath	c.1919	$25	$23	$28	$21

Bridal Wreath c.1920

Roanoke	c.1916	24	21	26	22

Roanoke c.1916

Roger Williams	c.1916	24	21	26	22

Roger Williams c.1915

Spartan	c.1914	25	22	28	24

Spartan c.1918

Van Buren	c.1915	27	24	30	23

Van Buren c.1915

MANCHESTER

Abraham Lincoln	c.1909	28	24	30	25

Abraham Lincoln N.L.P.

Amaryllis	1951	32	26	35	25

Amaryllis

American Beauty	1935	40	30	42	28

American Beauty

Pattern	Date of Issue	Dinner fork	Dessert knife	Dessert fork	Tea-spoon
Beacon	1936	$24	$22	$25	$19

Beacon

Beaux Art	c.1920	27	24	28	22

Beaux Art

Colannade	1936	36	30	40	26

Colonnade

Copenhagen	1936	30	25	35	23

Copenhagen 1936

Dixie	c.1920	28	26	30	22

Dixie

Doric	c.1920	28	26	32	22

Doric

Duke of Windsor	1937	38	30	35	28

Duke of Windsor 1937

Fleetwood	1934	28	25	30	23

Fleetwood

BAKER/MANCHESTER

Pattern	Date of Issue	Dinner fork	Dessert knife	Dessert fork	Tea-spoon
Gadroonette	1938	$40	$30	$42	$28

Gadroonette 1938

Pattern	Date of Issue	Dinner fork	Dessert knife	Dessert fork	Tea-spoon
Leonore	1939	26	24	28	21

Leonore 1939

| Manchester | c.1928 | 25 | 23 | 23 | 15 |

Manchester

| Mary Warren | c.1920 | 26 | 20 | 27 | 20 |

Mary Warren

| Mayflower | c.1915 | 24 | 20 | 22 | 19 |

Mayflower

| Park Avenue | 1931 | 35 | 28 | 38 | 24 |

Park Avenue

| Pilgrim | c.1932 | 28 | 24 | 30 | 24 |

Pilgrim

| Polly Lawton | 1935 | 26 | 23 | 28 | 22 |

Polly Lawton

| Plymouth | 1933 | 20 | 17 | 22 | 15 |

Plymouth

Pattern	Date of Issue	Dinner fork	Dessert knife	Dessert fork	Tea-spoon
Princess	c.1928	$25	$23	$27	$18

Princess

| Priscilla | c.1928 | 26 | 22 | 27 | 20 |

Priscilla

| Silverstream | 1934 | 25 | 20 | 24 | 18 |

Silverstream

| Southern Rose | 1933 | 30 | 25 | 34 | 25 |

Southern Rose

| Valenciennes | 1938 | 50 | 40 | 55 | 35 |

Valenciennes

| Vogue | 1932 | 22 | 20 | 24 | 18 |

Vogue

12

BAKER/MANCHESTER

''Never made in place settings, this was a short line of
sterling silver fancy serving pieces.'' Pierced handle

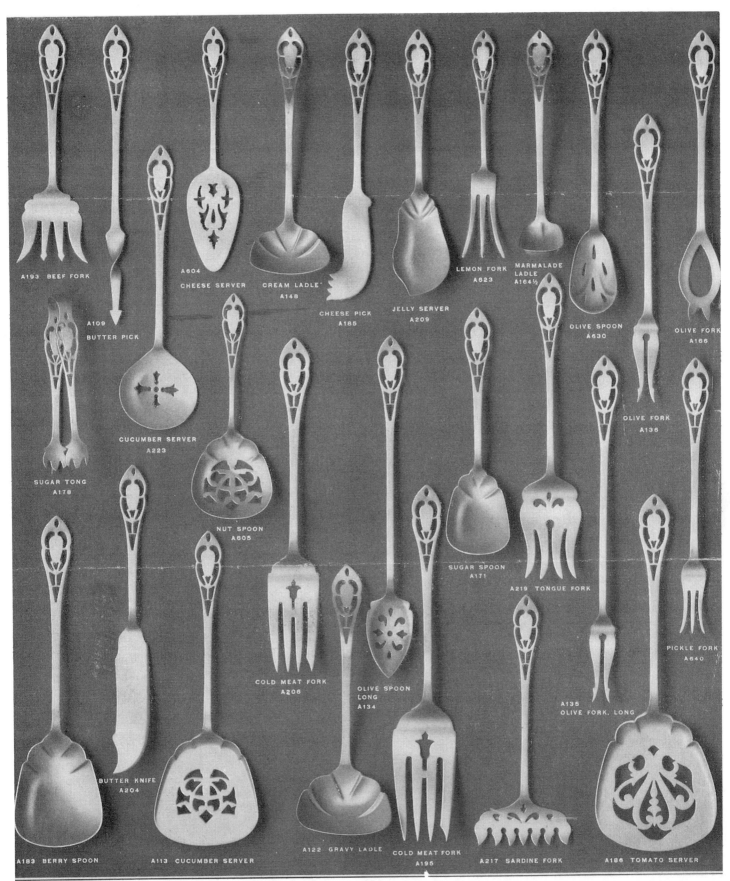

A193 BEEF FORK

A604
CHEESE SERVER

CREAM LADLE'
A148

CHEESE PICK
A185

JELLY SERVER
A209

LEMON FORK
A523

MARMALADE
LADLE
A164½

OLIVE SPOON
A630

OLIVE FORK
A166

A109
BUTTER PICK

CUCUMBER SERVER
A223

OLIVE FORK
A136

SUGAR TONG
A178

NUT SPOON
A605

SUGAR SPOON
A171

A219 TONGUE FORK

BUTTER KNIFE
A204

COLD MEAT FORK
A206

OLIVE SPOON
LONG
A134

PICKLE FORK
A640

A135
OLIVE FORK, LONG

A183 BERRY SPOON

A113 CUCUMBER SERVER

A122 GRAVY LADLE

COLD MEAT FORK
A195

A217 SARDINE FORK

A186 TOMATO SERVER

DOMINICK & HAFF

Dominick & Haff has been out of business as a separate entity since 1928 and as the pieces become harder to find this company's silver is attracting a highly sophisticated group of collectors which continues to grow. The name is a rather rarefied one. Some of the patterns are achieving a legendary appeal, the Medallion for example, which is coveted and costly. Renaissance, 1900, New King and Trianon pierced are all superior examples of the silversmith's art. As with all well made grape patterns, the old Grape of Dominick and Haff continues to be sought after. The Trianon Pierced is so desirable it has been reissued and "Labors of Cupid', called "1900" pattern in early catalogues is becoming one of the prima donnas of the silver world.

"D & H" as it is generally called, was almost 60 years old when Reed and Barton purchased the company in 1928, although its roots go back to the 1820s. At this juncture it is difficult to determine precisely the number of patterns issued by Dominick and Haff but Reed and Barton estimates "approximately 70". Of those 70 several were so outstanding reproductions or "reissues" have been made. After its absorption by Reed and Barton few new designs were issued and by the late 1930s the company had been phased out entirely as a separate unit.

Dominick and Haff is one of those companies whose history is inextricably intertwined with other manufacturers through buy-outs, reorganizations and absorptions. It is a tribute to the beauty of the patterns and the quality of the silver that the name has survived with such integrity. D & H had many popular patterns and the fact that sterling silver enjoyed such wide acceptance at the time makes finding some of the patterns eaiser than one would expect.

The company had its beginnings in New York; it moved to Newark, New Jersey, then to Taunton, Massachusetts. The date of its consolidation with Reed and Barton says more about the economy of the times than it does about the skills of the company, which encouraged wonderful design work and good, heavy quality silver with unusually sharply delineated die craftsmanship. It is definitely a fact that as we distance ourselves from the last days of D & H its patterns seem more alluring to collectors.

This was a very thorough and conscientious company. Its patterns have endured because it correctly interpreted the public taste of the times but it overdid variations of some of those designs to the point of boredom. The Queen Anne was produced in at least five incarnations with but minor differences. Overall the inventory went from the usual plain patterns to the usual ornate. D & H did such a spectacular design and production job on the ornate that they are the ones people now search for. The company also produced elaborate holloware and almost all of its silver shows fine workmanship and precise attention to detail. The Labors of Cupid pattern, for example, shows Cupid in a different attitude on each piece which guarantees the pattern will not become tedious and also must have been dear to the busy Victorian heart. The silver line produced by D & H after its acquisition by Reed and Barton was fairly mundane.

Dominick and Haff was a successor company to Gale, Dominick & Haff about 1870, although the history of the company was a long one reaching back into the first quarter of the 19th century and boasting connections with William Gale, a noted early American silversmith, noted enough to give Dominick & Haff added cachet in the field. Indeed H. Blanchard Dominick and Leroy Haff were in themselves an interesting and compatible pair. Haff had great business acumen and brought considerable skill to the operations of the company. Dominick with his French antecedents who had long been associated with the silver business brought this proficiency as well as his own great flair. Their diverse backgrounds in retailing and selling of silver as well as a solid foundation in the technical aspects of the business made the combination of Dominick and Haff a formidable one. The promotion and actual sale of its silver had an almost Madison Avenue importance to the company; great emphasis was put on retailing the merchandise and it was a large part of company policy. Promotion was considered very important and finding catalogues and advertisements of these old line companies not only becomes historically important but illustrates the scope and uncovers details which make any serious collector ecstatic. Reading enough of these ads shows us that the silver companies were primarily business oriented - Dominick & Haff certainly were.

The company neglected no opportunity. As with many other such manufacturers they sold large quantities of what is now called "hotel silver", but unlike many other silver companies D & H were extremely proud of this aspect of their production. In 1907 an advertisement boasts that "the order placed with us for the new Plaza Hotel, New York City, will be the finest and most extensive service of the kind ever produced." In the Edwardian years the great hotels were scenes of magnificent galas; the Plaza was one of the finest, so D & H felt justifiably honored. They considered themselves a "prestige" company and so we regard them today.

The story of the early years of Dominick & Haff fascinates us today almost as a tale of two companies. The early production is uneven as to design but the best of this work is almost unparalleled. The later output shows the lack of the dedication, and yes, flamboyance of some of the first efforts.

As to be expected of Mr. Dominick and Mr. Haff with their eye on production and business matters, the silver is definitively marked with the sterling standard 925 while the numbers in the diamond indicate the year the piece was made. We thank them for that.

Collectors should always be aware of D & H pieces, the best of them are going to be portable wealth.

DOMINICK & HAFF PRICES

Pattern	Date of Issue	Dinner fork	Dessert knife	Dessert fork	Tea-spoon
Acanthus	c.1895	$30	$28	$37	$24

Acanthus

Pattern	Date of Issue	Dinner fork	Dessert knife	Dessert fork	Tea-spoon
Basket of Flowers	1920	25	22	27	20

Basket of Flowers

Blossom	c.1902	65	60	47	35

Blossom

Century	c.1901	30	28	35	24

Century

Century No. 6 engraved	c.1901	35	32	38	26

Century No. 6

Charles II	1894	40	35	44	28

Charles II

Chippendale	c.1880	25	23	27	22

Chippendale

Pattern	Date of Issue	Dinner fork	Dessert knife	Dessert fork	Tea-spoon
Colonial Antique	c.1925	$25	$23	$27	$20

Colonial Antique

Contempora	1930	27	25	28	20

Contempora

Gothic	1900	50	45	54	30

Gothic

Grape	1895	55	50	57	35

Grape

King	c.1890	50	40	55	30

King

Labors of Cupid	1900	145	80	150	65

Other catalogues refer to this as "1900" pattern

Labors of Cupid

La France	1916	30	25	32	26

La France

Pattern	Date of Issue	Dinner fork	Dessert knife	Dessert fork	Tea-spoon
LaSalle	1928	$22	$20	$26	$22

LaSalle

Pattern	Date of Issue	Dinner fork	Dessert knife	Dessert fork	Tea-spoon
LaSalle, chased	1928	24	22	26	22

LaSalle Chased

Pattern	Date of Issue	Dinner fork	Dessert knife	Dessert fork	Tea-spoon
Lexington	1915	20	18	22	15

Lexington

Pattern	Date of Issue	Dinner fork	Dessert knife	Dessert fork	Tea-spoon
Louis XIV Old Style	1888	30	27	32	25

Old catalogues listed this as the complete name

Louis XIV Old Style

Pattern	Date of Issue	Dinner fork	Dessert knife	Dessert fork	Tea-spoon
Louis XIV, New	1913	32	27	35	28

Louis XIV, New

Pattern	Date of Issue	Dinner fork	Dessert knife	Dessert fork	Tea-spoon
Louis XVI, Old Style	1916	28	24	30	26

Louis XVI

Pattern	Date of Issue	Dinner fork	Dessert knife	Dessert fork	Tea-spoon
Louis XVI	1925	28	23	28	22

Louis XVI

Pattern	Date of Issue	Dinner fork	Dessert knife	Dessert fork	Tea-spoon
Marie Antoinette	1917	28	24	28	23

Marie Antoinette

Pattern	Date of Issue	Dinner fork	Dessert knife	Dessert fork	Tea-spoon
Marie Antoinette, Chased	1917	$28	$24	$30	$52

Marie Antoinette, Chased

Pattern	Date of Issue	Dinner fork	Dessert knife	Dessert fork	Tea-spoon
Martha Washington	1926	28	24	30	22

Martha Washington

Pattern	Date of Issue	Dinner fork	Dessert knife	Dessert fork	Tea-spoon
Mayflower	1911	22	20	25	19

Mayflower

Pattern	Date of Issue	Dinner fork	Dessert knife	Dessert fork	Tea-spoon
Mazarin	1892	48	38	42	30

Mazarin

Pattern	Date of Issue	Dinner fork	Dessert knife	Dessert fork	Tea-spoon
Medallion	1907	95	75	100	65

Pattern	Date of Issue	Dinner fork	Dessert knife	Dessert fork	Tea-spoon
New King	1898	55	45	58	35

New King

Pattern	Date of Issue	Dinner fork	Dessert knife	Dessert fork	Tea-spoon
No. 10	1896	40	35	45	30

No. 10

Pattern	Date of Issue	Dinner fork	Dessert knife	Dessert fork	Tea-spoon
Old English Antique and Old English Antique Hammered	1880 / 1880	25	22	28	20

Old English Antique

Pattern	Date of Issue	Dinner fork	Dessert knife	Dessert fork	Tea-spoon
Old English Antqiue No. 1		27	24	28	22

Old English Antique Hammered

16

DOMINICK & HAFF

Pattern	Date of Issue	Dinner fork	Dessert knife	Dessert fork	Tea-spoon
Pointed Antique	1895	$25	$22	$28	$22

Pointed Antique

Pointed Antique Hammered	1895	25	22	28	22

Pointed Antique Hammered

Pointed Antique No. 2 engraved	1895	26	23	30	24

Pointed Antique No. 2

Pointed Antique No. 3	c.1895	26	23	30	24

Pointed Antique No. 3

Priscilla	1916	24	22	26	20

Priscilla

Queen Anne, plain	c.1910 -1912	24	22	25	16

Queen Anne, plain

Queen Anne No. 11, engraved	c.1910 -1912	27	24	28	18

Queen Anne No. 11

Queen Anne No. 15, engraved	c.1910 -1912	28	25	30	21

Queen Anne No. 15

Pattern	Date of Issue	Dinner fork	Dessert knife	Dessert fork	Tea-spoon
Queen Anne No. 16, engraved	c.1910 -1912	$27	$24	$28	$18

Queen Anne No. 16

Queen Anne No. 18, engraved	c.1910 -1912	27	24	28	18

Queen Anne No. 18

Queen Elizabeth	1916	30	26	34	25

Queen Elizabeth

Renaissance 1894	1894	95	85	125	45

Renaissance

Ribbed Antique	c.1885	22	20	25	18

Ribbed Antique

Rococo	1888	45	40	48	30

Rococo

Seventeenth Century	c.1890	22	20	25	18

Seventeenth Century

1776	c.1890	25	22	28	20

the similarities between 1776 and Pointed Antique make it difficult to identify.

1776

DOMINICK & HAFF

Pattern	Date of Issue	Dinner fork	Dessert knife	Dessert fork	Tea-spoon
Tradition	1939	$26	$23	$30	$24

Bears a strong resemblance to Pointed Antique No. 2, engraved

Pattern	Date of Issue	Dinner fork	Dessert knife	Dessert fork	Tea-spoon
Trianon Pierced	c.1901	95	85	100	55

Trianon Pierced

Pattern	Date of Issue	Dinner fork	Dessert knife	Dessert fork	Tea-spoon
Victoria	1901	55	50	60	40

Victoria

Pattern	Date of Issue	Dinner fork	Dessert knife	Dessert fork	Tea-spoon
Virginia	1912	22	20	25	15

Virginia

Pattern	Date of Issue	Dinner fork	Dessert knife	Dessert fork	Tea-spoon
Washington		$30	$25	$32	$22

Washington

Pattern	Date of Issue	Dinner fork	Dessert knife	Dessert fork	Tea-spoon
Virginia No. 19, engraved		25	22	28	18

Virginia No. 19

Pattern	Date of Issue	Dinner fork	Dessert knife	Dessert fork	Tea-spoon
Virginia No. 20, engraved		27	23	30	21

Virginia No. 20

WILLIAM B. DURGIN CO.

Although it seems forever destined to be known as "The Durgin Division of Gorham" the Durgin Silver Company was in fact an early prestigious maker of sterling silver. William Durgin himself is a rather legendary figure in the annals of the industry, an industry which abounded with men of courage and daring. Durgin and his cohorts were the reincarnation of Horatio Alger.

An old newspaper account tells his story very well in the overblown language of the day: "Born in 1833 and raised in the shadow of the Great Stone Face that has stood ceaseless sentinel over the White Mountains through all the endless centuries, William B. Durgin acquired the productive energy, steadiness of purpose and business industry that has so frequently distinguished men of the soil. During the brief years at the country school young Durgin read and dreamed of the busy lives of men far beyond the little home of his nativity and while thus reading and dreaming he felt the constant urge to 'make something better of himself'."

Little Compton Village could not contain William Durgin for long. In the mode of old time American heroes at the age of 15 or 16 he made his way toward opportunity in the big city. The accounts talk of the "deprivation and toil that only a poor boy knows and appreciates", but somehow he scraped together his fare to Boston, "bid goodbye to his frugal mountain home" and walked the deeply wooded miles to the railroad station.

Although accounts talk of "much discouragement at first" Durgin never really veered from his goals. He soon "found himself apprenticed to a silversmith". That was the spur - the long hours and poor recompense disillusioned him about working for others. In 1853 Durgin and two fellow apprentices decided to found their own company. All were virtually penniless. In the parlance of the times, "these friends, these sturdy industrial pioneers, faced the great venture - that of starting a manufacturing business sans funds, sans credit, sans market".

Quite a trick, even then, and it would certainly be interesting to examine the account books of those first days." He set up shop in Concord" and bought the inventory of two smaller jewelry concerns. "Sans funds" must have meant poverty but not absolute destitution. Still contemporary history has it that prosperity did not come easily, but that "every obstacle simply proved a stepping stone to greater things."

The struggling business employed only one engraver, William F. Groves, originally from England. When Groves lost his life in a fire at his home, Durgin contacted John H. Harriott a skilled master engraver well-established in Boston. He recommended his brother James Harriott who must have been a man after Durgin's own heart. James Harriott was then a resident of New York "way up on 140th St." and the long commute to the downtown Whiting plant where he worked was becoming nerve wracking. He often found himself delayed in horse traffic to the point where he would return home at "10 or 11 at night", so he immediately accepted the offer to move to Concord. The fact that he knew nothing of Durgin or his business except what his brother had told him says much, either for his frustration or his gambling instinct. He remained with Durgin until the plant closed. And in later years his brother spoke of the "long struggle" Durgin had to make his business successful.

The companies were so interwoven with each other that employees moved back and forth and names have become a matter of confusion, for example, Harold H. Hamilton was for many years connected with the Durgin business as its New York representative but he resigned this position to become President of the Whiting Manufacturing Co. Ironically James Harriott was again associated with Whiting when in the 1920s Whiting moved to Providence to consolidate with Gorham, of which Durgin was then a "unit".

In spite of very long hours and hard work these men were devoted to their business and took a fierce personal pride in the company name.

Nothing seems to have fazed Durgin. In spite of very little money, he married early and his "good wife" was obviously a gem. Mrs. Durgin "cooked for, mended for and roomed the three partners in their humble home" so that all living expenses could be minimized until the fledgling business could get a solid start. In those days apparently all William possessed in the worldly sense was unimportant compared with his energy, his confidence in his ultimate success and his pride of craftsmanship.

Contemporary recollection has it that Durgin was an engaging person and one of strictest integrity. His notes indicate that even on his very first purchase as a businessman (a few tools) he paid the debt the day before it was due. This became one of his trademarks, ever after any debt he incurred was paid before the due date. The business, started so confidentially and with anticipation did well for years but after the Civil War this business, as with most others, foundered. William Durgin possessed pride in abundance, but none of it was based on vanity. When the silver trade took a tremendous downturn after the War he went - sample bag in hand - back to Boston and he sold piece by piece, if necessary, to obtain cash.

The economy worsened and so did the silver business. All the partners were in a "state of despair". At that point Good Fortune seemed to smile on Durgin. Jordan Marsh & Co. offered him $10,000 to produce a line of silver plate for them. At a time when most business would accommodate to anything that would produce revenue Durgin's pride in his own sterling silver was so great he seemed insulted and "calmly" turned down the offer. It is difficult for us today to understand this kind of response, this breed of man, the old entrepreneurs really lived and loved their product. It was not simply a way to build a fortune. The impoverished but ambitious 16 year old dreamer had matured into a man to match his mountain. Among fellow silver makers he became a hero, someone who would never, under any circumstances, sacrifice ''quality'' Eventually by perserverance, excellent management and the most rigid economies the factory endured and again prospered.

In its time William Durgin was an outstanding name in American Silver but the family connection was lost when William and his son who had become a vital part of the business both died in the same year 1905. Gorham then acquired the company and in 1931 moved it out of Concord.

Although the Gorham Company acquired financial interest in 1905, Durgin was operated as a separate firm by THE SILVERSMITHS CO. and THE SILVERSMITHS STOCK COMPANY from 1906 to 1923. It actually merged with Gorham in 1923 and of course moved to Providence in 1931. THE SILVERSMITHS CO. AND SILVERSMITHS STOCK CO. were holding companies chartered in New York in 1906-1907 and tended the Gorham Co. interest in Durgin. When Gorham took over Durgin some patterns continued to be produced under the Durgin name but this practice was discontinued about 1939 or 1940.

Many of the early patterns of this company are so scarce that one could move about the silver world for many years without seeing an example. Those which do exist are beginning to be avidly collected. One of the reasons it is so difficult to find patterns by Durgin is the fact that as early as the 1930s, the company issued the following directive:

''The Durgin Company, in recently listing some of the earlier products of William B. Durgin find the following patterns, many of which are obsolete and can no longer be reproduced. Anyone possessing such silver can classify it as bordering on the antique and almost priceless. The list of flatware patterns, now obsolete, follow: Athenian, Albion, Antique, Bouquet, Bug, Bridal, Cheltenham, Cattail, Dartmouth, Empress Josephine, Honeysuckle, Jonquil, Marie Antoinette, Medallion, Magnolia, Orleans, Orange Blossom, Olive, Revere, (special treatment Windsor) Renaissance, Scroll, Strawberry, Twist, Tulip, Undine, Victoria, (New Scroll) and Winthrop.'' So many of these patterns are so scarce photographs are not possible. But it proves that Durgin was a very active maker of fine silver in many different patterns. All the silver is of good weight and the diversity of patterns indicate a progressive attitude toward design, for example the ''New Art'' pattern which was already out of production by 1922 was a masterful tribute to Art Nouveau.

It is entertaining to speculate on this man William Durgin, well liked and respected, so obviously affable and gregarious but with that particular inner drive which carried him and his company to success, spinning gold from straw, as the fairy tale has it. As with many old line companies the personality and talents of the founder remain fixed in our mind long after the company has disappeared.

Although not a household name outside the silver world, Durgin's work lives on in the many truly magnificent patterns his company produced. Although scarce, which is somewhat ironic in view of Durgin's great nationwide success, a sampling of some of these patterns - the florals; Hearaldic; New Art; Marchal Niel; Dauphin; the distinctive Medallion and Fleur de Lis can only whet the collector's appetite.

William Durgin, the individual may not have imprinted his name into the American consciousness, but he certainly imprinted it on some exquisite silver.

DURGIN PRICES

Pattern	Date of Issue	Dinner fork	Dessert knife	Dessert fork	Tea-spoon

Many pieces of Durgin silverware are finished with gold wash. This increases the price.

Pattern	Date of Issue	Dinner fork	Dessert knife	Dessert fork	Tea-spoon
Antique Sheaf	c.1893	$37	$30	$40	$27

Antique Sheaf

Pattern	Date of Issue	Dinner fork	Dessert knife	Dessert fork	Tea-spoon
Arts & Crafts	1906	25	20	28	20

Arts & Crafts

Pattern	Date of Issue	Dinner fork	Dessert knife	Dessert fork	Tea-spoon
Bead	1893	$27	$24	$29	$21

Bead

Pattern	Date of Issue	Dinner fork	Dessert knife	Dessert fork	Tea-spoon
Bradford	1909	27	24	29	21

Bradford

Pattern	Date of Issue	Dinner fork	Dessert knife	Dessert fork	Tea-spoon
Chatham and Chatham, hammered	1915	25	22	28	22

Chatham

INDEX

For 65 or Chatham Tea Set and Hollow Ware, see pages 322–323

Chatham Index showing vast number of pieces available in 1922.

DURGIN

Pattern	Date of Issue	Dinner fork	Dessert knife	Dessert fork	Tea-spoon
Chatham No. 3, engraved	1915	$32	$25	$30	$25

Chatham No. 3, engraved

Pattern	Date of Issue	Dinner fork	Dessert knife	Dessert fork	Tea-spoon
Chatham No. 4, chased	1915	32	25	30	25

Chatham No. 4, chased

Chrysanthemum	1893	55	40	60	35

Chrysanthemum

Colfax	1922	30	25	32	26

Colfax

Cromwell	1893	40	32	45	30

Cromwell

Dartmouth	1917	38	30	40	26

Dartmouth

Dauphin	1897	60	50	65	38

Dauphin

Dolly Madison	1904	24	20	26	18

Dolly Madison

Pattern	Date of Issue	Dinner fork	Dessert knife	Dessert fork	Tea-spoon
Dolly Madison, engraved	1904	$27	$22	$29	$20

Dolly Madison, engraved

Du Barry	1901	75	60	80	39

Du Barry

Empire	1895	85	70	95	40

Empire

English Antique	1887	25	24	28	18

English Antique

English Tip c.1880		27	22	28	18

English Tip

Essex	1911	27	24	30	22

Essex

Essex No. 5, engraved	1911	30	26	32	24

Essex No. 5, engraved

Fairfax	1910	32	28	35	25

Gorham has been listing Fairfax as a Gorham pattern since the 1930s.

Fairfax

DURGIN

Pattern	Date of Issue	Dinner fork	Dessert knife	Dessert fork	Tea-spoon
Fairfax No. 1, engraved	1910	$32	$25	$35	$25

Fairfax No. 1, engraved

Pattern	Date of Issue	Dinner fork	Dessert knife	Dessert fork	Tea-spoon
Fairfax No. 2, engraved,	Same prices as Fairfax No. 1 engraved				

Fairfax No. 2, engraved

Pattern	Date of Issue	Dinner fork	Dessert knife	Dessert fork	Tea-spoon
Fairfax No. 4 - B engraved,	Same prices as Fairfax No. 1 engraved				

Fairfax No. 4 - B, engraved

Pattern	Date of Issue	Dinner fork	Dessert knife	Dessert fork	Tea-spoon
Fiddle	1850s	30	25	32	25

Fiddle

Pattern	Date of Issue	Dinner fork	Dessert knife	Dessert fork	Tea-spoon
Fleur de Lis	1886	45	35	48	30

Fleur de Lis

Pattern	Date of Issue	Dinner fork	Dessert knife	Dessert fork	Tea-spoon
French Antique	c.1870 -1875	28	25	30	25

French Antique

Pattern	Date of Issue	Dinner fork	Dessert knife	Dessert fork	Tea-spoon
Hampshire	1906	$45	$35	$50	$30

Hampshire

Pattern	Date of Issue	Dinner fork	Dessert knife	Dessert fork	Tea-spoon
Hunt Club	1931	27	22	28	22

Although originally released as a Durgin Division pattern, early on this was heavily advertised as a Gorham pattern.

Hunt Club

Pattern	Date of Issue	Dinner fork	Dessert knife	Dessert fork	Tea-spoon
Iris	1900	85	80	95	40

Iris

Pattern	Date of Issue	Dinner fork	Dessert knife	Dessert fork	Tea-spoon
Lenox	1912	28	24	30	20

Lenox

Pattern	Date of Issue	Dinner fork	Dessert knife	Dessert fork	Tea-spoon
Louis XV	1891	65	50	70	38

Louis XV

Pattern	Date of Issue	Dinner fork	Dessert knife	Dessert fork	Tea-spoon
Madame Royale	1897	55	45	50	32

Madame Royale

Pattern	Date of Issue	Dinner fork	Dessert knife	Dessert fork	Tea-spoon
Marechal Niel	1896	$75	$60	$85	$40

Marechal Niel

Pattern	Date of Issue	Dinner fork	Dessert knife	Dessert fork	Tea-spoon
Medallion	1870	125	85	140	65
Navarre	1909	30	27	34	23

Navarre

| New Art | 1899 | 90 | 75 | 85 | 60 |

New Art

| New Queens | 1900 | 55 | 40 | 65 | 32 |

New Queens

| New Standish | 1905 | 35 | 30 | 38 | 27 |

New Standish

| New Vintage | 1904 | 65 | 50 | 65 | 40 |

New Vintage

Pattern	Date of Issue	Dinner fork	Dessert knife	Dessert fork	Tea-spoon
No. 19, plain	1912	$25	$20	$28	$15

No. 19, plain

| No. 19, B | 1912 | 25 | 20 | 28 | 15 |

No. 19 - B

| No. 19, C | 1912 | same prices as B | | | |

No. 19 - C

| No. 19, E and No. 19 G | | same prices as B | | | |

No. 19 - E

No. 19 - G

| Old Standish | 1901 | 24 | 20 | 27 | 14 |

Old Standish

| Princess Patricia | 1927 | 24 | 20 | 27 | 14 |

Princess Patricia

DURGIN

Pattern	Date of Issue	Dinner fork	Dessert knife	Dessert fork	Tea-spoon
Regent	1901	$65	$55	$68	$32

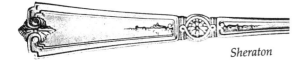

Regent

Pattern	Date of Issue	Dinner fork	Dessert knife	Dessert fork	Tea-spoon
Shell	c.1892	30	24	35	20

Shell

Pattern	Date of Issue	Dinner fork	Dessert knife	Dessert fork	Tea-spoon
Sheraton (later listed as Victorian)	1918	28	22	30	22

Sheraton

Pattern	Date of Issue	Dinner fork	Dessert knife	Dessert fork	Tea-spoon
Tip Sheaf	1887	40	30	45	30

Gorham later advertised this as Sheaf of Wheat

Tip Sheaf

Pattern	Date of Issue	Dinner fork	Dessert knife	Dessert fork	Tea-spoon
Watteau	1891	35	30	38	27

Watteau

Pattern	Date of Issue	Dinner fork	Dessert knife	Dessert fork	Tea-spoon
Wellington	1908	35	30	38	22

Wellington

Pattern	Date of Issue	Dinner fork	Dessert knife	Dessert fork	Tea-spoon
Wentworth	1902	25	20	28	15

Wentworth

Pattern	Date of Issue	Dinner fork	Dessert knife	Dessert fork	Tea-spoon
Wentworth, engraved	1902	$28	$23	$30	$20

Wentworth, engraved

Pattern	Date of Issue	Dinner fork	Dessert knife	Dessert fork	Tea-spoon
Wentworth No. 1822, chased		30	25	35	24

Wentworth

Pattern	Date of Issue	Dinner fork	Dessert knife	Dessert fork	Tea-spoon
Wentworth, hammered and chased wreath		35	28	38	27

Wentworth, hammered and chased wreath

Pattern	Date of Issue	Dinner fork	Dessert knife	Dessert fork	Tea-spoon
Wentworth No. 18211, chased		35	30	40	28

Wentworth No. 18211, chased

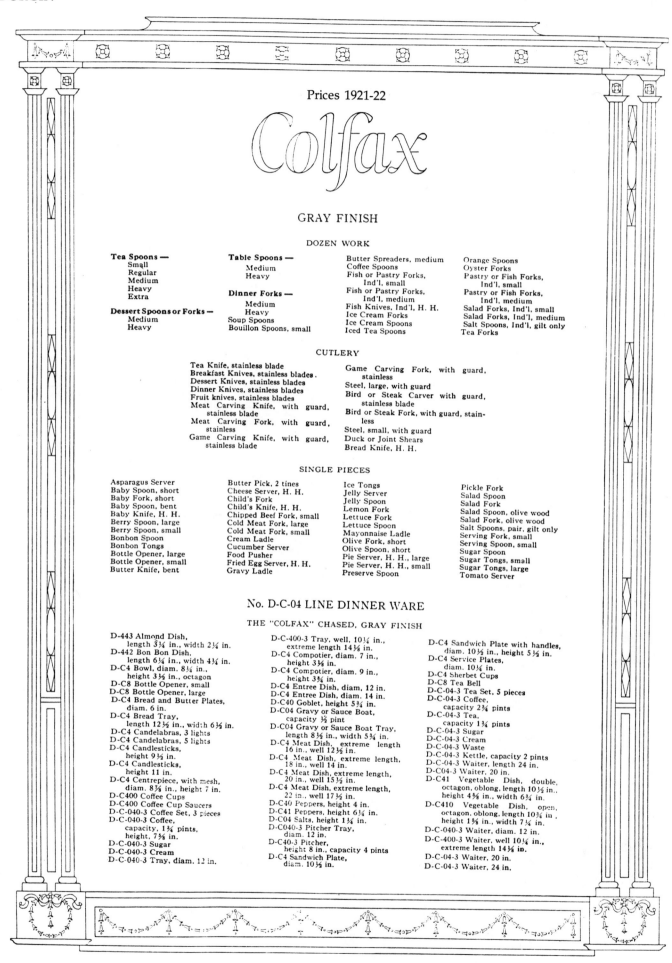

Prices 1921-22

Colfax

GRAY FINISH

DOZEN WORK

Tea Spoons —
- Small
- Regular
- Medium
- Heavy
- Extra

Dessert Spoons or Forks —
- Medium
- Heavy

Table Spoons —
- Medium
- Heavy

Dinner Forks —
- Medium
- Heavy
- Soup Spoons
- Bouillon Spoons, small

Butter Spreaders, medium
Coffee Spoons
Fish or Pastry Forks, Ind'l, small
Fish or Pastry Forks, Ind'l, medium
Fish Knives, Ind'l, H. H.
Ice Cream Forks
Ice Cream Spoons
Iced Tea Spoons

Orange Spoons
Oyster Forks
Pastry or Fish Forks, Ind'l, small
Pastry or Fish Forks, Ind'l, medium
Salad Forks, Ind'l, small
Salad Forks, Ind'l, medium
Salt Spoons, Ind'l, gilt only
Tea Forks

CUTLERY

Tea Knife, stainless blade
Breakfast Knives, stainless blades
Dessert Knives, stainless blades
Dinner Knives, stainless blades
Fruit knives, stainless blades
Meat Carving Knife, with guard, stainless blade
Meat Carving Fork, with guard, stainless
Game Carving Knife, with guard, stainless blade

Game Carving Fork, with guard, stainless
Steel, large, with guard
Bird or Steak Carver with guard, stainless blade
Bird or Steak Fork, with guard, stainless
Steel, small, with guard
Duck or Joint Shears
Bread Knife, H. H.

SINGLE PIECES

Asparagus Server
Baby Spoon, short
Baby Fork, short
Baby Spoon, bent
Baby Knife, H. H.
Berry Spoon, large
Berry Spoon, small
Bonbon Spoon
Bonbon Tongs
Bottle Opener, large
Bottle Opener, small
Butter Knife, bent

Butter Pick, 2 tines
Cheese Server, H. H.
Child's Fork
Child's Knife, H. H.
Chipped Beef Fork, small
Cold Meat Fork, large
Cold Meat Fork, small
Cream Ladle
Cucumber Server
Food Pusher
Fried Egg Server, H. H.
Gravy Ladle

Ice Tongs
Jelly Server
Jelly Spoon
Lemon Fork
Lettuce Fork
Lettuce Spoon
Mayonnaise Ladle
Olive Fork, short
Olive Spoon, short
Pie Server, H. H., large
Pie Server, H. H., small
Preserve Spoon

Pickle Fork
Salad Spoon
Salad Fork
Salad Spoon, olive wood
Salad Fork, olive wood
Salt Spoons, pair, gilt only
Serving Fork, small
Serving Spoon, small
Sugar Spoon
Sugar Tongs, small
Sugar Tongs, large
Tomato Server

No. D-C-04 LINE DINNER WARE

THE "COLFAX" CHASED, GRAY FINISH

D-443 Almond Dish, length 3¼ in., width 2¼ in.
D-442 Bon Bon Dish, length 6¼ in., width 4¼ in.
D-C4 Bowl, diam. 8¼ in., height 3½ in., octagon
D-C8 Bottle Opener, small
D-C8 Bottle Opener, large
D-C4 Bread and Butter Plates, diam. 6 in.
D-C4 Bread Tray, length 12½ in., width 6½ in.
D-C4 Candelabras, 3 lights
D-C4 Candelabras, 5 lights
D-C4 Candlesticks, height 9½ in.
D-C4 Candlesticks, height 11 in.
D-C4 Centrepiece, with mesh, diam. 8⅞ in., height 7 in.
D-C400 Coffee Cups
D-C400 Coffee Cup Saucers
D-C-040-3 Coffee Set, 3 pieces
D-C-040-3 Coffee, capacity, 1¾ pints, height, 7⅝ in.
D-C-040-3 Sugar
D-C-040-3 Cream
D-C-040-3 Tray, diam. 12 in.

D-C-400-3 Tray, well, 10¼ in., extreme length 14⅛ in.
D-C4 Compotier, diam. 7 in., height 3½ in.
D-C4 Compotier, diam. 9 in., height 3¾ in.
D-C4 Entree Dish, diam. 12 in.
D-C4 Entree Dish, diam. 14 in.
D-C40 Goblet, height 5¾ in.
D-C04 Gravy or Sauce Boat, capacity ½ pint
D-C04 Gravy or Sauce Boat Tray, length 8½ in., width 5¾ in.
D-C4 Meat Dish, extreme length 16 in., well 12½ in.
D-C4 Meat Dish, extreme length, 18 in., well 14 in.
D-C4 Meat Dish, extreme length, 20 in., well 15½ in.
D-C4 Meat Dish, extreme length, 22 in., well 17½ in.
D-C40 Peppers, height 4 in.
D-C41 Peppers, height 6¼ in.
D-C04 Salts, height 1¼ in.
D-C040-3 Pitcher Tray, diam. 12 in.
D-C40-3 Pitcher, height 8 in., capacity 4 pints
D-C4 Sandwich Plate, diam. 10½ in.

D-C4 Sandwich Plate with handles, diam. 10½ in., height 5½ in.
D-C4 Service Plates, diam. 10¼ in.
D-C4 Sherbet Cups
D-C8 Tea Bell
D-C-04-3 Tea Set, 5 pieces
D-C-04-3 Coffee, capacity 2¾ pints
D-C-04-3 Tea, capacity 1¾ pints
D-C-04-3 Sugar
D-C-04-3 Cream
D-C-04-3 Waste
D-C-04-3 Kettle, capacity 2 pints
D-C-04-3 Waiter, length 24 in.
D-C04-3 Waiter, 20 in.
D-C41 Vegetable Dish, double, octagon, oblong, length 10½ in., height 4⅝ in., width 6¾ in.
D-C410 Vegetable Dish, open, octagon, oblong, length 10¾ in., height 1⅝ in., width 7¼ in.
D-C-040-3 Waiter, diam. 12 in.
D-C-400-3 Waiter, well 10¼ in., extreme length 14⅛ in.
D-C-04-3 Waiter, 20 in.
D-C-04-3 Waiter, 24 in.

DU BARRY

Alphabetical List of Articles

100 Asparagus Fork
101 Asparagus Tongs
102 Berry Fork
103 Berry Spoon, small
104 Berry Spoon
105 Bouillon Spoon
106 Bouillon Ladle
107 Bonbon Spoon
108 Bonbon Tongs or Sugar, small
109 Butter Knife, small, bent
110 Butter Knife, large, bent
111 Butter Knife, flat
112 Butter Spreader, medium, No. 2
113 Butter Spreader, large, No. 2
114 Butter Spreader, tea handle
115 Butter Spreader, H.H.
116 Butter Pick, gimlet
117 Butter Pick, 2-tine
118 Caddy Spoon
119 Cake Lifter or Waffle Server
120 Cake Knife, saw blade
121 Carving Set, 5-piece
122 Carving Set, 3-piece (bird)
123 Chocolate Spoon, small
124 Chocolate Spoon, large
125 Chocolate Muddler
126 Cheese Knife
127 Cheese Scoop, small
128 Cheese Scoop, medium
129 Cheese Scoop, large
130 Chip Beef Fork, small
131 Chip Beef Fork, large
132 Child's Spoon
133 Child's Knife, flat
134 Child's Fork
135 Coffee Spoon
136 Cold Meat Fork
137 Cold Meat Fork, or Individual Fish Fork, small
138 Cracker Server
139 Cream Ladle
140 Croquette Server, small
141 Croquette Server, large
142 Crumb Knife
143 Cucumber Server, small
144 Cucumber Server, large
145 Dessert Knife, H.H.
146 Egg Spoon
147 Envelope Knife
148 Fish Knife and Fork, medium
149 Fish Knife and Fork, large
150 Fish Knife, Individual
151 Food Pusher
152 Fried Oyster Server
153 Fruit Knife, flat
154 Fruit Knife, H.H.
155 Fruit or Child's Fork, H.H.
156 Gravy Dish Spoon
157 Gravy Ladle

158 Horseradish Spoon, small
159 Horseradish Spoon, large
160 Ice or Nut Spoon
161 Ice-Cream Fork
162 Ice-Cream Spoon
163 Ice-Cream Server
164 Ice-Cream Slicer, H.H.
165 Ice-Cream Slicer
166 Iced Teaspoon, small
167 Iced Teaspoon, large
168 Ice Tongs, large
169 Jelly Knife, No. 6
170 Jelly Spoon
171 Lettuce Fork, large
172 Lettuce Fork, small
173 Lemon Fork
174 Medium Knife, H.H.
175 Mustard Spoon
176 Olive Spoon, long
177 Olive Spoon, short
178 Olive Fork, short
179 Olive Fork, long
180 Orange Spoon
181 Orange Knife, H.H.
182 Oyster Fork, long
183 Oyster Fork, short
184 Oyster Ladle
185 Pap Spoon
186 Pastry Fork
187 Pea Server
188 Pickle Fork, short
189 Pickle Fork, long
190 Pickle Knife
191 Pie Knife
192 Pie Knife, English blade
193 Pie Server, H.H., large
194 Pie Server, H.H., small
195 Punch Ladle
196 Salt Spoon
197 Salad Fork and Spoon, large
198 Salad Fork and Spoon, small
199 Salad Fork, Individual
200 Sardine Fork
201 Sardine Tongs
202 Sherbet Spoon
203 Soup Spoon
204 Soup Ladle
205 Sugar Spoon
206 Sugar Sifter, small
207 Sugar Sifter, No. 3
208 Sugar Tongs, medium
209 Teaspoon, Five O'clock
210 Tea or Child's Knife, H.H.
211 Terrapin Fork
212 Toast Fork
213 Tomato Server
214 Vegetable Spoon
215 Vegetable Fork

THE ESSEX   Prices 1921

DOZEN WORK

Tea Spoons
Small $13.50
Regular 16.50
Medium 22.00
Heavy 25.00
Extra 32.00

Dessert Spoons or Forks
Medium 38.00
Heavy 45.00

Table Spoons or Forks —
Medium 38.00
Heavy 61.00

Soup Spoons 38.00

The Above prices are per dozen.

CUTLERY

Tea knife,
  Stainless Blades, each 2.75
Breakfast Knives,
  Stainless blades, doz 38.00
Dessert Knives,
  Stainless Blades, doz 34.00
Medium or Dinner Knives,
  Stainless Blades, doz 42.00
Fruit Knives,
  Stainless Blades, doz 32.00
Orange Knives,
  Plated Blades, doz 32.00
Meat Carving Knife, with
  guard, Stainless Blade 9.50
Meat Carving Fork, with
  guard, Stainless Blade 9.50
Game Carving Knife with
  guard, Stainless Blade 9.50
Game Carving Fork with
  guard, Stainless blade 9.50
Steel, large, with guard 8.50
Bird or Steak Carver, with
  guard, Stainless 4.75
Bird or Steak Fork, with
  guard, Stainless 4.75
Steel, small, with guard 4.25
Steak Set, small, 2 pcs.
  Stainless 8.00
Broiler Set, 2 pcs. Stainless 5.50
Duck or Joint Shears 10.50
Carver's Asst. or Joint Fork 8.50
Baby Knife, H.H. 2.00
Bread Knife, H.H. 4.00
Cheese Server, H.H. 2.75
Child's Knife, H.H. 2.75
Fried Egg Server, H.H. 3.50
Ice Cream Slicer, H.H. 6.50
Pie Server, H.H. large 4.75
Pie Server, H.H. small 3.50

DOZENS

	Plain	Gift
Boullion Spoons	$21.00	$24.00
Butter Spreaders	25.00	
Chocolate Spoons	17.00	19.00
Coffee Spoons	11.00	12.50
Fish Forks, Ind'l, sm.	33.00	36.00
Fish Forks, Ind'l, lg.	56.00	60.00

	Plain	Gift
Fish Knives, Ind'l, sm.	$74.00	$80.00
Ice Cream Forks	30.00	33.00
Ice Cream Spoons	30.00	33.00
Iced Tea Spoons	30.00	33.00
Orange Spoons	29.00	32.00
Oyster Forks	17.00	18.50
Pastry Forks	34.00	37.00
Salad Forks, Ind'l small	33.00	36.00
Salad Forks, Ind'l large	56.00	60.00
Salt Spoons, Ind'l		7.50
Tea Forks	33.00	

PAIRS

	Plain	Gift
Fish Knife	12.50	14.00
Fish Fork	9.00	10.00
Lettuce Fork	4.75	5.50
Lettuce Spoon	4.75	5.50
Salad Spoon	6.50	7.50
Salad Fork	6.50	7.50
Salad Spoon and Fork Olive wood bowl and Tines	7.50	
Serving Fork, small	8.50	9.50
Serving Spoons, See Table Spoons		

SINGLE PIECES

	Plain	Gift
Asparagus Server	15.50	16.00
Baby Fork, short	2.00	
Baby Spoon, short	2.00	
Baby Spoon, bent	2.00	
Baby knife, H.H.	2.00	
Berry Spoon, lg.	9.00	9.50
Berry Spoon, sm.	6.50	7.00
Bonbon Spoon	2.00	2.25
Bonbon Tongs	2.50	2.75
Butter Knife, bent	4.25	
Butter Pick, 2 tines	2.00	
Child's Fork	2.75	
Chipped Beef Fork, small	3.00	3.25
Cold Meat Fork large	6.50	7.00
Cold Meat Fork, small	4.75	5.00
Cream Ladle	3.00	3.50
Cucumber Server	5.00	5.50
Food Pusher	2.00	
Gravy Ladle	6.50	7.00
Honey Server	2.75	3.00
Ice or Nut Spoon	9.00	9.50
Jelly Spoon	4.75	5.00
Lemon Fork	1.25	1.50
Mayonnaise Ladle	2.75	3.00
Olive Fork, short	2.50	2.75
Olive Spoon, short	2.50	2.74
Oyster Ladle	18.00	19.00
Pastry Server	16.50	17.00
Preserve Spoon	6.50	7.00
Pickle Fork	2.75	3.00
Pie Knife	10.50	11.50
Salt Spoon	1.25	1.50
Sugar Spoon	2.50	1.50
Sugar Tongs, large	3.00	3.25
Sugar Tongs, small	2.50	2.75
Tomato Server	8.50	9.00

FAIRFAX

INDEX

THE NEW FAIRFAX TEA SET AND HOLLOW WARE, SEE PAGE 122

FESSENDEN & CO.
Providence, Rhode Island

Fessenden is not a name any but the most dedicated silver collectors are aware of, but almost uniformly their patterns are lovely and beautifully crafted. The company was founded in 1858 but as early as 1900 some of their patterns were out of production and finding them today is not easy. Their floral examples — Tulip, Narcissus and others are stunning in their beauty and patterns such as Marie Louise, Newport and Avon are well worth searching for. In general, their patterns show outstanding design work, but the designers, as usual, are the unsung heroes, although records indicate that John H. Harmstone was designing for the company in 1920 and patent applications were being made in 1921.

The actual chronology and factory sites of these old companies is fairly easy to track, what is difficult is unravelling the tangled skein of relationships of the companies themselves, who used whose dies and who sold what to whom. Certainly the names Whiting and Manchester are tied to the Fessenden Company. An early trade paper says. ''The firm of Fessenden & Co. was established by William B. Fessenden in 1858 when he moved to Providence after having been in business with W.D. Whiting at North Attleboro for several years. Mr. Fessenden engaged in business for himself in the Calendar Building and remained there for 4 years before moving. When Thomas Fessenden, a son of the founder joined the firm and took strong hold, William Fessenden left the company. Two of the Manchesters of the old silver family joined Fessenden, one in the 1860s and one about a decade later. Fessenden and Company went out of business in the early 1920s, either 1922 or 1923. Fessenden then ceased to be an active name in American silver, but it had been around for a very long time. A Fessenden was working in silver in Newport, Rhode Island as early as 1845 and claimed descent from the silversmith to Elizabeth I of England.

Although collectors do not display passion at mention of the Fessenden name it is a vastly undervalued company. Some patterns are spectacular — Tulip, McKinley, Marie Louise and Newport for example. The output was small compared with many larger companies so collectors do not have a huge body of choice, however the Fessenden mark is distinctive and so is some of its silver.

Ⓕ STERLING ⓒⓄ

Pattern	Date of Issue	Dinner fork	Dessert knife	Dessert fork	Tea-spoon
Alice	c.1888	$40	$35	$42	$30

Alice

Pattern	Date of Issue	Dinner fork	Dessert knife	Dessert fork	Tea-spoon
Antique	c.1880	26	24	28	23

Antique

Pattern	Date of Issue	Dinner fork	Dessert knife	Dessert fork	Tea-spoon
Avon	c.1888	38	32	40	30

Avon

Pattern	Date of Issue	Dinner fork	Dessert knife	Dessert fork	Tea-spoon
Daisy	c.1900	$45	$40	$48	$32

Daisy

Pattern	Date of Issue	Dinner fork	Dessert knife	Dessert fork	Tea-spoon
Graeco	c.1912	38	30	40	28

Graeco

Pattern	Date of Issue	Dinner fork	Dessert knife	Dessert fork	Tea-spoon
Greenwich	c.1890	35	30	38	28

Greenwich

Pattern	Date of Issue	Dinner fork	Dessert knife	Dessert fork	Tea-spoon	Pattern	Date of Issue	Dinner fork	Dessert knife	Dessert fork	Tea-spoon
La Provence	c.1900	$42	$35	$45	$32	Old Rose	c.1890	$38	$35	$40	$30

La Provence

Old Rose

Langdon	c.1915	25	23	26	23	Tremont	c.1910	30	28	32	26

Langdon

Tremont

Marie Louise	c.1905	50	42	55	32	Tulip	c.1915	75	60	80	55

Marie Louise

Tulip

McKinley	c.1900	65	48	65	38

McKinley

Narcissus	c.1915	70	50	75	50

Narcissus

Newport	c.1905	45	35	48	35

Newport

Old Boston	c.1880	30	26	32	28

Old Boston

GORHAM COMPANY

For sheer number of patterns issued The Gorham Company is a colossus. It is also one of the oldest American silver companies having its first pattern in 1831 or 1832, and as with most of the old companies it has a tangled corporate history. It existed until 1989 as a subsidiary of Textron, Inc., a conglomerate but in January, 1989 Gorham was sold to DANSK INTERNATIONAL DESIGNS, LTD. which for its short tenure continued to offer many of the desirable sterling patterns made by Gorham which continued to be marked with the Gorham name. In July, 1990, Brown-Forman Corp., of Louisville, Kentucky purchased Dansk and subsequently its subsidiary, Gorham. Many of the fine older patterns have been eliminated from the line but some are still available by special order.

Still Jabez Gorham is probably whirling in his grave. He was another of those pioneers in the industry, who learned the trade the hard way. It was this background in the rigorous apprentice system of early 19th century America which is directly responsible for the world-wide prominence Gorham later achieved. These apprentices learned well and were trained in skills not only in their main trade but in peripheral areas as well. Thus, although he made his debut as an independent entrepreneur in 1818 as a jeweler he was also wise enough to trade on the expertise of one Henry Webster, a silversmith, and added Webster's excellent spoons to his inventory as early as 1831. The silver spoons sold so well Gorham elevated Webster to a partnership and began a long history of acquisition and expansion. Jabez whose large picture adorned the foyer of the Gorham Silver Company in Providence must have gazed with incredulity at what his little venture had wrought.

The Gorham Company has ever been adaptable and as with all successful companies it was the ability of the leaders to sense changing times and tastes which kept it in the forefront. Machinery, the new machinery powered by steam excited John Gorham, Jabez' son. In 1847 and his early 20s he was open to "progress" and in his position as foreman he was impressed with the potential of the new steam engine to power the machinery. When his father retired in 1847 John really expanded his horizons. His purchase and adaptation of this machinery was probably the single factor which made Gorham a premier maker of silver. It took the obscure little company and transformed it into a prestigious manufacturer. This took courage and foresight as well as intelligence.

John Gorham "a doer" then hired George Wilkinson as designer. Wilkinson alone is responsible for many of the earlier beautiful patterns which moved Gorham toward its eminence not only among other makers, but among consumers. Quality being more or less equal, silver companies did, and still do, stand or die on the strength of their pattern designs.

The Gorham Company survived the terrible years of the Civil War but not without compromise. It accommodated by producing large quantities of electro-plated ware in order to cut back on the use of silver. This early foray into plating ceased before 1900 and it was not until the 1960s that Gorham again emphasized silver plated items.

The company actually adopted the sterling standard in 1868 as well as its well known trademark of the lion - the English hallmark for sterling; and anchor - for the state of Rhode Island; and the capital 'G' for the company name. Interestingly, before 1861 the trademark lion faces right. As Gorham expanded and cornered a large share of the market, it also moved into its "Golden Age of Craftsmanship". The ornate, often magnificent patterns made then are eagerly sought after today. Because of this enduring popularity Dansk Ltd. has recently reactivated the following patterns: Mythologique, Mothers, Adam, Colfax, Dauphin, Roanoke, Old Orange Blossom and Bead. Dansk also promised "that all active products produced today are under the same Gorham name." All the silver manufactured under the Dansk auspices was made in Smithfield, Rhode Island, in what Dansk called "the best silver manufacturing facility in the United States, which Gorham had built approximately three years ago."

Jabez Gorham himself was a progressive company manager and in his son those qualities of willingness to expand and change were magnified. For a very long time 'Gorham' in the silver world became an almost generic term for quality, prosperity and expansion. The fact that the great Gorham Company is now in a somewhat diminished position must disturb the shades of the men who charted its early course and added so many other companies to their own - Whiting, Durgin, Alvin, Kerr, Mt. Vernon, Mauser, Hayes & McFarland, McChesney, and as late as 1959 The Quaker Silver Co., in 1960 The Friedman Silver Co. of Brooklyn and in 1961 Graff, Washbourne & Dunn another old company. In the American silver consciousness only Whiting, Durgin, Alvin and to a much lesser extent, Mt. Vernon, survived. By 1961 Gorham had become so large it matured into a corporation, then in 1967 Textron, Inc., a conglomerate, acquired Gorham and ever after all printed matter bore not only the Gorham name but the Textron name as well. The pointers were indeed surfacing and by the late 1970s Gorham, as with so many other distinctive American companies, was somewhat unsettled. So in January, 1990 Gorham becomes a legend and collectors would do well to look diligently for its many exquisite patterns which can only gain value and prestige as time passes. "Archives" is such a final-sounding word, but indeed, we are told that the "Archives of the Gorham Silver Company" now rest at Brown University in Providence, Rhode Island as part of the John Hay Library.

Some of Gorham's patterns are benchmarks in the production of American Silver, its Chantilly pattern issued in 1895 is consistently on lists of most wanted patterns. Arguably it is the most popular silver pattern ever issued by any company. Buttercup, Medallion, Versailles, among others continue to attract, and Mythologique is masterful. The early, very plain patterns are wonderfully crafted examples of American taste in the early 19th century and should be cherished by collectors. In this age of passion for folk art, they are prime examples of the simple, uncluttered tastes of our ancestors, and they are almost woefully underpriced.

Dansk seems a company which intended to do well by the Gorham name but in this revolving world which is now American sterling silver, Dansk itself was purchased in July of 1990 by Brown-Forman Corp. of Louisville, Kentucky, the rapidly diversifying distillers of Jack Daniel's, Canadian Mist and Southern Comfort. Gorham, a Dansk subsidiary, was also acquired by the same company.

The judgment of future generations on Gorham's magnificent silver will not rest on whatever paths Brown-Forman may choose for it. The quality and distinction of many of its patterns, the very diversity of its early output, the large role of the company in the industrial and social development of the United States are all secure.

Indeed, "gorham" the word rather than the company name is almost generic of silver, American silver. Regardless of the ultimate disposition of Gorham Silver Company as an entity by Brown-Forman, the name is safely embedded in the American psyche.

GORHAM PRICES

Pattern	Date of Issue	Dinner fork	Dessert knife	Dessert fork	Tea-spoon	Pattern	Date of Issue	Dinner fork	Dessert knife	Dessert fork	Tea-spoon
Albermarle	1894	$32	$25	$35	$18	Baronial	1973	$60	$50	$65	$40

Albermarle

Baronial

Alencon Lace	1965	45	35	48	32	Beaumont	1915	32	28	35	26

Alencon Lace

Beaumont

Andante	1957	38	30	40	28	Blithe Spirit	1960	30	25	34	25

Andante

Blithe Spirit

Antique	c.1875	25	19	28	14	Buckingham	1910	40	32	45	30

Antique

Buckingham

Atlanta	1904	45	32	48	32	Buttercup	1899	55	45	58	38

Atlanta

Buttercup

Balzac	1908	42	35	45	35	Cambridge	1899	42	35	45	30

Balzac

Cambridge

Baronial Old	1897	38	25	50	20	Camellia	1941	34	28	35	27

Designed by James Russell Price

Baronial, Old

Camellia

33

Pattern	Date of Issue	Dinner fork	Dessert knife	Dessert fork	Tea-spoon
Celeste	1956	$28	$25	$32	$24

Celeste

Pattern	Date of Issue	Dinner fork	Dessert knife	Dessert fork	Tea-spoon
Cellini	1915	35	28	40	28

Cellini

Pattern	Date of Issue	Dinner fork	Dessert knife	Dessert fork	Tea-spoon
Chantilly	1895	55	45	60	35

Chantilly

Pattern	Date of Issue	Dinner fork	Dessert knife	Dessert fork	Tea-spoon
Chelmsford	1911	37	26	39	28

Chelmsford

Pattern	Date of Issue	Dinner fork	Dessert knife	Dessert fork	Tea-spoon
Chesterfield	1908	45	35	48	28

Chesterfield

Pattern	Date of Issue	Dinner fork	Dessert knife	Dessert fork	Tea-spoon
Chippendale	1890	38	30	45	28

Chippendale

Pattern	Date of Issue	Dinner fork	Dessert knife	Dessert fork	Tea-spoon
Christina	1935	35	28	38	28

Christina

Pattern	Date of Issue	Dinner fork	Dessert knife	Dessert fork	Tea-spoon
Chrysanthemum	c.1885	$38	$30	$40	$28

Chrysanthemum

Pattern	Date of Issue	Dinner fork	Dessert knife	Dessert fork	Tea-spoon
Classic Bouquet	1972	40	32	45	30

Classic Bouquet

Pattern	Date of Issue	Dinner fork	Dessert knife	Dessert fork	Tea-spoon
Classique	1961	35	30	40	30

Pattern	Date of Issue	Dinner fork	Dessert knife	Dessert fork	Tea-spoon
Clermont	1915	32	26	35	27

Clermont

Pattern	Date of Issue	Dinner fork	Dessert knife	Dessert fork	Tea-spoon
Cluny	c.1880	55	36	60	30

Designed by F. Antoine Heller

Cluny

Pattern	Date of Issue	Dinner fork	Dessert knife	Dessert fork	Tea-spoon
Colfax	1922	27	24	29	24

Colfax

Pattern	Date of Issue	Dinner fork	Dessert knife	Dessert fork	Tea-spoon
Colonial	1885	32	25	37	25

Colonial

GORHAM

Pattern	Date of Issue	Dinner fork	Dessert knife	Dessert fork	Tea-spoon
Colonial Eagle	1960	$30	$24	$34	$26

Colonial Eagle

Pattern	Date of Issue	Dinner fork	Dessert knife	Dessert fork	Tea-spoon
Corinthian	1871	34	26	38	28

Corinthian

Pattern	Date of Issue	Dinner fork	Dessert knife	Dessert fork	Tea-spoon
Cottage	1861	26	23	28	18

Cottage

Pattern	Date of Issue	Dinner fork	Dessert knife	Dessert fork	Tea-spoon
Covington	1914	36	28	38	25

Covington

Covington hammered

Covington engraved

Pattern	Date of Issue	Dinner fork	Dessert knife	Dessert fork	Tea-spoon
Cromwell	1900	32	25	34	26

Cromwell

Pattern	Date of Issue	Dinner fork	Dessert knife	Dessert fork	Tea-spoon
Crown Baroque	1975	$75	$55	$85	$45

Crown Baroque

Pattern	Date of Issue	Dinner fork	Dessert knife	Dessert fork	Tea-spoon
Golden Crown Baroque	1975	78	58	88	48

Golden Crown Baroque

Pattern	Date of Issue	Dinner fork	Dessert knife	Dessert fork	Tea-spoon
Decor	1953	60	48	65	40

Decor

Pattern	Date of Issue	Dinner fork	Dessert knife	Dessert fork	Tea-spoon
Dolly Madison	1929	25	21	28	20

Dolly Madison

Pattern	Date of Issue	Dinner fork	Dessert knife	Dessert fork	Tea-spoon
Edgemont and Edgemont Gold	1987	50	40	55	38
	1987	60	50	65	40

Edgemont

Pattern	Date of Issue	Dinner fork	Dessert knife	Dessert fork	Tea-spoon
Edgeworth	1922	27	22	30	19

Edgeworth

Pattern	Date of Issue	Dinner fork	Dessert knife	Dessert fork	Tea-spoon
English Gadroon	1939	$37	$28	$40	$20

English Gadroon

Pattern	Date of Issue	Dinner fork	Dessert knife	Dessert fork	Tea-spoon
Esprit	1963	25	20	27	16

Esprit

Etruscan by William C. Codman	1913	40	30	37	28

Etruscan

Etruscan engraved	1913	42	32	45	29

Etruscan, engraved

Eventide	1936	25	20	28	19

Eventide

Fanshawe designed by Alex H. Staf	1922	28	23	30	22

Fanshawe

Firelight	1959	25	19	28	21

Firelight

Pattern	Date of Issue	Dinner fork	Dessert knife	Dessert fork	Tea-spoon
Fleury	1909	$40	$36	$45	$30

Florentine	1901	50	35	55	30

Florentine

Gold Cipher	1952	30	25	32	25

Gold Cipher

Gold Tip	1952	30	25	32	25

Gold Tip

Golden Scroll	1977	38	32	40	30

Golden Scroll

Golden Snowflake	1952	30	25	32	25

Golden Snowflake

Golden Stardust	1952	30	25	32	25

Golden Stardust

Golden Wheat	1952	35	26	38	25

Golden Wheat

GORHAM

Pattern	Date of Issue	Dinner fork	Dessert knife	Dessert fork	Tea-spoon
Gorham	c.1880	$27	$23	$28	$20

Gorham

Pattern	Date of Issue	Dinner fork	Dessert knife	Dessert fork	Tea-spoon
Gossamer	1965	28	24	30	20
Gossamer, engraved	1966	28	24	30	20

Gossamer

Pattern	Date of Issue	Dinner fork	Dessert knife	Dessert fork	Tea-spoon
Governor's Lady	1937	25	20	28	19
Governor's Lady, engraved A & B	1937	25	20	28	17

Governer's Lady

Pattern	Date of Issue	Dinner fork	Dessert knife	Dessert fork	Tea-spoon
Greenbrier	1938	27	21	29	14

Greenbrier

Pattern	Date of Issue	Dinner fork	Dessert knife	Dessert fork	Tea-spoon
Griswold	1922	30	23	34	18

Griswold

Pattern	Date of Issue	Dinner fork	Dessert knife	Dessert fork	Tea-spoon
Hamilton	1908	22	18	22	19

Hamilton

Pattern	Date of Issue	Dinner fork	Dessert knife	Dessert fork	Tea-spoon
Hazelmere	1914	28	23	30	24

Hazelmere

Pattern	Date of Issue	Dinner fork	Dessert knife	Dessert fork	T spo
Hunt Club	1930	$30	$27	$32	$25

Hunt Club

Pattern	Date of Issue	Dinner fork	Dessert knife	Dessert fork	T spo
Imperial Chrysanthemum	1894	65	50	65	46

Imperial Chrysanthemum

Pattern	Date of Issue	Dinner fork	Dessert knife	Dessert fork	T spo
Jefferson	1907	24	21	28	19

Jefferson

Pattern	Date of Issue	Dinner fork	Dessert knife	Dessert fork	T spo
King Edward	1936	42	32	48	30

King Edward

Pattern	Date of Issue	Dinner fork	Dessert knife	Dessert fork	T spo
King George	1894	38	26	42	28

King George

Pattern	Date of Issue	Dinner fork	Dessert knife	Dessert fork	T spo
Knickerbocker, engraved	c.1870	24	20	28	22

Knickerbocker

	Date of Issue	Dinner fork	Dessert knife	Dessert fork	Tea-spoon

Pattern	Date of Issue	Dinner fork	Dessert knife	Dessert fork	Tea-spoon

Pattern	Date of Issue	Dinner fork	Dessert knife	Dessert fork	Tea-spoon
...Washington designed by George Wilkinson	1876	$95	$70	$100	$45

Lady Washington

| La Modele | 1909 | 40 | 32 | 45 | 28 |

La Modele

| Lancaster | 1897 | 44 | 32 | 55 | 27 |

Lancaster

| Lansdowne | 1917 | 38 | 30 | 42 | 30 |

Lansdowne

| Late Georgian designed by Frederick R. Woodward of Attleboro, Mass. | 1934 | 35 | 30 | 40 | 30 |

Late Georgian

| LaScala designed by Peter C. Gavette | 1964 | 65 | 50 | 72 | 40 |

LaScala

| Leaf Twist | c.1890 | 65 | 45 | 65 | 36 |

Leaf Twist

| Lenox | 1897 | $32 | $24 | $38 | $25 |

Lenox

| Lily of the Valley designed by James Russell Price | 1950 | 45 | 34 | 48 | 30 |

Lily of the Valley

| Luxembourg | 1893 | 80 | 65 | 90 | 40 |

Luxembourg

| Lyric | 1940 | 30 | 23 | 32 | 21 |

Lyric

| Marie Antoinette | 1891 | 75 | 60 | 80 | 45 |

Marie Antoinette

| Martha Washington | 1907 | 27 | 21 | 29 | 19 |

Marth Washington

GORHAM

Pattern	Date of Issue	Dinner fork	Dessert knife	Dessert fork	Tea-spoon
Medallion	1864	$150	$100	$185	$65

Medallion

Pattern	Date of Issue	Dinner fork	Dessert knife	Dessert fork	Tea-spoon
Medici, old	c.1880	85	65	90	48

Medici, Old

Pattern	Date of Issue	Dinner fork	Dessert knife	Dessert fork	Tea-spoon
Medici	1971	65	45	70	50

Medici

Pattern	Date of Issue	Dinner fork	Dessert knife	Dessert fork	Tea-spoon
Golden Medici	1971	68	48	72	54

Golden Medici

Pattern	Date of Issue	Dinner fork	Dessert knife	Dessert fork	Tea-spoon
Melrose	1908	35	27	38	24

Melrose

Pattern	Date of Issue	Dinner fork	Dessert knife	Dessert fork	Tea-spoon
Melrose	1948	39	29	40	25

Melrose

Pattern	Date of Issue	Dinner fork	Dessert knife	Dessert fork	Tea-spoon
Modern American	1928	$30	$25	$34	$22

Modern American

Pattern	Date of Issue	Dinner fork	Dessert knife	Dessert fork	Tea-spoon
Montclair	1908	45	35	50	30

Montclair

Pattern	Date of Issue	Dinner fork	Dessert knife	Dessert fork	Tea-spoon
Mothers	1875	25	22	27	24
Mothers, hammered	c.1875	27	24	29	25
Mothers, engraved	1875	21	17	24	14

Mothers

Mothers, engraved

Pattern	Date of Issue	Dinner fork	Dessert knife	Dessert fork	Tea-spoon
Mythologique	1894	125	90	145	85

Designed by F. Antoine Heller

Mythologique

Pattern	Date of Issue	Dinner fork	Dessert knife	Dessert fork	Tea-spoon
Newcastle	1895	28	22	35	20

Newcastle

Pattern	Date of Issue	Dinner fork	Dessert knife	Dessert fork	Tea-spoon
Newport Scroll	1983	$50	$45	$65	$40

Newport Scroll

Pattern	Date of Issue	Dinner fork	Dessert knife	Dessert fork	Tea-spoon
New Tipt	c.1870	45	35	48	34

New Tipt

Pattern	Date of Issue	Dinner fork	Dessert knife	Dessert fork	Tea-spoon
Nocturne Designed by James Russell Price	1938	36	26	38	27

Nocturne

Pattern	Date of Issue	Dinner fork	Dessert knife	Dessert fork	Tea-spoon
Norfolk	1903	30	25	27	24

Norfolk

Pattern	Date of Issue	Dinner fork	Dessert knife	Dessert fork	Tea-spoon
Old Dominion	1912	28	22	32	20

Old Dominion

Pattern	Date of Issue	Dinner fork	Dessert knife	Dessert fork	Tea-spoon
Old English Tipt	1870	28	25	30	18
Old English Tipt, engraved (A)	1870	26	22	28	22

Old English Tipt

Pattern	Date of Issue	Dinner fork	Dessert knife	Dessert fork	Tea-spoon
Old French	1905	40	28	35	27

Old French

Pattern	Date of Issue	Dinner fork	Dessert knife	Dessert fork	Tea-spoon
Old London, engraved	1916	$28	$22	$30	$22

Old London, engraved

Pattern	Date of Issue	Dinner fork	Dessert knife	Dessert fork	Tea-spoon
Old London	1916	28	22	30	22

Old London

Pattern	Date of Issue	Dinner fork	Dessert knife	Dessert fork	Tea-spoon
Old Maryland	1885	27	21	30	15

Pattern	Date of Issue	Dinner fork	Dessert knife	Dessert fork	Tea-spoon
Old Masters designed by T. Antoine Heller	c.1885	155	85	165	85

Old Masters

Pattern	Date of Issue	Dinner fork	Dessert knife	Dessert fork	Tea-spoon
Paris	1900	100	75	135	65

Paris

Pattern	Date of Issue	Dinner fork	Dessert knife	Dessert fork	Tea-spoon
Pembroke	1895	28	24	30	21

Pembroke

Pattern	Date of Issue	Dinner fork	Dessert knife	Dessert fork	Tea-spoon
Plymouth	1900	24	21	28	16

Plymouth

GORHAM

Pattern	Date of Issue	Dinner fork	Dessert knife	Dessert fork	Tea-spoon
Plymouth	1911	$36	$32	$40	$26

Plymouth

Pattern	Date of Issue	Dinner fork	Dessert knife	Dessert fork	Tea-spoon
Poppy	c.1894	65	45	68	35

Poppy

Pattern	Date of Issue	Dinner fork	Dessert knife	Dessert fork	Tea-spoon
Portland	1904	36	30	40	28

Portland

Pattern	Date of Issue	Dinner fork	Dessert knife	Dessert fork	Tea-spoon
Portsmouth	1918	28	22	28	24

Portsmouth

Pattern	Date of Issue	Dinner fork	Dessert knife	Dessert fork	Tea-spoon
Raphael	1877	75	55	80	40

Raphael

Pattern	Date of Issue	Dinner fork	Dessert knife	Dessert fork	Tea-spoon
Regent	1892	48	36	50	32

Regent

Pattern	Date of Issue	Dinner fork	Dessert knife	Dessert fork	Tea-spoon
Roanoke	1913	$60	$40	$65	$36

Roanoke

Pattern	Date of Issue	Dinner fork	Dessert knife	Dessert fork	Tea-spoon
Roman	1855	26	23	28	18

this pattern was made in electroplate

Roman

Pattern	Date of Issue	Dinner fork	Dessert knife	Dessert fork	Tea-spoon
Rondo	1951	40	30	45	28

Rondo

Pattern	Date of Issue	Dinner fork	Dessert knife	Dessert fork	Tea-spoon
Rose Marie	1933	32	28	35	24

designed by Alex H. Staf

Rose Marie

Pattern	Date of Issue	Dinner fork	Dessert knife	Dessert fork	Tea-spoon
Rosemont	1915	42	32	48	30

Rosemont

GORHAM

Pattern	Date of Issue	Dinner fork	Dessert knife	Dessert fork	Tea-spoon
Rosette	1868	$50	$40	$55	$35

Rosette

Pattern	Date of Issue	Dinner fork	Dessert knife	Dessert fork	Tea-spoon
Rose Tiara	1963	36	30	38	26

Rose Tiara

Pattern	Date of Issue	Dinner fork	Dessert knife	Dessert fork	Tea-spoon
Royal Oak	1904	45	30	48	27

Royal Oak

Pattern	Date of Issue	Dinner fork	Dessert knife	Dessert fork	Tea-spoon
St. Cloud	c.1885	95	75	45	30

St. Cloud

Pattern	Date of Issue	Dinner fork	Dessert knife	Dessert fork	Tea-spoon
St. Dunstan	1916	42	36	45	25

St. Dunstan

Pattern	Date of Issue	Dinner fork	Dessert knife	Dessert fork	Tea-spoon
St. Dustan, chased	1917	54	38	48	27

St. Dustan, chased

Pattern	Date of Issue	Dinner fork	Dessert knife	Dessert fork	Tea-spoon
Sea Rose	1958	$27	$23	$30	$22

Sea Rose

Pattern	Date of Issue	Dinner fork	Dessert knife	Dessert fork	Tea-spoon
Sea Sculpture	1986	48	38	50	35

Sea Sculpture

Pattern	Date of Issue	Dinner fork	Dessert knife	Dessert fork	Tea-spoon
Secret Garden	1959	38	30	40	25

Secret Garden

Pattern	Date of Issue	Dinner fork	Dessert knife	Dessert fork	Tea-spoon
Shamrock V	1931	30	25	34	22

Shamrock V

Pattern	Date of Issue	Dinner fork	Dessert knife	Dessert fork	Tea-spoon
Sovereign designed by James Russell Price	1941	45	30	41	26

Sovereign

Pattern	Date of Issue	Dinner fork	Dessert knife	Dessert fork	Tea-spoon
Sovereign and Golden Sovereign	1968	65	40	70	40

Golden Sovereign

Hispania, now renamed sovereign was still being advertised under the original name in the 1970s.

GORHAM

Pattern	Date of Issue	Dinner fork	Dessert knife	Dessert fork	Tea-spoon
Spanish Tracery	1970	$45	$35	$45	$28

Spanish Tracery

Pattern	Date of Issue	Dinner fork	Dessert knife	Dessert fork	Tea-spoon
Spotswood	1912	40	30	42	29

Spotswood

Pattern	Date of Issue	Dinner fork	Dessert knife	Dessert fork	Tea-spoon
Stamford	1914	40	30	42	29

Stamford

Pattern	Date of Issue	Dinner fork	Dessert knife	Dessert fork	Tea-spoon
Stardust and Golden Stardust	1957	25	18	28	21

Stardust

Pattern	Date of Issue	Dinner fork	Dessert knife	Dessert fork	Tea-spoon
Strasbourg	1897	50	38	52	35

Strasbourg

Pattern	Date of Issue	Dinner fork	Dessert knife	Dessert fork	Tea-spoon
Swansea	1919	27	22	29	20

Swansea

Pattern	Date of Issue	Dinner fork	Dessert knife	Dessert fork	Tea-spoon
Swiss	1870	28	22	30	21

Swiss

Pattern	Date of Issue	Dinner fork	Dessert knife	Dessert fork	Tea-spoon
Theme	1954	$25	$20	$27	$16

Theme

Pattern	Date of Issue	Dinner fork	Dessert knife	Dessert fork	Tea-spoon
Tipt	1840	27	23	30	24

Tipt

Pattern	Date of Issue	Dinner fork	Dessert knife	Dessert fork	Tea-spoon
Touraine	1917	40	30	45	25

Touraine

Pattern	Date of Issue	Dinner fork	Dessert knife	Dessert fork	Tea-spoon
Tuileries	1906	45	35	48	29

Tuileries

Pattern	Date of Issue	Dinner fork	Dessert knife	Dessert fork	Tea-spoon
Versailles	1888	95	75	55	35

Versailles

Pattern	Date of Issue	Dinner fork	Dessert knife	Dessert fork	Tea-spoon
Vine	before 1910	45	30	50	28

Vine

Pattern	Date of Issue	Dinner fork	Dessert knife	Dessert fork	Tea-spoon
Virgiana	1905	45	32	48	30

Virgiana

Pattern	Date of Issue	Dinner fork	Dessert knife	Dessert fork	Tea-spoon
Weymouth	1914	$38	$32	$40	$28

Weymouth

| White Paisley | 1966 | 28 | 22 | 30 | 22 |

White Paisley

| Willow | 1954 | 24 | 20 | 26 | 21 |

Willow

| Wreath | 1911 | 35 | 32 | 38 | 27 |

Wreath

| Wyndham | 1911 | 38 | 30 | 38 | 26 |

Wyndham

| Zodiac | 1906 | 95 | 50 | 125 | 55 |

Zodiac

The Antique

These photos give an entirely new perspective to this pattern.

Table

Table

Dessert

Tea

The Atlanta
1904

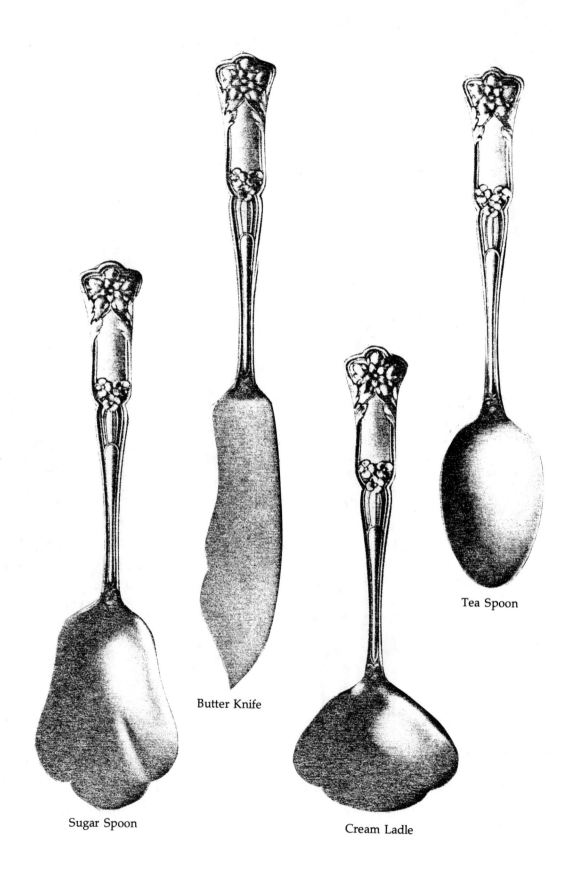

Sugar Spoon

Butter Knife

Cream Ladle

Tea Spoon

The Baronial

This pattern in point of design is pure Renaissance; is strong and massive, and embodying all the characteristics of that period. Hence this design will be appreciated by those who seek a pattern especially designed to suit massive surroundings.

LIST OF PIECES

SPOONS

Berry, large
Bonbon
Bouillon
Chocolate, large
Chocolate, small
Coffee
Confection
Cracker
Dessert
Egg
Gravy
Horse Radish
Ice
Ice Cream, large
Ice Cream, small
Jelly
Lettuce Salad
Mustard
Nut
Olive
Olive, long
Orange
Pap
Pea
Preserve
Salad, large
Salad, small
Salt
Serving
Sorbet
Soup
Sugar
Table
Tea
Vegetable

FORKS

Asparagus
Beef
Berry
Cheese
Cold Meat, large
Cold Meat, small
Dessert
Fish, large
Fish, small
Fish, Ind., large
Fish, Ind., small
Ice Cream, small
Lettuce
Olive

Olive, long
Oyster
Pastry
Pickle
Pie
Salad, large
Salad, small
Salad, Ind., large
Salad, Ind., small
Sardine
Serving
Table
Tea
Toast
Vegetable

KNIVES

Butter
Butter Spreader
Cake, flat
Cheese
Crumb, flat
Dessert, flat
Fish, large
Fish, small
Fish, Ind., large
Fish, Ind., small
Ice Cream Slicer, large, H.H.
Ice Cream Slicer, small flat
Jelly, large
Jelly, small
Macaroni
Pickle
Pie
Tea, flat
Waffle

CUTLERY

Dessert Knives, H.H.
Dessert Knives, H.H., unplated blades
Medium Knives, H.H.
Medium Knives, H.H., unplated blades
Tea Knives, H.H.

Fruit, H.H.
Orange, H.H.
Meat Carver
Meat Fork
Steel
Game Carver
Game Fork
Steak Carver
Steak Fork
Steak Steel
Joint Fork, large
Bone Holder
Knife Sharpener
Bird Knives
Bird Forks

LADLES AND SIFTERS

Cream Ladle, large
Cream Ladle, small
Gravy Ladle
Soup Ladle, large
Soup Ladle, small
Sugar Sifter, large
Sugar Sifter, small
Sugar Sifter, new style

SERVERS

Asparagus
Cake
Entree
Fried Oyster
Pie, H.H.
Saratoga Chips
Sliced Tomato, large
Sliced Tomato, small

MISCELLANEOUS

Asparagus Tongs
Asparagus Tongs, Ind.
Butter Pick
Cheese Scoop, large
Cheese Scoop, small
Chocolate Muddler
Food Pusher
Ice Tongs
Nut Picks
Sugar Tongs, large
Sugar Tongs, small

front view

back view

47

Baronial

Table

Table

Dessert

Dessert

Buckingham

This pattern is English in conception, belonging to the period of Wren and Chippendale, and may be traced back through this English style as all examples of this style may be traced back to the great decorative period of the transition between Louis XV and Louis XVI of France. This transition gave birth to and served as the inspiration for the masterpieces of decorative art of the 18th Century in England. So closely linked is the decorative art of this period in different countries, that an example such as this is equally appropriate in different surroundings, — for example, it is perfectly harmonious with the late Louis XV or early Louis XVI., with the English 18th Century or Chippendale, and with the Colonial.

LIST OF PIECES

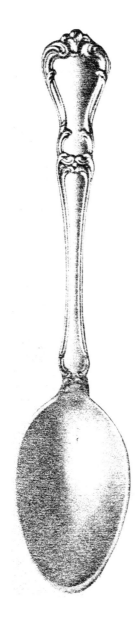

SPOONS
Baby
Berry
Bonbon
Bouillon
Chocolate
Coffee
Dessert
Gravy
Grape Fruit
Ice
Ice Cream
Iced Tea
Jelly
Mustard
Nut
Olive
Olive, long
Orange
Pap
Pea
Preserve
Salad, large
Salad, small
Salt
Serving
Sherbet
Soup
Sugar
Table
Tea

FORKS
Asparagus
Beef
Cold Meat, large
Cold Meat, extra
Dessert
Fish, large
Fish, small
Fish, Ind.
Ice Cream
Lettuce
Lemon

Olive
Olive, long
Oyster
Pastry
Ramekin
Salad, large
Salad, small
Salad, Ind.
Sardine
Serving
Table
Tea

KNIVES
Butter
Butter, small
Butter Spreaders
Crumb, flat
Fish, large
Fish, small
Fish, Ind.
Ice Cream Slicer, large, H.H.
Ice Cream Slicer, small flat
Ice Cream Slicer, steel blade
Jelly
Pie

CUTLERY
Dessert Knives, H.H.
Dessert Knives, H.H., unplated blades
Medium Knives, H.H.
Medium Knives, H.H., unplated blades
Tea Knives, H.H.
Fruit, H.H.
Orange, H.H.
Duck Shears
Meat Carver
Meat Fork
Steel Game Carver

Game Fork
Steak Carver
Steak Fork
Steak Steel
Joint Fork, large

LADLES AND SIFTERS
Bouillon Ladle
Cream Ladle, large
Cream Ladle, small
Gravy Ladle
Soup Ladle
Sugar Sifter, large

SERVERS
Asparagus
Cake
Cheese
Entree
Pie, H.H.
Saratoga Chips
Sliced Tomato, large
Sliced Tomato, small

MISCELLANEOUS
Asparagus Tongs, Ind.
Butter Pick
Cheese Scoop, large
Cheese Scoop, small
Food Pushers
Ice Tongs
Sandwich Tongs
Sugar Tongs, large
Sugar Tongs, small
Tea Maker

Buckingham

Dessert

Dessert

Table

Table

The Buttercup

The beautiful and familiar buttercup has been used as the principal decorative motif, avoiding in its treatment all crudity, yet retaining the conventional in flower and foliage.

In the handle every detail is brought out in strong relief.

In the decoration of the bowls and tines of the Fancy Pieces the designer has been most successful in producing an effect in harmony with the general design.

LIST OF PIECES

SPOONS

Baby
Bar
Berry, large
Berry, small
Bonbon
Bouillon
Breakfast
Chocolate
Coffee
Confection
Cracker
Dessert
Egg
Grape Fruit
Gravy
Honey
Horse Radish
Ice
Ice Cream
Iced Tea
Jelly
Lettuce Salad
Mustard
Nut
Olive
Olive, long
Orange
Pap
Pea
Preserve
Relish
Salad, large
Salad, small
Salt
Salt, Ind.
Serving
Sherbet
Sorbet
Soup
Sugar
Table
Tea
Vegetable

Fruit
Ice Cream
Lemon
Lettuce
Lettuce Salad
Olive
Olive, long
Oyster
Pastry
Pickle
Pie
Ramekin
Relish
Salad, large
Salad, small
Salad, Ind., large
Salad, Ind., small
Sardine
Serving
Table
Tea
Toast
Vegetable

KNIVES

Butter
Butter Spreaders
Butter Spreaders,
   steel blades
Cake, flat
Cheese
Crumb, flat
Dessert, flat
Fish, large
Fish, small
Fish, Ind.
Ice Cream Slicer,
   large, H.H.
Ice Cream Slicer,
   small, flat
Ice Cream Slicer,
   steel blade
Jelly, large
Macaroni
Pickle
Pie
Waffle

CUTLERY

Dessert Knives,
   H.H.
Dessert Knives,
   H.H., uplated
   blades
Medium Knives,
   H.H.
Medium Knives
   H.H., unplated
   blades

Tea Knives, H.H.
Fruit H.H.
Orange, H.H.
Duck Shears
Meat Carver
Meat Fork
Steel
Game Carver
Game Fork
Steak Carver
Steak Fork
Steak Steel
Joint Fork, large
Knife Sharpener
Bird Knives
Bird Forks

LADLES AND SIFTERS

Bouillon Ladle
Cream Ladle, large
Cream Ladle, small
Gravy Ladle
Mayonnaise Ladle
Punch Ladle
Soup Ladle, large
Soup Ladle, small
Sugar Sifter
Sugar Sifter, new
   style

SERVERS

Asparagus
Bouillon
Cake
Entree
Pie, H.H.
Saratoga Chips
Sliced Tomato,
   large
Sliced Tomato,
   small

MISCELLANEOUS

Asparagus Tongs
Asparagus Tongs,
   Ind.
Butter Pick
Cheese Scoop,
   large
Cheese Scoop,
   small
Chocolate Muddler
Food Pusher
Ice Tongs
Sandwich Tongs
Sugar Tongs, large
Sugar Tongs, small
Tea Maker

FORKS

Asparagus
Beef
Berry
Cold Meat, large
Cold Meat, small
Dessert
Fish, large
Fish, small
Fish, Ind., large
Fish, Ind., small

Buttercup

Dessert

Dessert

Table

Table

The Chantilly

The Chantilly is essentially a pattern that will appeal to those who seek in the family silver a certain simplicity with just enough ornament to relieve it of the appearance of plainness.

This is French in character of design and derives its name from the famous palace of Chantilly, situated some twenty odd miles from Paris. It is of the time of Louis XV. Silversmithing had greatly improved from the time of Louis XIV to the latter part of the reign of Louis XV, and this was a period of great refinement of taste in designs for silverware, furniture, and decoration.

LIST OF PIECES

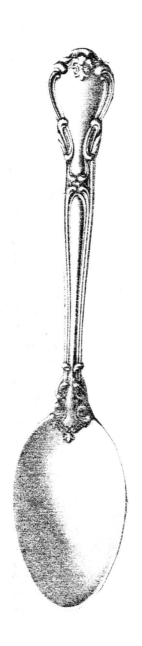

SPOONS

Baby
Berry, large
Berry, small
Bonbon
Bouillon
Chocolate
Coffee
Confection
Cracker
Dressing
Egg
Grape Fruit
Gravy
Honey
Horse Radish
Ice
Ice Cream
Iced Tea
Jelly
Lettuce Salad
Mustard
Nut
Olive
Olive, long
Orange
Pap
Pea
Preserve
Relish
Salad, large
Salad, small
Salt
Salt, Ind.
Serving
Sorbet
Sugar
Vegetable

FORKS

Asparagus
Beef
Beef, small
Berry
Cold Meat, large
Cold Meat, small
Cold Meat, extra
Fish, large
Fish, small
Fish, Ind., large
Fish, Ind., small
Ice Cream
Lettuce
Lettuce Salad
Olive

Olive, long
Oyster
Pastry
Pickle
Pie
Salad, large
Salad, small
Salad, Ind., large
Salad, Ind., small
Sardine
Serving
Tea
Vegetable

KNIVES

Butter
Butter Spreader
Cake
Cheese
Crumb
Dessert, flat
Fish, large
Fish, small
Fish, Ind.
Fruit, H.H.
Ice Cream Slicer, large, H.H.
Ice Cream Slicer, small, flat
Ice Cream Slicer, steel blade
Jelly
Orange, H.H.
Pickle
Pie
Waffle

CUTLERY

Dessert Knives, H.H.
Dessert Knives, H.H., unplated blades
Medium Knives, H.H.
Medium Knives, H.H., unplated blades
Tea Knives, H.H.
Duck Shears
Carving Knife
Carving Fork
Steel

Game Knife
Game Fork
Steak Carving Knife
Steak Carving Fork
Steak Steel
Joint Fork, large
Bone Holder
Knife Sharpener
Bird Knives
Bird Forks

LADLES AND SIFTERS

Bouillon Ladle
Cream Ladle, large
Cream Ladle, small
Gravy Ladle
Mayonnaise Ladle
Punch Ladle
Soup Ladle, large
Soup Ladle, small
Sugar Sifter

SERVERS

Asparagus
Cake
Cheese
Cucumber
Entree
Fried Oyster
Pie
Saratoga Chips
Sliced Tomato, large
Sliced Tomato, small

MISCELLANEOUS

Asparagus Tongs
Bonbon Tongs
Butter Pick
Cheese Scoop, large
Cheese Scoop, small
Chocolate Muddler
Food Pusher
Ice Tongs
Sandwich Tongs
Sugar Tongs, large
Sugar Tongs, small
Tea Maker
Cheese Scoop, large
Cheese Scoop, small

Chantilly

Table

Table

Dessert

Dessert

The Chesterfield

Out of the latter half of the XVIII century there are few figures more interesting than that of Lord Stanhope, Earl of Chesterfield, statesman, wit and man of fashion.

His epoch was marked in literature and art by a revival of the classical ideals. The excavations at Pompeii, begun in 1748, were revealing treasures of ancient art which public taste was eagerly turning to for inspiration. Silverware, furniture and decorative art in general were reverting to a style more austere and subdued than that which had preceded.

In its chaste and severely simple outline, the motif of the pattern is truly characteristic of the times. The decorative effect, obtained by a tasteful arrangement of husks, swags, Grecian border, and such motifs of the period, is most happy in producing a design thoroughly representative of Chesterfield and his epoch in elegance and refinement worthy of the period.

LIST OF PIECES

SPOONS

Berry, large, engraved
Berry, large, not engraved
Bonbon
Bouillon
Chocolate, large. To order only
Chocolate, small
Coffee
Confection, engraved
Confection, not engraved
Dessert
Egg
Grape Fruit
Gravy
Honey
Ice, engraved
Ice, not engraved
Ice Cream
Iced Tea
Jelly, engraved
Jelly, not engraved
Mustard
Nut, engraved
Nut, not engraved
Olive
Olive, long
Orange
Pap
Preserve, engraved
Preserve, not engraved
Salad
Salt
Serving
Sorbet
Soup
Sugar
Table
Tea

FORKS

Asparagus, engraved
Asparagus, not engraved
Beef
Berry
Cold Meat, large, engraved
Cold Meat, large not engraved
Cold Meat, small, engraved
Cold Meat, small, not engraved
Dessert
Fish, engraved
Fish, Ind., large
Fish, Ind., small
Fruit. To order only
Ice Cream
Lemon
Lettuce
Lettuce Salad
Jelly, engraved
Jelly, not engraved
Pickle
Pie, engraved
Pie, not engraved

CUTLERY

Dessert Knives, H.H.
Dessert Knives, H.H., unplated blades
Medium Knives, H.H.
Medium Knives, H.H., unplated blades
Tea Knives, H.H.
Fruit, H.H.
Orange, H.H.
Duck Shears
Meat Carver
Meat Fork
Steel Game Carver
Olive
Olive, long
Oyster
Pastry

Pickle
Ramekin
Salad
Salad, Ind., small
Salad, Ind., large
Sardine
Serving
Table
Tea

KNIVES

Butter
Butter, small
Butter Spreaders
Crumb, flat, engraved
Crumb, not engraved
Fish, engraved
Fish, Ind.
Ice Cream Slicer, large, H.H. engraved. Made to order only
Ice Cream Slicer, H.H., not engraved
Ice Cream Slicer, steel blade
Game Fork
Steak Carver
Steak Fork
Steak Steel
Joint Fork, large

LADLES AND SIFTERS

Cream Ladle, large
Cream Ladle, small
Gravy Ladle
Mayonnaise Ladle
Soup Ladle
Sugar Sifter, large
Sugar Sifter, small

SERVERS

Asparagus
Cake
Cucumber
Entree, engraved
Entree, not engraved
Fried Oyster, engraved

Pie, H.H.
Sliced Tomato, engraved
Sliced Tomato, not engraved

MISCELLANEOUS

Butter Pick
Cheese Scoop, large
Cheese Scoop, small
Food Pusher
Ice Tongs
Sandwich Tongs
Sugar Tongs
Tea Maker

Chesterfield

Table

Table

Dessert

Dessert

The Cromwell
Bright Finish

Is less ornate in design than many patterns on the market. In designing the spoon the endeavor was to get a plain, generous form with simple ornament, and no better period could be taken than that of the "Round Heads" of the latter period, plain, good, and solid.

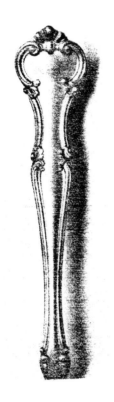

LIST OF PIECES

SPOONS
Berry, large
Bonbon
Bouillon
Chocolate, large
Chocolate, small
Coffee
Cracker
Dessert
Egg
Gravy
Ice
Ice Cream
Jelly
Mustard
Nut
Olive
Olive, long
Orange
Pap
Pea
Preserve
Salad, large
Salad, small
Salt
Serving
Sorbet
Soup
Sugar, large
Table
Tea
Vegetable

FORKS
Asparagus
Beef
Cold Meat, large
Cold Meat, small
Dessert
Fish, large
Fish, Ind., large
Fruit
Ice Cream
Lettuce
Lettuce Salad
Olive
Olive, long
Oyster
Pickle
Pie
Salad, large
Salad, small
Salad, Ind., large
Sardine
Serving
Tea
Table
Toast
Vegetable

KNIVES
Butter
Butter, small
Butter Spreaders,
Cake, flat
Crumb, flat
Fish, large
Fish, Ind., large
Ice Cream Slicer,
  large, H.H.
Ice Cream Slicer,
  small, flat
Jelly, large
Macaroni
Pickle
Pie
Waffle

CUTLERY
Dessert Knives,
  H.H.
Dessert Knives,
  H.H., unplated
  blades
Medium Knives,
  H.H.
Medium Knives
  H.H., unplated
  blades
Tea Knives, H.H.
Fruit H.H.
Orange Knives,
H.H.
Duck Shears
Meat Carver
Meat Fork
Steel
Game Carver
Game Fork
Steak Carver
Steak Fork
Steak Steel
Joint Fork, large
Bird Knives
Bird Forks

LADLES AND SIFTERS
Bouillon Ladle
Cream Ladle, large
Cream Ladle, small
Gravy Ladle
Punch Ladle
Soup Ladle, large
Soup Ladle, small
Sugar Sifter, small
Sugar Sifter, new
  style

SERVERS
Asparagus
Entree
Fried Oyster
Pie, H.H.
Saratoga Chips
Sliced Tomato,
  large

MISCELLANEOUS
Asparagus Tongs
Butter Pick
Cheese Scoop,
  large
Cheese Scoop,
  small
Chocolate Muddler
Food Pusher
Ice Tongs
Sugar Tongs, large

Cromwell

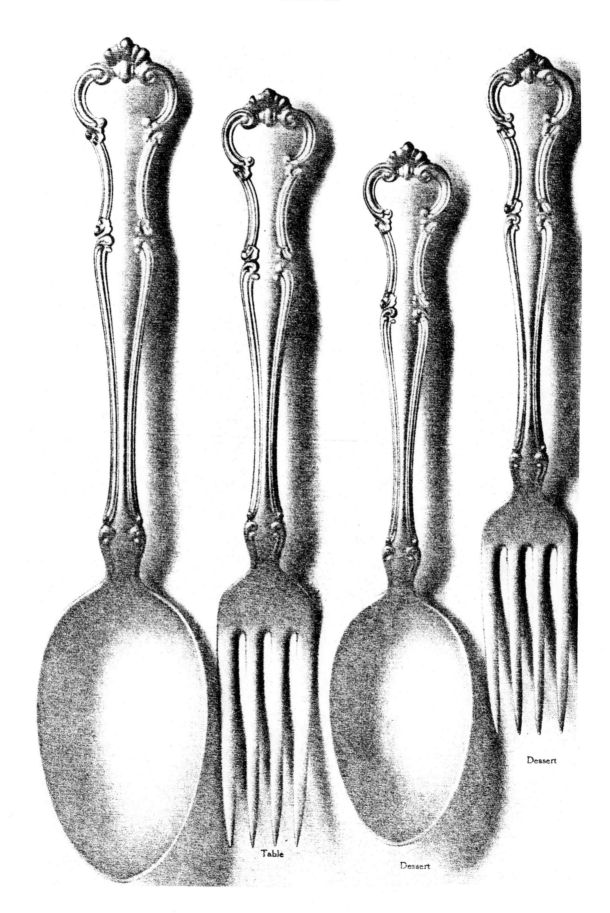

Table

Dessert

Dessert

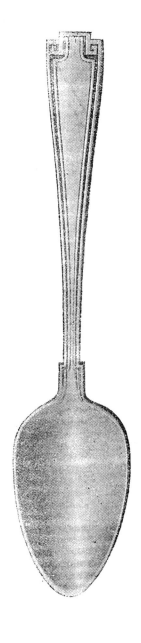

THE ETRUSCAN

PLAIN

Gray Finish

———

THIS pattern shows the influence of the classic revival under the brothers Adam in England which gave us so many of our cherished colonial treasures. The Greek Doric porches of our own houses, the pilasters and entrances of a slightly later date (1800 to 1820) with Greek Corinthian capitals and the fret or key, are among the finest examples that have come down to us. And this pattern, by careful study of both the spirit and detail, is clearly related to that period.

THE ETRUSCAN

PLAIN—GRAY FINISH

STERLING SILVER FLATWARE

RETAIL PRICE LIST

TRADE MARK

STERLING

GORHAM MFG. COMPANY

PROVIDENCE, R. I.

———

AUGUST 1, 1923

———

PRICES SUBJECT TO CHANGE
WITHOUT NOTICE

———

THE GORHAM COMPANY

REPRESENTING

GORHAM MFG. CO.	WM. B. DURGIN CO.
PROVIDENCE, R. I.	CONCORD, N. H.
WHITING MFG. CO.	THE WM. B. KERR CO.
BRIDGEPORT, CONN.	NEWARK, N. J.

———

OFFICES AT

NEW YORK, N. Y.	BOSTON, MASS.
5TH AVE. & 36 ST.	480 WASHINGTON ST.
ATLANTA. GA.	CHICAGO, ILL.
METROPOLITAN BUILDING	10 SO. WABASH AVE.

SAN FRANCISCO, CAL.
140 GEARY STREET

THE ETRUSCAN
Sterling Silver : Gray Finish

DOZEN WORK

TEA SPOONS
Small
Trade
Extra
Heavy
Massive

DESSERT SPOONS OR FORKS
Trade
Extra

TABLE SPOONS
Trade
Extra

TABLE FORKS
Trade
Extra

CUTLERY
Tea Knife
Breakfast Knives, H.H., Stainless blades
Dessert Knives, H.H., Stainless blades
Medium or Dinner Knives, H.H., Stainless blades
Meat Carving Knife, stainless blade
Meat Carving Fork, Stainless Carving Steel
Game Carving Knife, stainless blade
Game Carving Fork, Stainless
Steak Knife, stainless blade
Steak Fork, stainless
Steak Steel
Baby Knife
Bread Knife
Cheese Server
Child's Knife
Fried Egg Server
Fruit Knives, H.H.
Pie Server, H.H.
Pie Server, H.H., small
Duck Shears
Knife Sharpener, small

DOZENS
Bouillon
Butter Spreaders
Coffee Spoons
Fish Forks, Ind'l

Fish Knives, Ind'l
Grape Fruit Spoons
Ice Cream Forks
Ice Cream Spoons
Iced Tea Spoons
Orange Spoons
Oyster Forks
Pastry Forks
Ramekin Forks
Salad Forks, Ind'l
Salt Spoons, Ind'l
Sherbet Spoons

PAIRS
Fish Knife, large
Fish Fork, large
Salad Spoon, med.
Salad Fork, med.
Salad Spoon, small
Salad Spoon & Fork Olive Wood
Serving Spoon
Serving Fork
Serving Fork, small
Serving Spoon, small

SINGLE PIECES
Asparagus Fork
Baby Fork, large
Baby Fork, small
Baby Spoon, bent Hdl.
Baby Spoon, large
Baby Spoon, small
Baby Knife
Berry Spoon, large
Bonbon Spoon
Butter Knife, large
Butter Knife, small
Butter Pick
Child's Fork
Cold Meat Fork, med.
Cold Meat Fork, large
Cold Meat Fork, small
Cream Ladle, large
Cream Ladle, small

Food Pusher
Gravy Ladle
Honey Spoon
Ice Cream Slicer, large, H.H.
Ice Spoon
Ice Tongs, large
Ice Tongs, small
Jelly Server, small
Jelly Server, med.
Jelly Server, large
Jelly Spoon
Lemon Fork, small
Lettuce Fork
Marmalade Spoon
Mustard Spoon
Napkin Marker
Nut Spoon
Olive Spoon, short
Olive Fork, short
Pea Spoon
Pie Knife
Pickle Fork
Preserve Spoon, large
Preserve Spoon, small
Salt Spoon
Sandwich or Baked Potato Fork
Sardine Fork
Soup Ladle
Sugar Spoon
Sugar Tongs, large
Sugar Tongs, small
Tea Maker
Tomato Server, large
Tomato Server, small

The Florentine

For the motif of the Florentine pattern we are indebted to the great Renaissance movement in the early sixteenth century, when Italy gave to the world the most beautiful examples of architecture and decorations known as the Italian Renaissance, which for richness and grandeur has never been excelled. Typical of the beauty of this Italian style in both form and enrichment, the Florentine pattern suited to the taste of those who admire an elegant and massive style. In its outline and decoration it has every essential of a heavy weight ornate spoon.

front view

back view

LIST OF PIECES

SPOONS

Berry, large
Bonbon
Bouillon
Chocolate, large
Coffee
Confection
Cracker
Dessert
Gravy
Ice
Ice Cream, large
Jelly
Mustard
Olive
Orange
Pap
Pea
Preserve
Salad, large
Salt
Serving
Sugar
Table
Tea
Vegetable

Oyster
Pickle
Pie
Salad, large
Salad, Ind., large
Sardine
Table
Tea
Vegetable

KNIVES

Butter
Butter Spreader
Cake, flat
Crumb, flat
Fish, large
Fish, Ind., large
Ice Cream Slicer, small, flat
Ice Cream Slicer, large, H.H.
Jelly, large
Macaroni
Pie
Waffle

CUTLERY

Dessert Knives, H.H.
Dessert Knives, H.H., unplated blades
Medium Knives, H.H.
Medium Knives, H.H., unplated blades
Tea Knives, H.H.
Fruit, H.H.
Orange, H.H.

FORKS

Asparagus
Beef
Berry
Cold Meat, large
Dessert
Fish, large
Fish, Ind., large
Ice Cream, large
Lettuce
Lettuce Salad
Olive

Meat Carver
Meat Fork
Steel
Game Carver
Game Fork
Steak Carver
Steak Fork
Steak Steel
Joint Fork, large
Bird Knives
Bird Forks

LADLES AND SIFTERS

Cream Ladle, large
Gravy Ladle
Soup Ladle, large
Soup Ladle, small
Sugar Sifter, new style

SERVERS

Asparagus
Cake
Entree
Fried Oyster
Pie, H.H.
Saratoga Chips
Sliced Tomato, large

MISCELLANEOUS

Asparagus Tongs
Butter Pick
Cheese Scoop, large
Food Pusher
Ice Tongs
Sugar Tongs, large

Florentine

Table

Table

Dessert

Dessert

The Fleury
Gray Finish

The Fleury pattern derives its name from Andre Hercule de Fleury, who was made Prime Minister of France by Louis XV, in 1726. He was the immediate successor of the Duke of Bourbon whose wretched maladministration necessitated a change of government. A man of umblemished character and chaste ideals, Fleury did much to curb and refine the inclination to over-ornateness and exaggeration in all forms of decorative art, which the early period of the reign of Louis XV had brought about. Suggestive of the refinement of that period, with all the freedom of line and charm of floral decoration which have always appealed to the popular taste, the Fleury pattern has been happily conceived and most appropriately named. It will appeal at once to all who admire beauty of form and richness of decoration without sacrificing elegance and dignity.

LIST OF PIECES

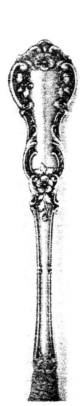

Tea Spoon
Back View

SPOONS

Berry, large,
Berry, small
Bonbon
Bouillon
Chocolate, large.
Chocolate, small
Coffee
Cracker
Dessert
Egg
Grape Fruit
Gravy
Ice
Ice Cream
Iced Tea
Jelly
Lettuce Salad
Mustard
Nut
Olive
Olive, long
Orange
Pap
Pea
Preserve Relish
Salad, large
Salad, small
Salt
Serving
Sherbet
Soup
Sugar
Table
Tea

FORKS

Asparagus, Beef
Beef, small
Berry
Child's
Cold Meat,
  large
Cold Meat,
  small
Cold Meat, extra
Dessert
Fish, large
Fish, small
Fish, Ind., large
Fish, Ind., small
Ice Cream
Lemon
Lettuce
Lettuce Salad

Olive
Olive, long
Oyster
Pastry
Ramekin
Relish
Salad, large
Salad, small
Salad, Ind., large
Salad, Ind., small
Sardine
Serving
Table
Tea

KNIVES

Breakfaast
Butter
Butter, small
Butter Spreaders
Child's
Crumb, flat Fish,
  large
Fish, small
Ice Cream Slicer,
  small, flat Ice
Cream Slicer,
  steel blade Jelly
Pickle
Pie
Waffle

CUTLERY

Dessert Knives,
  H.H.
Dessert Knives,
  H.H., unplated
  blades
Medium Knives,
  H.H.
Medium Knives,
  H.H., unplated
  blades
Tea Knives, H.H.
Fruit, H.H.
Orange, H.H.
Meat Carver
Meat Fork
Steel
Game Carver

Game Fork
Steak Carver
Steak Fork
Steak Steel
Joint Fork, large

**LADLES AND
SIFTERS**

Bouillon Ladle
Cream Ladle, large
Cream Ladle, small
Gravy Ladle
Mayonnaise Ladle
Punch Ladle
Soup Ladle
Sugar Sifter, new
  style

SERVERS

Bacon
Cake, H.H., steel
  blade
Cheese
Entree
Fried Oyster, Pie,
  H.H.
Saratoga Chip
Sliced Tomato,
  large
Sliced Tomato,
  small

MISCELLANEOUS

Asparagus Tongs
Asparagus Tongs,
  Ind.
Butter Pick
Cheese Scoop,
  large
Cheese Scoop,
  small
Food Pusher
Ice Tongs
Sandwich Tongs
Sugar Tongs, large
Sugar Tongs, small
Tea Maker

Fleury

The Hamilton

While not an absolutely plain pattern, the Hamilton has all the elements of elegance and simplicity which gave distinction to the work of the silversmith of the Georgian period. Fashioned after the best examples of that period, chaste and simple in outline, with its plainness relieved and enriched by the delicate thread border, it cannot fail to appeal to all who appreciate real beauty and refinement in silverware.

LIST OF PIECES

SPOONS

Berry
Bonbon
Bouillon
Chocolate
Child's
Coffee
Cracker
Dessert
Egg
Grape Fruit
Gravy
Honey
Ice
Ice Cream
Iced Tea
Jelly
Lettuce Salad
Mustard
Nut
Olive
Olive, long
Orange
Pap
Pea
Preserve
Salad, large
Salad, small
Salt
Serving
Sorbet
Soup
Sugar
Table
Tea

Ice Cream
Lemon
Lettuce
Lettuce Salad
Olive
Olive, long
Oyster
Ramekin
Salad, large
Salad, small
Salad, Ind.
Sardine
Serving
Table
Tea

KNIVES

Butter
Butter, small
Butter Spreaders, Child's
Fish
Fish, Ind.
Ice Cream Slicer, large, H.H.
Ice Cream Slicer, small, flat
Pie

CUTLERY

Dessert Knives, H.H.
Dessert Knives, H.H., unplated blades
Medium Knives, H.H.
Medium Knives H.H., unplated blades

FORKS

Asparagus
Beef
Child's
Cold Meat, large
Cold Meat, extra
Dessert
Fish, small
Fish, Ind.

Tea Knives, H.H.
Fruit H.H.
Orange, H.H. Meat
Carver
Meat Fork
Steel
Game Carver
Game Fork
Steak Carver
Steak Fork
Steak Steel
Joint Fork, large

LADLES AND SIFTERS

Cream Ladle, large
Cream Ladle, small
Gravy Ladle
Mayonnaise Ladle
Soup Ladle
Sugar Sifter, new style

SERVERS

Bacon
Cucumber
Entree
Jelly
Pastry
Pie
Saratoga Chips
Sliced Tomato
Waffle

MISCELLANEOUS

Asparagus Tongs
Asparagus Tongs, Ind.
Bonbon Tongs
Butter Pick
Cheese Scoop
Chocolate Muddler
Food Pusher
Ice Tongs
Sandwich Tongs
Sugar Tongs
Tea Makers

Hamilton

Dessert

Dessert

Table

Table

The King George

From the early Georgian days to the present time no style of spoon has been in so universal use both in Europe and America as the King George. Originated as its name suggests in the early reign of King George III, it was instantly acknowledged a standard and was universally adopted as such. Strong and bold in treatment both in shape and ornamentation and particularly adapted to a bright polish, it attracts and is admired by the popular taste, for a pattern rich and ornate without over-elaboration.

front view

LIST OF PIECES

SPOONS

Berry
Bonbon
Bouillon
Chocolate
Coffee
Confection
Dessert
Egg
Gravy
Ice
Ice Cream
Jelly
Mustard
Nut
Olive
Orange
Pap
Pea
Preserve
Salad, large
Salad, small
Salt
Serving
Sorbet
Soup
Sugar
Table
Tea
Oyster
Pastry
Pickle
Pie
Salad, large
Salad, small
Salad, Ind., large
Salad, Ind., small
Sardine
Serving
Table
Tea
Terrapin

KNIVES

Butter
Butter Spreaders
Crumb, flat
Fish
Fish, Ind.
Ice Cream Slicer, large, H.H.
Ice Cream Slicer, small, flat
Ice Cream Slicer, large, flat
Jelly
Pie
Waffle

FORKS

Asparagus
Beef
Berry, new style
Cheese
Cold Meat, large
Cold Meat, small
Dessert
Fish, large
Fish, Ind., large
Fish, Ind., small
Ice Cream
Olive

CUTLERY

Dessert Knives, H.H.
Dessert Knives, H.H., unplated blades
Medium Knives, H.H.
Medium Knives, H.H., unplated blades
Tea Knives, H.H.
Fruit, H.H.
Orange, H.H.

Meat Carver
Meat Fork
Steel
Game Carver
Game Fork
Steak Carver
Steak Fork
Steak Steel
Joint Fork, large
Bone Holder
Bird Knives
Bird Forks

LADLES AND SIFTERS

Cream Ladle, large
Cream Ladle, small
Gravy Ladle
Soup Ladle, large
Soup Ladle, small
Sugar Sifter, new style

SERVERS

Asparagus, new style
Entree
Fried Oyster
Pie, H.H.
Sliced Tomato

MISCELLANEOUS

Asparagus Tongs
Asparagus Tongs, Ind.
Bonbon Tongs
Butter Pick
Cheese Scoop, large
Cheese Scoop, small
Chocolate Muddler
Food Pusher
Ice Tongs
Sandwich Tongs
Sugar Tongs, large
Sugar Tongs, small

back view

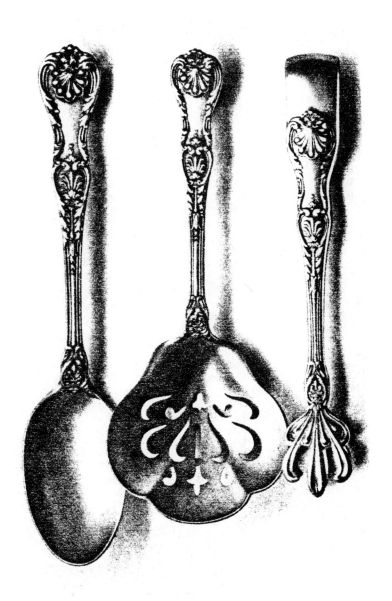

King George

Table

Table

Dessert

Dessert

La Modele

The designer's motif for this very elegant yet simple pattern is original in its form and treatment. The refined lines introduced and the slight ornamentation are of the twentieth century feeling, but with greater refinement than is generally used in the Art Nouveau style. The chaste outline and the simple, graceful lines are such that the name is particularly appropriate. Those who are looking for refinement and elegance in flatware cannot fail to be attracted to this pattern.

LIST OF PIECES

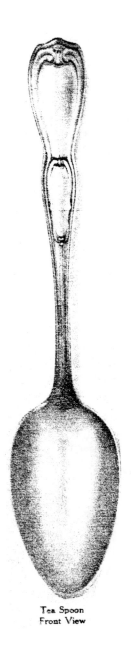

Tea Spoon
Front View

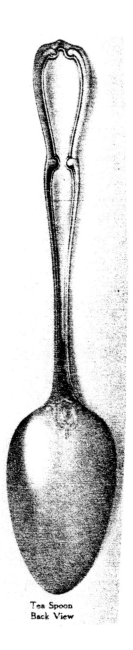

Tea Spoon
Back View

SPOONS
Baby
Berry, large,
Bonbon
Bouillon
Chocolate Coffee
Cracker
Gravy
Ice
Ice Cream
Iced Tea
Jelly
Lettuce Salad
Mustard
Nut
Olive
Olive, long
Orange
Pap
Pea
Preserve
Salad, large
Salad, small
Salt
Salt, Ind.
Serving
Sherbet
Sugar, large

FORKS
Asparagus
Beef
Berry
Cold Meat, large,
Cold Meat, small
Cold Meat, extra
Fish
Fish Ind.
Ice Cream
Lemon
Lettuce
Lettuce Salad
Olive
Olive, long
Oyster
Pastry
Ramekin
Salad, large
Salad, small
Salad, Ind.
Sardine
Serving
Tea

KNIVES
Butter
Butter, small
Butter Spreaders
Crumb, flat
Fish
Fish Ind.
Ice Cream Slicer, small, flat
Ice Cream Slicer, steel blade
Jelly
Pie

CUTLERY
Breakfast Knives, H.H., plated blades
Dessert Knives, H.H.
Dessert Knives, H.H., unplated blades
Medium Knives, H.H.
Medium Knives, H.H., unplated blades
Tea Knives, H.H.
Fruit, H.H.
Orange, H.H.
Duck Shears
Meat Carver
Meat Fork
Steel
Game Carver
Game Fork
Steak Carver
Steak Fork
Steak Steel
Joint Fork

LADLES AND SIFTERS
Bouillon Ladle
Cream Ladle, large
Cream Ladle, small
Gravy Ladle
Soup Ladle
Sugar Sifter, new style

SERVERS
Asparagus
Cake, all silver
Bacon
Cheese
Entree
Fried Oyster
Pie, H.H.
Saratoga Chip
Sliced Tomato, large
Sliced Tomato, small

DOZEN WORK
Tea Spoons, small size
Full size, Trade
Full size, Extra
Full size, Heavy
Dess. Spoons or forks
Trade
Extra
Table Spoons
Trade
Extra
Table Forks
Trade
Extra
Soup Spoons (Round Bowls)

MISCELLANEOUS
Butter Pick
Cheese Scoop
Food Pusher
Ice Tongs
Sandwich Tongs
Sugar Tongs, large
Sugar Tongs, small
Tea Maker

La Modele

Dessert

Dessert

Table

Table

The Lancaster

This pattern is essentially modern in design, introducing the bead pattern after the early Victorian design. The designer in this case has introduced the rose, giving the spoon a very modern appearance.

LIST OF PIECES

SPOONS

Berry, large
Berry, small
Bonbon
Bouillon
Chocolate
Coffee
Confection
Cracker
Dessert
Egg
Grape Fruit
Gravy
Horse Radish
Ice
Ice Cream
Iced Tea
Jelly
Lettuce Salad
Mustard
Nut
Olive
Olive, long
Orange
Pap
Pea
Preserve
Relish
Salad, large
Salad, small
Salt
Salt, Ind.
Serving
Sorbet
Soup
Sugar
Table
Tea

Pie
Ramekin
Relish
Salad, large
Salad, small
Salad, Ind., large
Salad, Ind., small
Sardine
Serving
Table
Tea
Toast
Vegetable

KNIVES

Butter
Butter Spreaders,
Cake, flat
Cheese
Crumb, flat
Fish, large
Fish, small
Fish, Ind.
Ice Cream Slicer,
   large, H.H.
Ice Cream Slicer,
   small, flat
Pie
Ice Cream Slicer,
   steel blade
Jelly, large
Jelly, small
Macaroni
Pickle
Pie
Waffle

CUTLERY

Dessert Knives,
   H.H.
Dessert Knives,
   H.H., unplated
   blades
Medium Knives,
   H.H.
Medium Knives
   H.H., unplated
   blades
Tea Knives, H.H.
Fruit H.H.
Orange, H.H. Meat
Duck Shears
Meat Carver
Meat Fork
Steel
Game Carver
Game Fork
Steak Carver
Steak Fork
Steak Steel
Joint Fork, large

Bone Holder
Knife Sharpener
Bird Knives
Bird Forks

LADLES AND SIFTERS

Bouillon Ladle
Cream Ladle, large
Cream Ladle, small
Gravy Ladle
Mayonnaise Ladle
Punch Ladle
Soup Ladle, large
Soup Ladle, small
Sugar Sifter, large
Sugar Sifter, small
Sugar Sifter,
   Tete-a-Tete

SERVERS

Asparagus
Cake
Cheese
Cucumber
Entree
Fried Oyster
Pie, H.H.
Saratoga Chips
Sliced Tomato,
   large
Sliced Tomato,
   small

MISCELLANEOUS

Asparagus Tongs
Asparagus Tongs,
   Ind.
Butter Pick
Cheese Scoop,
   large
Cheese Scoop,
   small
Chocolate Muddler
Food Pusher
Ice Tongs
Lobster Pick
Nut Picks
Nut Crack
Sandwich Tongs
Sugar Tongs, large
Sugar Tongs, small

FORKS

Asparagus
Beef
Beef, small
Berry
Cheese
Cold Meat, large
Cold Meat, small
Cold Meat, extra
Dessert
Fish, small
Fish, large
Fish Ind., large
Fish Ind., small
Ice Cream, large
Ice Cream, small
Lemon
Lettuce
Lettuce Salad
Olive
Olive, long
Oyster
Pastry
Pickle

Lancaster

THE LANSDOWNE

GRAY FINISH

STERLING SILVER
FLATWARE

RETAIL PRICE LIST

TRADE MARK

STERLING

GORHAM MFG. COMPANY

PROVIDENCE, R. I.

___

AUGUST 1, 1923

___

PRICES SUBJECT TO CHANGE
WITHOUT NOTICE

___

THE GORHAM COMPANY

REPRESENTING

GORHAM MFG. CO. PROVIDENCE, R. I.	WM. B. DURGIN CO. CONCORD, N. H.
WHITING MFG. CO. BRIDGEPORT, CONN.	THE WM. B. KERR CO. NEWARK, N. J.

___

OFFICES AT

NEW YORK, N. Y. 5TH AVE. & 36 ST.	BOSTON, MASS. 480 WASHINGTON ST.
ATLANTA, GA. METROPOLITAN BUILDING	CHICAGO, ILL. 10 SO. WABASH AVE.

SAN FRANCISCO, CAL.
140 GEARY STREET

THE LANSDOWNE

Gray Finish

THE Lansdowne is a pattern embodying the graceful elegancies which so distinguished the minor and domestic arts during the closing years of the Eighteenth Century, arts which, in England at least were so curiously dominated by the Brothers Adam.

TEA SPOONS
Small
Trade
Extra
Heavy
Massive

DESSERT SPOONS OR FORKS
Trade
Extra

TABLE SPOONS
Trade
Extra

TABLE FORKS
Trade
Extra
Soup spoons

CUTLERY
Tea Knife, stainless
Breakfast Knives, H.H., Stainless blades
Dessert Knives, H.H., Stainless blades
Medium or Dinner Knives, H.H., Stainless blades
Meat Carving Knife, stainless blade
Meat Carving Fork, Stainless
Carving Steel
Game Carving Knife, stainless blade
Game Carving Fork, Stainless
Steak Knife, stainless blade
Steak Fork, stainless
Steak Steel
Baby Knife
Bread Knife
Cheese Server
Child's Knife
Fried Egg Server
Fruit Knives,
Knife Sharpener, small

Pie Server, large
Pie Server, small
Duck Shears

DOZENS
Bouillon Spoons
Butter Spreaders
Coffee Spoons
Fish Forks, Ind'l
Fish Knives, Ind'l
Grape Fruit Spoons
Ice Cream Forks
Ice Cream Spoons
Iced Tea Spoons
Orange Spoons
Oyster Forks
Pastry Forks
Ramekin Forks
Salad Forks, Ind'l
Salt Spoons, Ind'l
Sherbet Spoons

PAIRS
Fish Knife
Fish Fork
Salad Spoon, small
Salad Fork, small
Salad Spoon, medium
Salad Fork, med.
Salad Spoon & Fork Olive Wood
Serving Spoon
Serving Fork

SINGLE PIECES
Asparagus Fork
Baby Fork
Baby Knife
Baby Spoon Baby Spoon, bent handle
Berry Spoon Bonbon Spoon
Butter Knife, large
Butter Knife, small

Butter Pick, either style
Child's Fork
Cold Meat Fork, med.
Cold Meat Fork, large
Cream Ladle, large
Cream Ladle, small
Food Pusher
Gravy Ladle
Honey Spoon
Ice Cream Slicer, large, H.H.
Ice Spoon
Ice Tongs
Jelly Server, small
Jelly Server, large
Jelly Spoon
Lemon Fork, small
Lettuce Fork
Marmalade Spoon
Mustard Spoon
Napkin Marker
Nut Spoon
Olive Spoon Olive Fork
Pea Spoon
Pie Knife
Pickle Fork
Preserve Spoon, small
Preserve Spoon, large
Salt Spoon
Sandwich or Baked Potato Fork
Sardine Fork
Soup Ladle
Sugar Spoon
Sugar Tongs, large
Sugar Tongs, small
Tea Maker
Tomato Server, large
Tomato Server, small

GORHAM

Lenox index showing vast number of pieces available.
(From 1921 catalog)

LENOX

INDEX

For 5 C or Lenox Tea Set and Hollow Ware, see page 222

The Mothers

There is always a charm and individuality about the old spoons which the early makers forged and wrought by hand. Absolutely plain, bright polished silverware is always rich and impressive and in our Mother's Pattern we have given this look of chasteness and dignity which the hand wrought spoon had. Designed from a very old pattern it is a perfect reproduction of the style our forefathers used and loved so well, and meets the demand in every way for a plain, bright finished Colonial pattern.

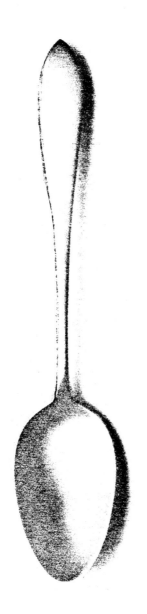

SPOONS

Berry
Bonbon
Bouillon
Chocolate
Coffee
Dessert
Honey
Ice Cream
Mustard
Olive
Preserve
Salad
Soup
Sugar
Table
Tea

FORKS

Beef
Cold Meat
Dessert
Fish
Fish, Ind.
Ice Cream
Lemon
Olive

Oyster
Ramekin
Salad
Salad, Ind.
Table
Tea

KNIVES

Butter
Butter Spreaders
Fish, small

CUTLERY

Dessert Knives, H.H.
Dessert Knives, H.H., unplated blades
Medium Knives, H.H.
Medium Knives, H.H., unplated blades
Tea Knives, H.H.
Meat Carver

Meat Fork
Steel
Game Carver
Game Fork
Steak Carver
Steak Fork
Steak Steel

LADLES

Cream Ladle, large
Gravy Ladle
Soup Ladle

SERVERS

Cheese Pie, H.H.
Sliced Tomato

MISCELLANEOUS

Food Pusher
Sugar Tongs

Mothers

Butter Spreader

Butter Knife

Oyster Fork

Chocolate Spoon

Food Pusher

Sugar Tongs,

Bouillon Spoon

Ramekin Fork

Olive, Spoon

Tea Fork

Cold Meat Fork

Beef Fork

Fish Knife

Tomato Server

Pie Server

Mythologique
1894

This beautiful pattern was designed by Mons. F. Antoine Heller, a distinguished French medalist, who has stamped it with his own individuality, seeming to have revived the best period of French Art, — that when Cellini in France, from 1540 to 1545, exerted such an overwhelming influence on the Goldsmith's Art in that country, and when all designs were extended in the Italian Style — Mythological subjects occupying almost exclusively their attention.

LIST OF PIECES

SPOONS

Berry, large,
Bonbon
Bouillon
Chocolate
Coffee
Confection
Cracker
Dessert
Egg
Gravy
Horse Radish
Ice
Ice Cream
Iced Tea
Jelly
Lettuce Salad
Mustard
Nut
Olive
Olive, long
Orange
Pap
Pea
Preserve
Salad, large
Salad, small
Salt
Serving
Sorbet
Soup
Sugar
Table
Tea
Vegetable

FORKS

Asparagus
Beef
Berry
Cheese
Cold Meat, large,
Cold Meat, small
Dessert
Fish, large
Fish, small
Fish Ind., large
Fish Ind., small
Ice Cream
Lettuce
Lettuce Salad

Olive
Olive, long
Oyster
Pastry
Pickle
Pie
Salad, large
Salad, small
Salad, Ind., large
Salad, Ind., small
Sardine
Serving
Table
Tea
Terrapin
Toast
Vegetable

KNIVES

Butter
Butter, small
Butter Spreaders
Cake, flat
Cheese
Crumb, flat
Dessert, flat
Fish, large
Fish, small
Fish Ind., large
Fish Ind., small
Ice Cream Slicer, large, H.H.
Ice Cream Slicer, small, flat
Jelly, large
Jelly, small
Macaroni
Pickle
Pie
Tea, flat
Waffle

CUTLERY

Dessert Knives, H.H.
Dessert Knives, H.H., unplated blades
Medium Knives, H.H.
Medium Knives, H.H., unplated blades

Tea Knives, H.H.
Fruit, H.H.
Duck Shears
Orange, H.H.
Meat Carver
Meat Fork
Steel
Game Carver
Game Fork
Steak Carver
Steak Fork
Steak Steel
Joint Fork, large
Bird Knives
Bird Forks

LADLES AND SIFTERS

Bouillon Ladle
Cream Ladle, large
Gravy Ladle
Mayonnaise Ladle
Punch Ladle
Soup Ladle, large
Soup Ladle, small
Sugar Sifter, large
Sugar Sifter, small

SERVERS

Asparagus
Cucumber
Entree
Fried Oyster
Pie, H.H.
Saratoga Chip
Sliced Tomato, large
Sliced Tomato, small

MISCELLANEOUS

Asparagus Tongs
Asparagus Tongs, Ind.
Butter Pick
Cheese Scoop, large
Cheese Scoop, small
Chocolate Muddler
Food Pusher
Ice Tongs
Sandwich Tongs
Sugar Tongs, large
Sugar Tongs, small

Mythologique

Dessert

Dessert

Table

Table

The Newcastle

The outline of this spoon is purely classic and is very much on the order of the old spoon made in early part of Queen Victoria's reign known as the ''Bead Antique.'' For lovers of good severe silverware this spoon will be highly appreciated. The treatment of the bead is entirely different from the Lancaster. In this case the bead has an incised line on either side, giving the desired severe appearance.

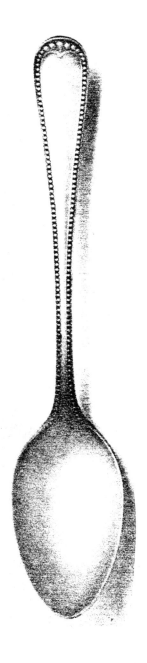

LIST OF PIECES

SPOONS

Berry, large
Berry, small
Bonbon
Bouillon
Chocolate, large
Chocolate, small
Coffee
Coffee, small
Confection
Cracker
Dessert
Egg
Gravy
Horse Radish
Ice
Ice Cream, large
Jelly
Lettuce Salad
Mustard
Nut
Olive
Olive, long
Orange
Pap
Pea
Preserve
Salad, large
Salad, small
Salt
Salt, Ind.
Serving
Soup
Sugar
Table
Tea
Vegetable

FORKS

Asparagus
Beef
Berry
Cheese
Cold Meat, large
Cold Meat, small
Cold Meat, extra
Dessert
Fish, small
Fish, large

Fish Ind., large
Fish Ind., small
Ice Cream
Lettuce
Lettuce Salad
Olive
Olive, long
Oyster
Pastry
Pickle
Pie
Salad, large
Salad, small
Salad, Ind., large
Salad, Ind., small
Sardine
Table
Tea
Toast
Vegetable

KNIVES

Butter
Butter, small Butter Spreader
Cake, flat
Cheese
Crumb, flat
Dessert, flat
Fish, large
Fish, small
Fish, Ind., large
Fish, Ind., small
Ice Cream Slicer, large, H.H.
Ice Cream Slicer, small, flat
Jelly, large
Jelly, small
Macaroni
Pickle
Pie
Tea, flat
Waffle

CUTLERY

Dessert Knives, H.H.
Dessert Knives, H.H., unplated blades
Medium Knives, H.H.
Medium Knives H.H., unplated blades

Tea Knives, H.H.
Fruit H.H.
Orange, H.H.
Meat Carver Meat Fork
Game Carver
Game Fork
Steak Carver
Steak Fork
Steak Steel
Joint Fork, large

LADLES AND SIFTERS

Cream Ladle, large
Cream Ladle, small
Gravy Ladle
Punch Ladle
Soup Ladle, large
Soup Ladle, small
Sugar Sifter, large
Sugar Sifter, small

SERVERS

Asparagus
Cucumber
Entree
Fried Oyster
Pie, H.H.
Saratoga Chips
Sliced Tomato, large
Sliced Tomato, small

MISCELLANEOUS

Asparagus Tongs
Butter Pick
Cheese Scoop, large
Cheese Scoop, small
Chocolate Muddler
Food Pusher
Ice Tongs
Nut Picks
Sugar Tongs, large
Sugar Tongs, small

Newcastle

Table

Table

Dessert

Dessert

The Norfolk
Bright Finish

The Norfolk is dignified by a chaste plainness, the ornament being entirely subsidiary to the express purpose of realizing a pattern whose lines shall accent its true beauty.

This pattern derives its name from the famous Duke of Norfolk, Premier Duke and Earl, and heredity Earl Marshal of Great Britain. Plain in its general impression, it is not lacking in distinction and in refinement.

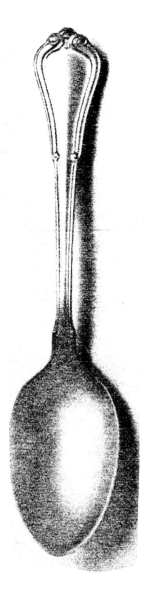

SPOONS

Baby
Berry, large
Berry, small
Bonbon
Bouillon
Chocolate, small
Coffee
Confection
Cracker
Dessert
Egg
Grape Fruit
Gravy
Honey
Horse Radish
Ice Cream, large
Iced Tea
Jelly
Lettuce Salad
Mustard
Nut
Olive
Olive, long
Orange
Pap
Pea
Preserve
Relish
Salad, large
Salad, small
Salt
Serving
Sorbet
Soup
Sugar
Table
Tea
Vegetable

FORKS

Asparagus
Beef
Beef, small
Berry
Cold Meat, large
Cold Meat, small
Dessert
Fish, large
Fish, small
Fish, Ind., large
Fish, Ind., small
Ice Cream, large
Lettuce Salad
Olive
Olive, long
Oyster
Pastry
Pickle
Pie
Ramekin
Relish
Salad, large
Salad, small
Salad, Ind., large
Salad, Ind., small
Sardine
Serving
Table
Tea
Vegetable

KNIVES

Butter
Butter, small
Butter Spreader
Cake, flat
Cheese
Crumb, flat
Dessert, flat
Fish, small
Fish, large
Fish, Ind., large
Ice Cream Slicer, small, flat
Ice Cream Slicer, large, H.H.
Ice Cream Slicer, steel blade
Jelly, small
Pickle
Pie
Waffle

CUTLERY

Dessert Knives, H.H.
Dessert Knives, H.H., unplated blades
Medium Knives, H.H.
Medium Knives, H.H., unplated blades
Tea Knives, H.H.
Fruit, H.H.

Orange, H.H.
Meat Carver
Meat Fork
Steel
Game Carver
Game Fork
Steak Carver
Steak Fork
Steak Steel
Joint Fork, large
Bone Holder
Bird Knives
Bird Forks

LADLES AND SIFTERS

Bouillon Ladle
Cream Ladle, large
Cream Ladle, small
Gravy Ladle
Punch Ladle
Soup Ladle, large
Soup Ladle, small
Sugar Sifter, large
Sugar Sifter, small

SERVERS

Asparagus
Cheese
Entree
Fried Oyster
Pie, H.H.
Saratoga Chip
Sliced Tomato, large
Sliced Tomato, small

MISCELLANEOUS

Asparagus Tongs
Asparagus Tongs, Ind.
Butter Pick
Cheese Scoop, large
Cheese Scoop, small
Chocolate Muddler
Food Pusher
Ice Tongs
Sandwich Tongs
Sugar Tongs, large
Sugar Tongs, small

Norfolk

Table   Table   Dessert   Dessert

The Old French
Bright Finish

XVIIIth Century French; is a very chaste and elegant spoon. The old spoons of this character were forged and wrought, the bowls being deeper and more blunt at the toe. This spoon conforms with the original outline of the old spoons, this Company being fortunate in the possession of one made about the period 1708. Our designer has improved it to suit all modern requirements. The elegance of its simplicity makes it a pattern of the very first order. It is offered in a very complete number of pieces.

LIST OF PIECES

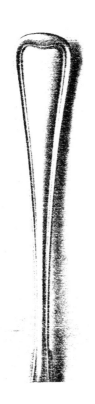

SPOONS

Baby
Berry
Bonbon
Bouillon
Chocolate
Coffee
Cracker
Dessert
Dressing
Egg
Gravy
Ice
Ice Cream
Iced Tea
Jelly
Lettuce Salad
Mustard
Nut
Olive
Olive, long
Orange
Pap
Pea
Preserve
Relish
Salad, large
Salad, small
Salt
Serving
Sorbet
Soup
Sugar
Table
Tea

FORKS

Asparagus
Beef
Cold Meat, large,
Cold Meat, small
Dessert
Fish, large
Fish, small
Fish Ind., large
Fish Ind., small
Ice Cream
Lemon
Lettuce
Lettuce Salad

Olive
Olive, long
Oyster
Pastry
Pickle
Ramekin
Relish
Salad, large
Salad, small
Salad, Ind., large
Salad, Ind., small
Sardine
Serving
Table
Tea
Toast

KNIVES

Butter
Butter, small
Butter Spreaders
Crumb, flat
Fish, large
Fish, small
Fish Ind., large
Ice Cream Slicer, large, H.H.
Ice Cream Slicer, small, flat
Jelly
Macaroni
Pickle
Pie
Waffle

CUTLERY

Dessert Knives, H.H.
Dessert Knives, H.H., unplated blades
Medium Knives, H.H.
Medium Knives, H.H., unplated blades
Tea Knives, H.H.
Fruit, H.H.
Duck Shears
Orange, H.H.
Meat Carver
Meat Fork
Steel
Game Carver

Game Fork
Steak Carver
Steak Fork
Steak Steel
Joint Fork, large
Bird Knives
Bird Forks
Bone Holder
Knife Sharpener

LADLES AND SIFTERS

Bouillon Ladle
Cream Ladle, large
Cream Ladle, small
Gravy Ladle
Punch Ladle
Soup Ladle, large
Soup Ladle, small
Sugar Sifter, large
Sugar Sifter, small

SERVERS

Asparagus
Cheese
Entree
Fried Oyster
Pie, H.H.
Saratoga Chip
Sliced Tomato, large
Sliced Tomato, small

MISCELLANEOUS

Asparagus Tongs
Asparagus Tongs, Ind.
Butter Pick
Cheese Scoop, large
Cheese Scoop, small
Chocolate Muddler
Food Pusher
Ice Tongs
Nut Picks
Sandwich Tongs
Sugar Tongs, large
Sugar Tongs, small
Tea Maker

THE OLD FRENCH

BRIGHT FINISH

STERLING SILVER
FLATWARE

RETAIL PRICE LIST

TRADE MARK

STERLING

GORHAM MFG. COMPANY
PROVIDENCE, R. I.

AUGUST 1, 1923

PRICES SUBJECT TO CHANGE
WITHOUT NOTICE

THE GORHAM COMPANY
REPRESENTING

GORHAM MFG. CO.	WM. B. DURGIN CO.
PROVIDENCE, R. I.	CONCORD, N. H.
WHITING MFG. CO.	THE WM. B. KERR CO.
BRIDGEPORT, CONN.	NEWARK, N. J.

OFFICES AT

NEW YORK, N. Y.
5TH AVE. & 36 ST.

BOSTON, MASS.
480 WASHINGTON ST.

ATLANTA. GA.
METROPOLITAN BUILDING

CHICAGO, ILL.
10 SO. WABASH AVE.

SAN FRANCISCO, CAL.
140 GEARY STREET

THE OLD FRENCH
Bright Finish

XVIIIth Century French; is a very chaste and elegant spoon. The old spoons of this character were forged and wrought, the bowls being deeper and more blunt at the toe. This spoon conforms with the original outline of the old spoons, this Company being fortunate in the possession of one made about the period 1708. Our designer has improved it to suit all modern requirements. The elegance of its simplicity makes it a pattern of the very first order. It is offered in a very complete number of pieces.

DOZEN WORK
TEA SPOONS

Trade
Extra
Heavy
Massive

DESSERT
SPOONS OR
FORKS

Heavy
Massive

TABLE SPOONS

Heavy
Massive

TABLE FORKS

Heavy
Massive

Soup spoons

CUTLERY

Tea Knife
Breakfast Knives,
   stainless blades
Dessert Knives,
   H.H., Stainless
   blades
Medium or
Dinner Knives,
   stainless blades
Meat Carving
   Knife, stainless
   blade
Meat Carving
   Fork, Stainless
Carving Steel
Game Carving
   Knife, stainless
   blade
Game Carving
   Fork, Stainless
Steak Knife,
   stainless blade
Steak Fork,
   stainless
Steak Steel
Baby Knife
Bread Knife
Cheese Server,
   small
Child's Knife,
   H.H.
Fried Egg
Server, H.H.
Fruit Knives,
   H.H.
Pie Server, H.H.

Pie Server, H.H.
Pie Server, H.H.,
   small
Duck Shears

DOZENS

Bouillon Spoons
Butter Spreaders,
   sm.
Coffee Spoons
Fish Forks, Ind'l,
   small
Fish Knives,
   Ind'l, large
Fish Knives,
   Ind.'l, H.H.
Grape Fruit
   Spoons
Ice Cream Forks,
   sm.
Ice Cream
   Spoons, sm.
Iced Tea Spoons
Orange Spoons
Oyster Forks, sm.
Pastry Forks
Ramekin Forks
Salad Forks,
   Ind'l, small
Salad Forks,
   Ind'l, small

PAIRS

Fish Knife, small
Fish Knife, large
Fish Fork, small
Fish Fork, large
Salad Spoon,
   small
Salad Fork, small
Salad Spoon,
   medium
Salad Fork, med.
Salad Spoon &
   Fork, Olive
   Wood
Serving Spoon
Serving Fork

SINGLE PIECES

Asparagus Fork
Baby Fork, large

Baby Fork, small
Baby Knife
Baby Spoon, large
Baby Spoon, small
Berry Spoon
Bonbon Spoon
Butter Knife, large
Butter Knife,
   small
Butter Pick
Child's Fork
Cold Meat Fork,
   med.
Cold Meat Fork,
   large
Cream Ladle,
   large
Cream Ladle,
   small
Food Pusher
Gravy Ladle
Ice Cream Slicer,
   large, H.H.
Ice Spoon
Ice Tongs
Jelly Server, small
Jelly Spoon
Lemon Fork
Lettuce Fork
Marmalade Spoon
Mustard Spoon
Napkin Marker
Nut Spoon
Olive Spoon, short
Olive Fork, short
Pea Spoon
Pie Knife
Pickle Fork
Preserve Spoon,
   small
Preserve Spoon,
   large
Salt Spoon
Sandwich or Baked
   Potato Fork
Sardine Fork
Soup Ladle
Sugar Spoon
Sugar Tongs,
   large
Sugar Tongs,
   small
Tea Maker
Tomato Server,
   large
Tomato Server,
   small

Old French

Table

Table

Dessert

Dessert

THE PLYMOUTH

BRIGHT FINISH

STERLING SILVER FLATWARE

RETAIL PRICE LIST

TRADE MARK

STERLING

GORHAM MFG. COMPANY

PROVIDENCE, R. I.

AUGUST 1, 1923

PRICES SUBJECT TO CHANGE
WITHOUT NOTICE

THE GORHAM COMPANY

REPRESENTING

GORHAM MFG. CO.
PROVIDENCE, R. I.

WM. B. DURGIN CO.
CONCORD, N. H.

WHITING MFG. CO.
BRIDGEPORT, CONN.

THE WM. B. KERR CO.
NEWARK, N. J.

OFFICES AT

NEW YORK, N. Y.
5TH AVE. & 36 ST.

BOSTON, MASS.
480 WASHINGTON ST.

ATLANTA, GA.
METROPOLITAN BUILDING

CHICAGO, ILL.
10 SO. WABASH AVE.

SAN FRANCISCO, CAL.
140 GEARY STREET

THE PLYMOUTH

Bright Finish

❧HIS attractive design has been specially prepared to meet the insistent demands for a flatware pattern to be used with the Gorham Plymouth Line of Dinner and Tea Ware, which has proved so popular.

The rich effect of the square edge, the simplicity of outline and refinement of decoration have been so successfully combined that the result is a pattern which not only harmonizes perfectly with the Plymouth Line of Dinner Ware, but is appropriate for use with any other Colonial or Old English bright finish ware.

A radical departure has been made in the bowls of the fancy pieces, which, while in accord with the general spirit of the design, affords a most attractive novelty in construction and appearance.

In addition to the spoons and forks a complete assortment of fancy pieces is included.

STERLING
SILVER
DOZEN WORK

TEA SPOONS
Small
Trade
Extra
Heavy
Massive

DESSERT
SPOONS OR
FORKS
Trade
Extra

TABLE SPOONS
Trade
Extra

TABLE FORKS
Trade
Extra
Soup spoons

CUTLERY
Tea Knife
Breakfast Knives, stainless blades
Dessert Knives, H.H., Stainless blades
Medium or Dinner Knives, H.H., stainless blades
Meat Carving Knife, stainless blade
Meat Carving Fork, Stainless
Carving Steel
Game Carving Knife, stainless blade
Game Carving Fork, Stainless
Steak Knife, stainless blade
Steak Fork, stainless blade
Steak Steel
Baby Knife, large
Bread Knife
Cheese Server
Child's Knife
Fried Egg Server, H.H.
Fruit Knives
Pie Server, H.H., large

Pie Server, H.H., small
Pie Server, H.H.,
Duck Shears

DOZENS
Bouillon Spoons
Butter Spreaders
Butter Spreaders, H.H.
Coffee Spoons
Fish Forks, Ind'l,
Fish Knives, Ind'l, H.H.
Grape Fruit Spoons
Ice Cream Forks
Ice Cream Spoons
Iced Tea Spoons
Orange Spoons
Oyster Forks, sm.
Pastry Forks
Ramekin Forks
Salad Forks, Ind'l
Salt Spoons, Ind'l
Sherbet Spoons

PAIRS
Fish Knife
Fish Fork
Salad Spoon, med.
Salad Fork, med.
Salad Spoon, small
Salad Fork, small
Salad Spoon & Fork, Olive Wood
Serving Spoon
Serving Fork

SINGLE PIECES
Asparagus Fork
Baby Fork, large

Baby Spoon, large
Baby Knife, large
Baby Spoon, bent handle
Baby Spoon, small
Baby Fork, small
Bonbon Spoon
Butter Knife, small
Butter Pick
Child's Fork
Cold Meat Fork, small
Cold Meat Fork, medium
Cold Meat Fork, large
Cream Ladle, large
Cream Ladle, small
Food Pusher
Gravy Ladle
Ice Cream Slicer, H.H.
Ice Spoon
Ice Tongs
Jelly Server, small
Jelly Server, large
Jelly Spoon, small
Lemon Fork
Lettuce Fork
Marmalade Spoon
Mustard Spoon
Napkin Marker
Nut Spoon
Olive Spoon, short
Olive Fork, short
Pea Spoon
Pickle Fork
Pie Knife
Preserve Spoon, small
Preserve Spoon, large
Salt Spoon
Sandwich or Baked Potato Fork
Sardine Fork
Soup Ladle
Sugar Spoon, large
Sugar Tongs, small
Sugar Tongs, large
Tomato Server, large
Tomato Server, small

Plymouth Pattern — Asparagus Server, Beef Fork, Berry Spoon and Table Spoon

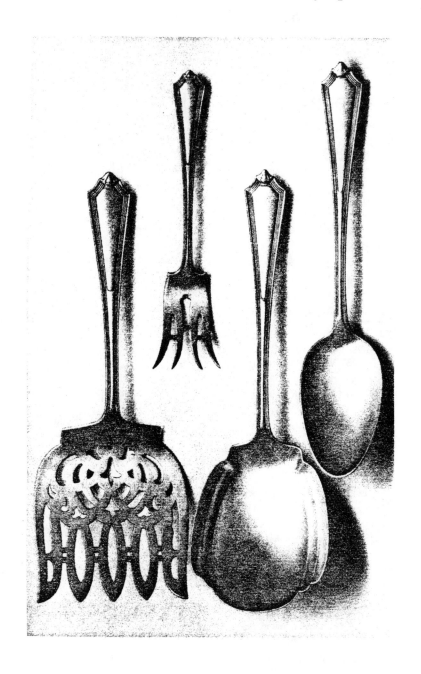

The Portland
1094

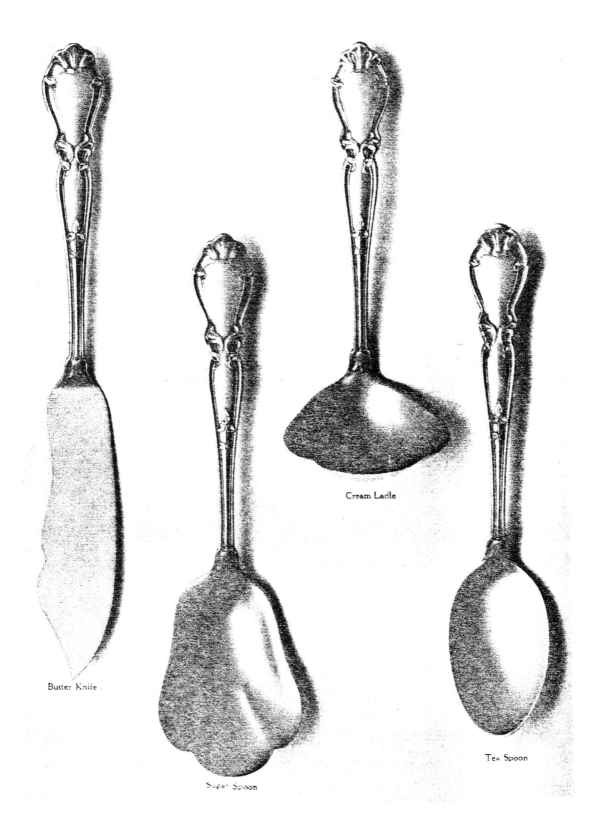

Butter Knife

Sugar Spoon

Cream Ladle

Tea Spoon

THE PORTSMOUTH

BRIGHT or GRAY FINISH
STERLING SILVER
FLATWARE
RETAIL PRICE LIST

TRADE MARK

STERLING

GORHAM MFG. COMPANY
PROVIDENCE, R. I.

AUGUST 1, 1923

PRICES SUBJECT TO CHANGE
WITHOUT NOTICE.

THE GORHAM COMPANY
REPRESENTING

GORHAM MFG. CO.   WM. B. DURGIN CO.
PROVIDENCE, R. I.   CONCORD, N. H.

WHITING MFG. CO.   THE WM. B. KERR CO.
BRIDGEPORT, CONN.   NEWARK, N. J.

OFFICES AT

NEW YORK, N. Y.   BOSTON, MASS.
5TH AVE. & 36 ST.   480 WASHINGTON ST.

ATLANTA, GA.   CHICAGO, ILL.
METROPOLITAN BUILDING   10 SO. WABASH AVE.

SAN FRANCISCO, CAL.
140 GEARY STREET

THE PORTSMOUTH
Bright or Gray Finish

RELYING for what must surely prove its attractive qualities mainly upon the exquisite simplicity of its line, upon its characteristic pointed handles and its quaint molded collars, the Portsmouth appropriately takes its name from one of the oldest Colonial cities in the country.

Quiet and old fashioned even beyond a majority of the old New England towns, Portsmouth stands in the eyes of the rest of the United States as typical of all communities which date lovingly back to pre-Revolutionary days.

STERLING SILVER DOZEN WORK

TEA SPOONS
Small
Trade
Extra
Heavy
Massive

DESSERT SPOONS OR FORKS
Trade
Extra

TABLE SPOONS
Trade
Extra

TABLE FORKS
Trade
Extra
Soup spoons

CUTLERY
Tea Knife
Breakfast Knives, H.H., stainless blades Dessert Knives, H.H., Stainless blades
Medium or Dinner Knives, H.H., stainless blades
Meat Carving Knife, stainless blade
Meat Carving Fork, Stainless
Carving Steel
Game Carving Knife, stainless blade
Game Carving Fork, Stainless
Steak Knife, stainless blade
Steak Fork, stainless blade
Steak Steel
Baby Knife
Bread Knife
Cheese Server
Child's Knife
Fried Egg Server
Fruit Knives
Pie Server, H.H.

Pie Server, H.H., small
Duck Shears

DOZENS
Bouillon Spoons
Butter Spreaders
Coffee Spoons
Fish Forks, Ind'l, large Fish Knives, Ind'l, H.H.
Grape Fruit Spoons
Ice Cream Forks
Ice Cream Spoons
Iced Tea Spoons
Orange Spoons
Oyster Forks
Pastry Forks
Ramekin Forks
Salad Forks, Ind'l, large
Salt Spoons, Ind'l
Sherbet Spoons

PAIRS
Fish Knife
Fish Fork
Salad Spoon, med.
Salad Fork, med.
Salad Spoon, small
Salad Fork, med.
Salad Spoon & Fork, Olive Wood
Serving Spoon
Serving Fork

SINGLE PIECES
Asparagus Fork
Baby Fork, large
Baby Fork, small
Baby Spoon, large
Baby Spoon, small
Baby Knife
Baby Spoon, bent handle

Berry Spoon
Bonbon Spoon
Butter Knife, small
Butter Knife, large
Butter Pick, 2 tines
Butter Pick, Gimlet
Child's Fork
Cold Meat Fork, large
Cold Meat Fork, medium
Cream Ladle, large
Cream Ladle, small
Food Pusher
Gravy Ladle
Ice Cream Slicer, large, H.H.
Ice Spoon
Ice Tongs
Jelly Server, small
Jelly Server, large
Jelly Spoon
Lemon Fork
Lettuce Fork
Marmalade Spoon
Mustard Spoon
Napkin Marker
Nut Spoon
Olive Spoon, short
Olive Fork, short
Pea Spoon
Pickle Fork
Pie Knife
Preserve Spoon, small
Preserve Spoon, large
Salt Spoon
Sandwich or Baked Potato Fork
Sardine Fork
Soup Ladle
Sugar Spoon
Sugar Tongs, small
Sugar Tongs, large
Tea Maker
Tomato Server, large
Tomato Server, small

Royal Oak

In this pattern the designer has used to the fullest advantage the oak leaf's beautiful and highly characteristic lines. The pattern is especially distinguished by its substantial weight and dignified solidity of appearance.

It is pre-eminently adapted by its richness of effect and weight to take place among the special selection of Family Silver.

While distinctly a pattern appealing to the demand for something out of the ordinary, it is yet extremely reasonable in price.

Tea Spoon
Back View

SPOONS

Berry, large
Bonbon
Bouillon
Chocolate, large
Coffee
Confection
Cracker
Dessert
Egg
Gravy
Honey
Horse Radish
Ice
Ice Cream, large
Jelly
Mustard
Nut
Olive
Olive, long
Orange
Pap
Pea
Preserve
Salad, large
Salad, small
Salt
Sorbet
Soup
Sugar
Table
Tea
Vegetable

Olive, long
Oyster
Pastry
Pickle
Pie
Salad, large
Salad, small
Salad, Ind., large
Salad, Ind., small
Sardine
Table
Tea
Toast
Vegetable

FORKS

Asparagus
Beef
Beef, small
Cold Meat, large
Cold Meat, small
Cold Meat, extra
Dessert
Fish, large
Fish, small
Fish, Ind., large
Fish, Ind., small
Ice Cream
Lettuce
Olive

KNIVES

Butter
Butter Spreader
Cake, flat
Cheese
Crumb, flat
Fish, small
Fish, large
Fish, Ind., large
Ice Cream Slicer, small, flat
Ice Cream Slicer, large, H.H.
Jelly, large
Macaroni
Pickle
Pie
Waffle

CUTLERY

Dessert Knives, H.H.
Dessert Knives, H.H., unplated blades
Medium Knives, H.H.
Medium Knives, H.H., unplated blades
Tea Knives, H.H.
Fruit, H.H.

Orange, H.H.
Meat Carver
Meat Fork
Steel
Game Carver
Game Fork
Steak Carver
Steak Fork
Steak Steel
Joint Fork, large
Bone Holder
Knife Sharpener
Bird Knives
Bird Forks

LADLES AND SIFTERS

Cream Ladle, large
Cream Ladle, small
Gravy Ladle
Mayonnaise Ladle
Punch Ladle
Soup Ladle, large
Soup Ladle, small
Sugar Sifter, new style

SERVERS

Asparagus
Cucumber
Entree
Fried Oyster
Pie, H.H.
Saratoga Chip
Sliced Tomato, large
Sliced Tomato, small

Royal Oak

Dessert

Dessert

Table

Table

THE ST. DUNSTAN

CHASED, GRAY FINISH

STERLING SILVER FLATWARE

RETAIL PRICE LIST

TRADE MARK

STERLING

GORHAM MFG. COMPANY

PROVIDENCE, R. I.

AUGUST 1, 1923

PRICES SUBJECT TO CHANGE WITHOUT NOTICE

THE GORHAM COMPANY

REPRESENTING

GORHAM MFG. CO. PROVIDENCE, R. I.	WM. B. DURGIN CO. CONCORD, N. H.
WHITING MFG. CO. BRIDGEPORT, CONN.	THE WM. B. KERR CO. NEWARK, N. J.

OFFICES AT

NEW YORK, N. Y. 5TH AVE. & 36 ST.	BOSTON, MASS. 480 WASHINGTON ST.
ATLANTA, GA. METROPOLITAN BUILDING	CHICAGO, ILL. 10 SO. WABASH AVE.

SAN FRANCISCO, CAL.
140 GEARY STREET

STERLING SILVER DOZEN WORK

TEA SPOONS
Small
Heavy
Massive

DESSERT SPOONS OR FORKS
Massive
Soup spoons

CUTLERY
Tea Knife
Breakfast Knives, stainless blades
Dessert Knives, H.H., Stainless blades
Medium or Dinner Knives, stainless blades
Meat Carving Knife, stainless blade
Meat Carving Fork, Stainless
Carving Steel
Game Carving Knife, stainless blade
Game Carving Fork, Stainless
Steak Knife, stainless blade
Steak Fork, stainless
Steak Steel
Cheese Server
Child's Knife
Fruit Knives, H.H.
Pie Server, H.H.

DOZENS
Bouillon Spoons
Butter Spreaders
Coffee Spoons
Fish Forks, Ind'l, large
Fish Knives, Ind'l, H.H.
Grape Fruit Spoons
Ice Cream Forks
Ice Cream Spoons
Iced Tea Spoons
Orange Spoons
Oyster Forks
Pastry Forks
Ramekin Forks
Salad Forks, Ind'l

PAIRS
Fish Knife
Fish Fork
Salad Spoon
Salad Fork
Serving Spoon
Serving Fork

SINGLE PIECES
Asparagus Fork
Berry Spoon
Bonbon Spoon
Butter Knife
Butter Pick, 2 tines
Child's Fork
Cold Meat Fork, large
Cream Ladle Gravy Ladle
Ice Cream Slicer, H.H.
Jelly Spoon
Lemon Fork
Mustard Spoon

Olive Spoon, short
Olive Fork, short
Pie Knife
Preserve Spoon Salt Spoon
Sardine Fork
Soup Ladle
Sugar Spoon
Sugar Tongs, small
Sugar Tongs, large
Tomato Server

THE ST. DUNSTAN
CHASED
Gray Finish

AS ITS name implies, the St. Dunstan is a pattern which, by its massive strength and virile outlines, recalls the handiwork of the silversmiths of olden times. In addition to these noble qualities, however, it is characterized by a refinement and delicacy of detail and finish which are only rendered possible by the ingenious appliances at the service of the modern silversmith.

GORHAM

The Strasbourg
Bright Finish

Rococo in style of design, the ornament being less ornate than most of the work of that period. The ornamentation is continued upon the bowls and tines of the fancy pieces, producing and effect of richness and finish not otherwise obtainable.

SPOONS

Berry, large
Berry, small
Bonbon
Bouillon
Chocolate, large
Chocolate, small
Coffee
Confection
Cracker
Dessert
Egg
Grape Fruit
Gravy
Horse Radish
Ice
Ice Cream, large
Ice Cream, small
Iced Tea
Jelly
Lettuce Salad
Mustard
Nut
Olive
Olive, long
Orange
Pap
Pea
Preserve
Relish
Salad, large
Salad, small
Salt
Salt, Ind.
Serving
Sorbet
Soup
Sugar, large
Sugar, small
Table
Tea
Vegetable

Ice Cream, small
Lettuce
Lettuce Salad
Olive
Olive, long
Oyster
Pastry
Pickle
Pie
Ramekin
Relish
Salad, large
Salad, small
Salad, Ind., large
Salad, Ind., small
Sardine
Serving
Table
Tea
Toast
Vegetable

KNIVES

Butter
Butter Spreaders
Cake, flat
Cheese
Child's
Crumb, flat
Dessert, flat
Fish, large
Fish, small
Fish Ind., large
Fish Ind., small
Ice Cream Slicer,
   large, H.H.
Ice Cream Slicer,
   small, flat
Ice Cream Slicer,
   steel blade
Jelly, large
Jelly, small
Macaroni
Pickle
Pie
Tea, flat
Waffle

FORKS

Asparagus
Beef
Beef, small
Berry
Berry
Cheese
Child's
Cold Meat,
   large,
Cold Meat,
   small
Cold Meat, extra
Dessert
Fish, large
Fish, small
Fish Ind., large
Fish Ind., small
Ice Cream, large

CUTLERY

Dessert Knives,
   H.H.
Dessert Knives,
   H.H., unplated
   blades
Medium Knives,
   H.H.
Medium Knives,
   H.H., unplated
   blades
Tea Knives, H.H.

Fruit, H.H.
Duck Shears
Orange, H.H.
Meat Carver
Meat Fork
Steel
Game Carver
Game Fork
Steak Carver
Steak Fork
Steak Steel
Joint Fork, large
Bird Knives
Bird Forks
Bone Holder
Knife Sharpener

LADLES AND SIFTERS

Bouillon Ladle
Cream Ladle, large
Cream Ladle, small
Gravy Ladle
Mayonnaise Ladle
Punch Ladle
Soup Ladle, large
Soup Ladle, small
Sugar Sifter, large
Sugar Sifter, small
Sugar Sifter,
Tete-a-Tete

SERVERS

Asparagus
Cake
Cheese
Cucumber
Entree
Fried Oyster
Pie, H.H.
Saratoga Chip
Sliced Tomato,
   large
Sliced Tomato,
   small

MISCELLANEOUS

Asparagus Tongs
Asparagus Tongs,
   Ind.
Bonbon Tongs
Butter Pick
Cheese Scoop,
   large
Cheese Scoop,
   small
Chocolate Muddler
Food Pusher
Ice Tongs
Nut Picks
Sandwich Tongs
Sugar Tongs, large
Sugar Tongs, small

96

Strasbourg

Dessert

Dessert

Table

The Tipt
c.1845

Table

Table

Dessert

Dessert

Tea

The Tuileries
1906
Gray Finish

The design of this spoon is of the best period of the reign of Louis XVI, showing an elegance and simplicity of style and an entirely new outline of handle.

The classic treatment of ornament of this period appeals to the growing refinement in taste in our own country at the present time which has shown its aversion to examples of that period of unrest in decorative art characterized by an overloaded ornament.

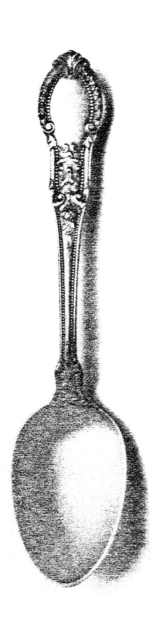

LIST OF PIECES

SPOONS

Berry
Bonbon
Bouillon
Chocolate
Coffee
Dessert
Egg
Gravy
Ice
Ice Cream
Iced Tea
Jelly
Mustard
Nut
Olive
Olive, long
Orange
Pap
Pea
Preserve
Relish
Salad, large
Salad, small
Salt
Serving
Sorbet
Soup
Sugar
Table
Tea

FORKS

Asparagus
Beef, large
Beef, small
Cold Meat, large
Cold Meat, small
Dessert
Fish, small
Fish, large

Fish Ind., large
Fish Ind., small
Ice Cream
Lettuce
Olive
Olive, long
Oyster
Patty
Pickle
Relish
Salad, large
Salad, small
Salad, Ind., large
Salad, Ind., small
Sardine
Table
Tea
Terrapin
Toast

KNIVES

Butter, large
Butter Spreader
Crumb, flat
Fish, large
Fish, small
Fish, Ind., large
Fruit, H.H.
Ice Cream Slicer,
    large, H.H.
Ice Cream Slicer,
    small, flat
Ice Cream Slicer,
    steel blade
Jelly
Orange, H.H.
Pickle
Pie
Waffle

CUTLERY

Dessert Knives,
    H.H.
Dessert Knives,
    H.H., unplated
    blades
Medium Knives,
    H.H.
Medium Knives
    H.H., unplated
    blades

Tea Knives, H.H.
Meat Carver
Meat Fork
Meat Steel
Game Carver
Game Fork
Steak Carver
Steak Fork
Steak Steel
Joint Fork, large
Knife Sharpener
Duck Shears
Bird Knives
Bird Forks

LADLES AND SIFTERS

Bouillon Ladle
Cream Ladle, large
Cream Ladle, small
Gravy Ladle
Soup Ladle, large
Soup Ladle, small
Sugar Sifter, new
    style

SERVERS

Asparagus
Cheese
Cucumber
Entree
Fried Oyster
Pie, H.H.
Saratoga Chips
Sliced Tomato,
    large
Sliced Tomato,
    small

MISCELLANEOUS

Asparagus Tongs
Asparagus Tongs,
    Ind.
Bonbon Tongs
Butter Pick
Cheese Scoop,
    large
Cheese Scoop,
    small
Chocolate Muddler
Food Pusher
Ice Tongs
Nut Cracks
Nut Pick
Sugar Tongs, large

Tuileries

Table

Table

Dessert

Dessert

The Versailles
Gray Finish
Of the Period of Louis XV

This design embodies the characteristics of the ornate and luxurious decorative work of that interesting period of French history.

The names chosen by the Gorham Company for many of its spoon work designs recognize the intimate relation between historical events and the progress of art.

Names such as Versailles, Cluny, Medici, Fontainebleau, and Luxembourg recall brilliant epochs in the art and literature of France and Italy.

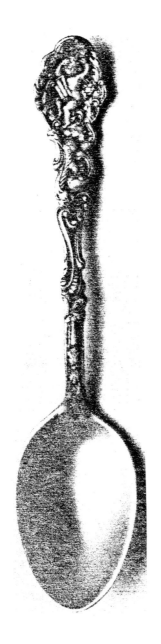

SPOONS

Berry
Bonbon
Bouillon
Chocolate
Coffee
Confection
Cracker
Dessert
Egg
Gravy
Horse Radish
Ice
Ice Cream
Jelly
Mustard
Nut
Olive
Olive, long
Orange
Pap
Pea
Preserve
Salad, large
Salad, small
Salt
Serving
Sorbet
Soup
Sugar
Table
Tea
Vegetable

FORKS

Asparagus
Beef
Berry
Cheese
Cold Meat, large
Cold Meat, small
Dessert
Fish, large
Fish, small
Fish, Ind., large
Fish, Ind., small
Ice Cream
Lettuce
Lettuce Salad
Olive

Olive, long
Oyster
Pastry
Pickle
Pie
Salad, large
Salad, small
Salad, Ind., large
Salad, Ind., small
Sardine
Table
Tea
Terrapin
Toast
Vegetable

KNIVES

Butter
Butter, small
Butter Spreaders
Cake, flat
Cheese
Crumb, flat
Dessert, flat
Fish, small
Fish, large
Fish, Ind.
Ice Cream Slicer, small, flat
Ice Cream Slicer, large, H.H.
Jelly, large
Jelly, small
Macaroni
Pickle
Pie
Tea, flat
Waffle

CUTLERY

Dessert Knives, H.H.
Dessert Knives, H.H., unplated blades
Medium Knives, H.H.
Medium Knives, H.H., unplated blades
Tea Knives, H.H.
Fruit, H.H.

Orange, H.H.
Duck Shears
Meat Carver
Meat Fork
Steel
Game Carver
Game Fork
Steak Carver
Steak Fork
Steak Steel
Joint Fork, large
Bird Knives
Bird Forks

LADLES AND SIFTERS

Bouillon Ladle
Cream Ladle
Gravy Ladle
Punch Ladle
Soup Ladle, large
Soup Ladle, small
Sugar Sifter, large
Sugar Sifter, small

SERVERS

Asparagus, H.H.
Asparagus, flat
Cucumber
Entree
Fried Oyster
Pie, H.H.
Saratoga Chip
Sliced Tomato, large
Sliced Tomato, small

MISCELLANEOUS

Asparagus Tongs
Asparagus Tongs, Ind.
Butter Pick
Cheese Scoop, large
Cheese Scoop, small
Chocolate Muddler
Food Pusher
Ice Tongs
Sandwich Tongs
Sugar Tongs, large
Sugar Tongs, small

Versailles

Table

Table

Dessert

Dessert

The Wreath
Gray Finish

From the Declaration of Independence the style in America became of a more monumental description and the United States became to possess certain characteristic national traits of their own. In presenting this new spoon the designer has kept the form and decoration as purely Colonial as possible on so small a service, and for a public requiring a refined and simple outline this spoon should meet the requirement of modern Colonial surroundings.

SPOONS

Berry
Bonbon
Bouillon
Chocolate
Coffee
Dessert
Ice Cream
Mustard
Olive
Preserve
Salad
Salt
Soup
Sugar
Table
Tea

FORKS

Beef
Cold Meat
Dessert
Fish
Fish, Ind.
Ice Cream
Lemon
Olive
Oyster
Ramekin
Salad
Salad, Ind.
Table
Tea

KNIVES

Butter
Butter Spreaders
Fish, small

KNIVES

Butter
Butter Spreaders
Fish, small

CUTLERY

Dessert Knives,
    H.H.
Dessert Knives,
    H.H., unplated
    blades
Medium Knives,
    H.H.
Medium Knives,
    H.H., unplated
    blades
Tea Knives, H.H.
Fruit
Orange
Steak Carver
Steak Fork
Steak Steel

LADLES

Cream Ladle
Gravy Ladle
Soup Ladle

SERVERS

Cheese
Pie, H.H.
Sliced Tomato,

MISCELLANEOUS

Food Pusher
Sugar Tongs

Wreath

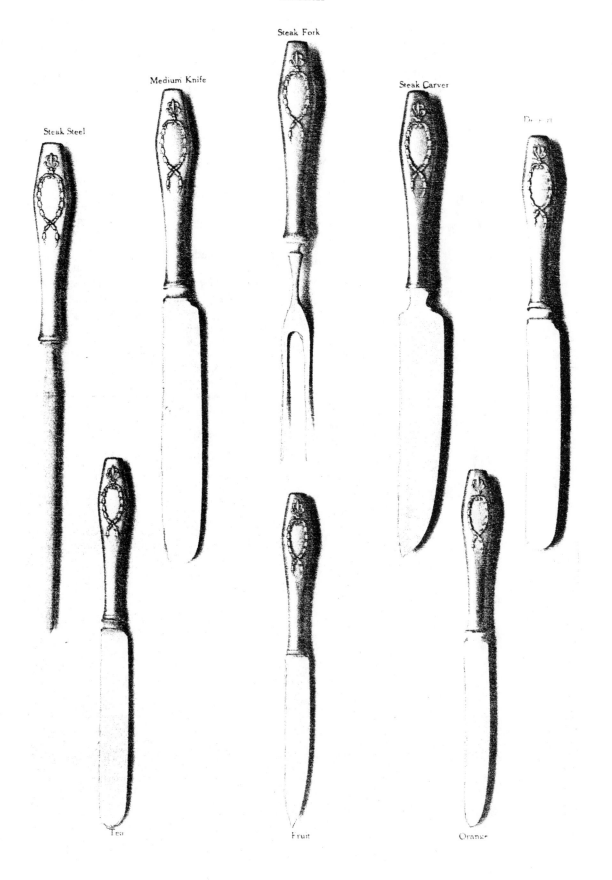

Steak Fork

Medium Knife

Steak Carver

Steak Steel

Dessert

Tea

Fruit

Orange

Wreath

Table

Table

Dessert

Dessert

To lovers of American silver the words are ominous..."What was once the largest silver company in the world......" That company is International Silver of Meriden, Connecticut. The year 1988.

In September of that year Insilco Corp., which owned International Silver, changed hands and moved much of the business to East Boston, Massachusetts and marketed some of International Silver Company and Wallace flatware. Much of it is foreign made.

But it was a very long road indeed from the pathway in Hartford, Connecticut to Meriden, from the humble workshop of the Rogers Brothers to the great and powerful International Silver Company in Meriden.

When International was formed in 1898 it became the largest manufacturer of silver in the world. The concept under which it was formed was, and is, an interesting manifestation of amalgamation in which the various companies existing under the umbrella name of the International Silver Company continued to use their own marks. These companies, many of which were composed of other companies previously absorbed and consolidated into more agressive companies, thus maintained their own identities. Some of these marks continued in use for a very long time while at the same time International used its own corporate mark on the silver it made. In 1968 International, parent to so many other silver companies, became itself part of a large conglomorate, Insilco Corp. In 1986, the Insilco Corp. of which International had became a subsidiary sold International and in 1988 Insilco itself changed hands. There is speculation that International will leave Meriden completely in the future.

From 1847 to 1985 International and its satellites have given us not only beautiful collectible silver but the stability of the company has exuded a vigorous air of commitment to the community, a sense of pride in its long history, and in its superlative craftsmanship. It has also been a company favored in its historian, Mr. Edmund Hogan, who has had a sense of awareness of the role the company has played in this country's history. The company has a complete record in dated sample spoons on its entire sterling pattern production, a commentary on the ability of the company officers to move with the times to be aware of the past and acknowledge responsibility to the future. In 1987 International celebrated its 50th birthday—a testimonial to the still vibrant skills and ingenuity of our American craftsmen.

One hundred fifty years ago the Rogers Brothers introduced the Olive pattern, the first plated pattern ever made in America. It was simplicity itself and geared to the housewife who wanted something useful, pretty and available at a reasonable cost. Collectors, all lovers of the metal itself, still have the same priorities today.

Given the quality of the metal itself, combine it with the standards of this great silver company, study the inventive designs of many of the patterns and it is evident that silver marked INTERNATIONAL will probably survive into infinity.

JOAN OF ARC, and PRELUDE have consistently been in the top 10 most preferred of all sterling patterns although there are others which command much attention because the company produced such exquisite patterns of superior design from its earliest days. The floral patterns of the early 1900s are almost without equal. The earliest of all, Kings, still blends well with any table setting, it is traditional yet in no way old fashioned. That is the true test of design—will it endure? All the early patterns of International are commendable. The very plain, sometimes ordinary-looking patterns characteristic of most of the original issues of the silver companies were by-passed by International since it began producing under that name at a much later date. So even the earliest patterns - Kings, Kenilworth, Dresden - the entire early production is tasteful, decorative and endearingly timeless. International has pursued an aggressive advertising campaign throughout its history and as a result has become an instantly recognizable name in silver. Some of the advertising itself is famous, the graphics have always been sharp and memorable. The ads are a chronicle of changes in taste and development of the culture.

In 1981 International discontinued its holloware line when it sold its Webster-Wilcox subdivision to Oneida and concentrated on flatware production. Plated flatware became almost half the company's business, sterling about ⅓ of the total production. This is a significant figure, as scarcity begins to become a factor, as it has in this case, prices will surely rise and pieces will become harder to find.

The story of International Silver reads like the story of America itself. It is the saga of enterprise and skill, of young ambitious entrepreneurs and the very large part the travelling peddlar played in the opening of the new markets. It is also the story of the many companies which preceded the formation of International itself. Not all of them produced sterling but all of them were organized by the old-time hard working, hopeful American manufacturer. It reads like a fairy tale. .....

Once upon a time there were two brothers, Rogers by name, who had a friend named Wilcox, Horace Wilcox. Horace was that almost mystical figure in history, the lone travelling peddlar. The Rogers Brothers were the first makers of cheap, innovative spoons. They used the newly discovered processes of electroplating over nickel silver. Spoons they made, and spoons by the cartload Horace Wilcox sold. He made their fortunes. But it is to the Rogers Brothers that we owe the first silverplate pattern ever made; it was called OLIVE, it was hugely popular and it made the date of issue 1847 forever part of the American consciousness.

International in the guise of its various companies has done everything. It has supplied tableware to shipping lines, hotels, restaurants, airlines, fine tableware for the home in almost every metal plus a tremendous variety of holloware. Collectors should be alert to some of the late production of the company. Often as time passes this newer ware becomes the most difficult to find.

A list of the companies which comprised International at its inception reads like a "Who's Who of American silver." Even a partial roster includes many famous old names. Webster and Son, Derby Silver Co., Simpson, Hall and Miller, Watrous, Barbour Silver Co., Holmes and Edwards, Forbes Silver Co., among others. The list is long and illustrious.

As were many of the founders of International. Much as in the earliest days of the republic and like the colonial silversmiths, the organizers of International and their heirs believed strongly in public service and several held public office. Horace Wilcox himself, that practical visionary, served as Mayor. The original founders of Meriden Brittania

Company left behind a legacy of public libraries, railroads, memberships in state legislatures, terms as Mayors of Meriden, Conn., endowments for homes for the aged and orphans and countless other worthwhile reminders of their existence, besides the really great silver they produced. These men felt a serious obligation to involve themselves for the public good.

International silver has been the sum of its parts. It was a bit like building a mighty structure - a very strong base, the best of materials, fine workmanship, good design and overall a pleasure to look upon. That is really what International Silver represents - a coming together of many entities, well-organized and directed, producing the beautiful, useful things which Americans wanted, and all at affordable prices. Indeed it was International which first began to advertise ''buy a three piece setting and get one free'' in 1957. This started a trend which did not augur well for the American silver companies. Those which did not participate in this price cutting and were able to maintain their price structures, fared better in the long run. But give high marks to International for trying to make their silver more affordable and thus available.

The changing nature of International is a warning to collectors and lovers of American silver; this wondrous flatware will not always be easy to find nor so inexpensively acquired.

INTERNATIONAL PRICES

Pattern	Date of Issue	Dinner fork	Dessert knife	Dessert fork	Tea-spoon
Abbotsford	1907	$52	$32	$48	$35
Acanthus	1917	30	24	30	24
Adanac	1910	38	32	42	29
Alexandria	1915	28	25	30	23

Pattern	Date of Issue	Dinner fork	Dessert knife	Dessert fork	Tea-spoon
Althea	1910	$55	$35	$58	$32
Andover	1919	28	25	30	23
Angelique designed by Edward J. Conroy	1959	40	30	42	28
Autumn	c.1912	28	25	28	23

Pattern	Date of Issue	Dinner fork	Dessert knife	Dessert fork	Tea-spoon
Avalon	1900	$60	$50	$65	$35
Autocrat	1923	24	20	27	18
Berkeley Colonial	1915	32	26	35	24
Beverly	1910	30	25	35	23
Blossom Time	1950	24	19	26	16
Brandon	1913	28	25	30	22

Pattern	Date of Issue	Dinner fork	Dessert knife	Dessert fork	Tea-spoon
Breton Rose	1954	$37	$29	$40	$27
Bridal Veil	1950	38	28	38	26
Brocade	1950	38	28	38	26
Cambridge & Luzon (same pattern)	1899	30	26	34	24
Cameo	1936	28	22	30	23
Carvell	1923	32	27	34	26

Pattern	Date of Issue	Dinner fork	Dessert knife	Dessert fork	Tea-spoon

Pattern	Date of Issue	Dinner fork	Dessert knife	Dessert fork	Tea-spoon

Charmaine — $55 $48 $60 $32

Colonial Hammered — 1923 $35 $30 $38 $28

Charmont — c.1910 30 25 34 25

Colonial Shell — 1941 26 24 28 22
Designed by Alfred G. Kintz

Chester — 1900 48 40 48 32

Continental — 1934 25 22 28 21

Chesterfield — 1914 35 30 38 23

Courtship — 1936 28 22 28 18

Chimes — 1938 25 20 27 19

Coventry — 1916 32 28 35 26

Cloeta — 1905 70 48 75 40

Crown Princess — 1949 45 35 47 29

Pattern	Date of Issue	Dinner fork	Dessert knife	Dessert fork	Tea-spoon
Dawn Rose	1969	$28	$24	$30	$21

Pattern	Date of Issue	Dinner fork	Dessert knife	Dessert fork	Tea-spoon
Davenport	1913	27	22	28	19

Pattern	Date of Issue	Dinner fork	Dessert knife	Dessert fork	Tea-spoon
Deerfield/Beacon Hill Same Pattern	1913	25	20	28	20

Pattern	Date of Issue	Dinner fork	Dessert knife	Dessert fork	Tea-spoon
Desire designed by Edward J. Conroy	1955	30	26	32	25

Pattern	Date of Issue	Dinner fork	Dessert knife	Dessert fork	Tea-spoon
Devonshire	1914	38	30	40	25

Pattern	Date of Issue	Dinner fork	Dessert knife	Dessert fork	Tea-spoon
Diana	1900	50	40	55	32

another example of the sample spoon kept by the company with pattern name and date in bowl

Pattern	Date of Issue	Dinner fork	Dessert knife	Dessert fork	Tea-spoon
Dorchester, Old	1910	$30	$25	$35	$23

Pattern	Date of Issue	Dinner fork	Dessert knife	Dessert fork	Tea-spoon
Dorchester, New	1910	27	24	28	22

Pattern	Date of Issue	Dinner fork	Dessert knife	Dessert fork	Tea-spoon
Doris	1907	40	30	42	30

Pattern	Date of Issue	Dinner fork	Dessert knife	Dessert fork	Tea-spoon
Dresden	1899	40	32	45	30

Pattern	Date of Issue	Dinner fork	Dessert knife	Dessert fork	Tea-spoon
DuBarry	1968	85	70	90	40

Pattern	Date of Issue	Dinner fork	Dessert knife	Dessert fork	Tea-spoon
Duchesse	1907	50	40	55	35

Pattern	Date of Issue	Dinner fork	Dessert knife	Dessert fork	Tea-spoon
Edgewood	1909	$48	$40	$50	$36
1810	1930	35	30	40	27
1810 engraved		37	32	42	29
Elegance	1934	32	26	34	24
Elsinore	1931	35	30	35	27
Empress	1932	50	40	55	30

Empress designed by Alfred G. Kintz

Pattern	Date of Issue	Dinner fork	Dessert knife	Dessert fork	Tea-spoon
Empress Eugenie	1933	$35	$28	$38	$25
Enchanted Rose	1954	40	30	42	28
Enchantress	1937	30	26	34	26
Florence	1903	35	28	37	25
Florentine	1912	32	28	35	24
Fontaine	1924	38	30	40	27

Fontaine designed by Frederick William Stark

Pattern	Date of Issue	Dinner fork	Dessert knife	Dessert fork	Tea-spoon
Frontenac	1903	$85	$70	$85	$40
Gadroon designed by Gilbert L. Crowell, Jr.	1933	45	38	47	30
Georgian Maid	1923	32	26	35	25
Governor Bradford	1913	25	22	28	22
Governor Warren	1918	25	22	28	22
Grand Recollection	1956	35	26	37	26

Pattern	Date of Issue	Dinner fork	Dessert knife	Dessert fork	Tea-spoon
Grand Regency	1969	$50	$42	$55	$35
Grand Trianon	1975	48	40	50	35
Irene	1902	30	24	32	24
Ivy	1911	40	32	45	28
Jeanne D'Arc	1905	60	40	62	35
John Winthrop	1911	26	22	28	25

Pattern	Date of Issue	Dinner fork	Dessert knife	Dessert fork	Tea-spoon
Joan of Arc	1940	$48	$40	$48	$30
Joy	1952	40	30	42	28
Kenilworth	1887	40	30	45	30
Kensington, Old	1912	30	26	34	24
Kensington, New	1912	28	24	30	22
King Louis	1971	85	75	90	40

Pattern	Date of Issue	Dinner fork			
Lady Betty	1920				
LaFrance	1907	40	30	45	27
Lambeth Manor	1952	47	40	48	29
LaRochelle	1909	40	28	47	26
LaStrada	1972	65	50	68	35
Golden LaStrada		68	54	70	38

Pattern	Date of Issue	Dinner fork	Dessert knife	Dessert fork	Tea-spoon
Leichester	1911	$40	$30	$45	$27

| Lenox | 1929 | 29 | 25 | 30 | 23 |

| Litchfield | 1898 | 38 | 30 | 42 | 24 |

| Lorraine | 1917 | 40 | 30 | 45 | 28 |

| Marathon, Old | 1909 | 35 | 27 | 38 | 26 |

| Marcell | 1907 | 45 | 30 | 48 | 30 |

Pattern	Date of Issue	Dinner fork	Dessert knife	Dessert fork	Tea-spoon
Mademoiselle designed by Siro R. Toffolon	1964	$37	$28	$38	$27

| Madrid | 1927 | 30 | 24 | 34 | 24 |

| Margaret, Old | 1907 | 35 | 30 | 38 | 26 |

| Margaret, New | 1912 | 35 | 32 | 38 | 28 |

| Maintenon | 1933 | 40 | 32 | 45 | 29 |

| Martel | 1925 | 27 | 23 | 29 | 22 |

INTERNATIONAL

Pattern	Date of Issue	Dinner fork	Dessert knife	Dessert fork	Tea-spoon
May Melody designed by Robert L. Doerfler	1952	$35	$28	$36	$25

Pattern	Date of Issue	Dinner fork	Dessert knife	Dessert fork	Tea-spoon
Moonbeam	1948	$32	$26	$34	$24

Miami	1900	65	55	75	38

Moonglow	1938	32	26	34	24

Mille Fleur	1904	70	50	75	38

Napoleon	1910	28	24	30	23

Minuet	1925	30	25	24	23

Nassau	1900	70	60	80	35

Minuet, engraved	1925	28	26	30	25

Nathan Hale	1912	55	40	58	35

Minuet, carved	1925	28	26	30	25

New Marathon	1912	32	23	30	25

Pattern	Date of Issue	Dinner fork	Dessert knife	Dessert fork	Tea-spoon
Norse	1937	$50	$40	$52	$32
Northern Lights	1946	50	40	52	32
Nosegay	1938	36	30	38	26
Old Charleston	1951	42	35	45	27
Old English	1917	25	20	27	19
Old Hampshire	1913	32	27	35	26

Pattern	Date of Issue	Dinner fork	Dessert knife	Dessert fork	Tea-spoon
Orange Blossom	1924	$35	$28	$38	$25
Orchid	1929	30	24	34	26
Ormond	1900	50	42	55	35
Our Empire	1907	45	32	48	30
Pansy	1909	45	32	48	30
Pantheon	1920	35	30	38	25

Pattern	Date of Issue	Dinner fork	Dessert knife	Dessert fork	Tea-spoon	Pattern	Date of Issue	Dinner fork	Dessert knife	Dessert fork	Tea-spoon
Patria	1918	$28	$24	$30	$23	Puritan	1912	$25	$23	$27	$22
Pine Spray	1957	27	23	29	23	Queen's Lace	1949	47	38	50	30
Pine Tree	1927	30	27	32	25	Quincy	1917	30	27	32	24
Prelude	1939	50	42	55	39	Radiant Rose	1938	42	30	45	28
Primrose	1936	65	50	75	35	Revere	1898	48	40	50	32
Processional designed by Lillian M.V. Helander	1947	48	42	52	30	Rhapsody, Old designed by Ernest T. Beck	1931	37	30	39	28

Pattern	Date of Issue	Dinner fork	Dessert knife	Dessert fork	Tea-spoon
Rhapsody, New	1957	$40	$32	$45	$27

Pattern	Date of Issue	Dinner fork	Dessert knife	Dessert fork	Tea-spoon
Richelieu	1935	85	60	95	40

Richmond	1910	32	25	36	22

Riviera	1936	40	30	45	28

Romance of the Stars	1959	30	26	35	23

Designed by Robert L. Doerfler

Romance Rose		30	24	28	19

Rosalind	1908	$37	$28	$40	$24

This is the same pattern which was issued under the name Wild Rose in 1939

Rosalind, New	1921	30	25	34	23

Rose Ballet	1962	30	26	35	23

Designed by John C. Engelman

Royal Danish	1939	55	50	60	37

Salem	1928	30	26	35	25

Sculptured Beauty	1957	48	40	50	36

Pattern	Date of Issue	Dinner fork	Dessert knife	Dessert fork	Tea-spoon
Sedan	1919	$32	$25	$36	$24

Pattern	Date of Issue	Dinner fork	Dessert knife	Dessert fork	Tea-spoon
Silver Rhythm	1953	$26	$21	$28	$21

| Serenity | 1940 | 34 | 26 | 38 | 26 |

| Simplicity | 1936 | 28 | 24 | 30 | 24 |

| Shirley | 1910 | 28 | 22 | 28 | 22 |

| Snowflake | 1966 | 25 | 20 | 28 | 20 |

| Silhouette | 1957 | 35 | 28 | 36 | 25 |

Designed by Siro R. Toffolon

| Sonja | 1937 | 40 | 30 | 42 | 28 |

| Silver Masterpiece | 1963 | 65 | 60 | 70 | 40 |

| Southern Colonial | 1945 | 48 | 38 | 50 | 30 |

| Silver Melody | 1955 | 45 | 40 | 47 | 32 |

| Splendor | 1939 | 30 | 26 | 32 | 25 |

Pattern	Date of Issue	Dinner fork	Dessert knife	Dessert fork	Tea-spoon
Spring Bouquet	1940	$30	$26	$32	$24
Spring Glory	1941	45	35	48	30
Springtime	1935	65	50	75	38
Stratford designed by S.H. Miller	1902	65	48	70	36
Styvesant	1916	28	25	30	24
Swan Lake designed by Robert L. Doerfler	1960	55	45	60	38

Pattern	Date of Issue	Dinner fork	Dessert knife	Dessert fork	Tea-spoon
Theseum	1922	$35	$25	$38	$24
Torchlight	1954	36	30	38	26
Tradewinds	1975	45	38	48	30
Golden Tradewinds	1975	50	40	52	35
Tranquility	1947	40	32	42	30

Designed by Lillian M.V. Hilander

Pattern	Date of Issue	Dinner fork	Dessert knife	Dessert fork	Tea-spoon
Trianon designed by Alfred G. Kintz	1921	50	40	52	36

Pattern	Date of Issue	Dinner fork	Dessert knife	Dessert fork	Tea-spoon
Trousseau	1935	$32	$26	$34	$22
designed by Alfred G. Kintz					

Pattern	Date of Issue	Dinner fork	Dessert knife	Dessert fork	Tea-spoon
Warwick	1898	$40	$32	$45	$28

Trumbull	1908	32	26	32	22

Wayfield					30
lightweight sterling, made in teaspoons only					

Valencia	1965	38	28	38	25

Wedding Bells	1948	40	35	42	27

Vandyke, plain	1910	35	30	38	26

Wedgwood	1924	38	32	40	28
designed by Alfred G. Kintz					

Vision	1961	46	35	48	30

Wellesley	1912	45	35	48	30

Wakefield	c.1919				32
lightweight sterling, made in teaspoons only					

Westfield					26
lightweight sterling, made in teaspoons only					

Pattern	Date of Issue	Dinner fork	Dessert knife	Dessert fork	Tea-spoon
Westminister	1915	$35	$25	$38	$26

Pattern	Date of Issue	Dinner fork	Dessert knife	Dessert fork	Tea-spoon
Winchester	1902	$50	$40	$54	$35

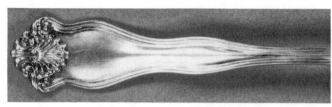

Whitfield   c.1920   26
lightweight sterling, made in teaspoons only

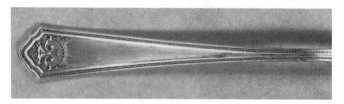

Windmere	1939	28	25	30	24

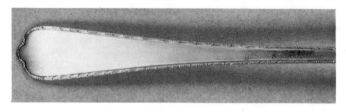

Whitehall   1938   45   40   50   32
Another pattern named WHITEHALL was produced in 1914 but was not made in all pieces.

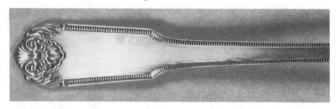

Wingfield   c.1910   25
lightweight sterling, made in teaspoons only

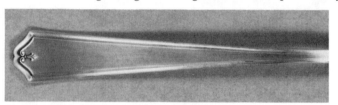

Alfred G. Kintz designed many patterns of International over a long period of time. Among his designs are:

Brandon	Pantheon
Elsinore	Prelude
Elegance	Rosalind
Enchantress	Riche Lieu
Georgian Maid	Royal Danish
Joan of Arc	Sedan
Lady Betty	Splendor
Masterpiece	Theseum
Monogram	Wild Rose
Northern Lights	
Old English	
Orchid	

Wickfield   c.1910   32
lightweight sterling, made in teaspoons only

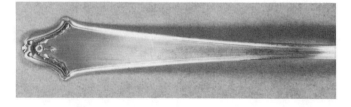

Wild Rose	1948	48	35	50	28

Designed by Alfred G. Kintz

Others who designed for International Frederick E. Pretat, Gustave Strohhaker, Thomas Lashar, William F. Mowry, and Inacio Carlos Barrousse. All of these men as well as Kintz and Beck created many designs for International during the 1920s and 30s. During the 1950s with their entirely characteristic designs of the times, Robert L. Doerfler, Edward J. Conroy, Lillian V. Hellender as well as John Leech, Leslie Brown and Orville W. Lucas were very active designers.

THE KIRK STIEFF COMPANY
Samuel Kirk and Sons

The Silversmiths of Kirk have a long and legandary history. The company is forever linked with the city of Baltimore and memorable events of early America.

Baltimore City lies 200 miles from the Atlantic ocean in a natural basin and a visitor to the city in its beginning days could stand in its center, look around, view the commanding harbor and easily understand the reason for its existence and rapid growth. Even at the start of the 19th century it was a place of great affluence, a place the Spanish first saw and admired but which the English eventually colonized.

Into this fertile land of bustle and prosperity came Samuel Kirk, a direct descendant of two of England's oldest silversmithing and banking families. Born of Quakers in Doylestown, Pennsylvania, he had completed his apprenticeship by this year of 1815, he was 20 years old, full of confidence and afire with ambition.

His choice of Baltimore as the location for his first small shop was daring. It was a sophisticated place, he was an inexperienced businessman. He hoped to mingle with names now legendary in American history for Baltimore itself was founded on land owned by Charles Carroll of Carrollton, a signer of the Declaration of Independence. It probably never crossed Kirk's mind that his name would someday be as well known as Carroll's and it was not until 1961 that the connection was honored when Kirk Silver issued the Carrollton pattern. But Kirk had an almost unlimited sense of certainty that he would succeed even in this heady atmosphere.

Twenty two years after its founding, Baltimore had 25 houses in its environment. Most of them were not truly opulent but the Irishman, John Stevenson, a medical doctor who realized the potential of the location gave impetus to other business with his own flourishing import venture. So when Samuel Kirk opened his small store, even though the economy was somewhat depressed in the aftermath of war, the arts flourished in Baltimore. Rembrandt Peale had opened his museum, the Continental Congress had met there, on a small scale even gaslight had arrived. It was this small, multi-faceted city which Kirk decided was ready for his wares. He meant to produce the highest quality merchandise from his very first effort and, to him Baltimore was the perfect niche. Samuel Kirk arrived with his skills finely honed, his apprenticeship to James Howell, a Philadelphia silversmith having taught him all he felt he needed to know.

Baltimore was the only city in American with a formal system of Assay for silver. Between 1814 and 1830 Maryland law stipulated that silver made in those years had to contain 900 parts pure silver. The other hundred parts of alloy were added for strength. Kirk certainly was aware of these strict laws as he began his business. He considered himself a Southern silversmith.

Indeed he fitted well into his new milieu. He was young, he was industrious in a city which thrived on industry, he was in the right place at the right time, he was imaginitive and skilled in his work. He was a man of integrity and he was committed to fine quality. He made useful silver objects with his own hands and they had a wonderful feeling of solidity and style. He gave satisfaction to his customers, he prospered and his silver has survived and his company became the oldest practicing silversmiths in America. This testifies to his taste and competence.

Kirk is revered for his revival of the art of Repousse (meaning "raised in relief") a European technique no longer much practiced, which he began making in 1822. It was then, and still is, a difficult exacting hand process which makes possible very elaborate designs. Kirk's Repousse is fabled, but then much of his silver spans the country's history. Yet prices on the older pieces remain modest and do not reflect the quality and historic connotations. Any collector who is not diligently trying to find Vintage Kirk is missing the opportunity to own genuine Americana in the true folk art spirit. This silver reflects the handwork of our forefathers and has the added value of the metal itself.

While the Kirk name remains synonomous with Baltimore silver it has achieved world-wide status. It is, without doubt, some of the finest silver made by anyone, at anytime, anywhere in the world. It is an unfortunate fact that the Civil War took its toll of much precious Kirk silver and since the overall production never equalled that of some of the large silver companies, probably much of the early Kirk has been lost. But the Kirk Company managed to survive wars, natural disasters, depression and recession and unlike most other silver companies in the United States did not find it necessary until 1979 to absorb other companies or to merge with other companies to bolster business.

Many of the great names of American history have done business with Kirk. Robert E. Lee, Jefferson Davis, The Carrolls, the Astors, the Roosevelts, even the White House could all claim ownership of early Kirk silver. Lafayette, himself, stopped by to order a pair of silver goblets. When Betsy Patterson married Jerome Bonaparte, brother of Napoleon, she ordered her silver from Kirk. The names of current collectors and owners of this silverware is equally long and illustrious. The company's past accomplishments have prompted very successful national tours of its representative silver.

Today Kirk continues to contribute to the American home with elegance and artistry. It has never wavered from young Samuel Kirk's concept - to make something magnificently beautiful accented by the metal itself and worked into utilitarian forms. The Maryland Historical Society considers that Kirk is part of the heritage of Maryland and of America itself. It is a stunning heritage indeed, and makes Kirk almost unique in the annals of American business.

Each piece of Kirk silver starts with a handmade steel die carved with minute detail. When engraving is called for the design it is applied after the piece had been shaped by hand cutting the pattern onto a blank surface. Hand work is involved in every piece of Kirk and all pieces are polished three times, first with pumice and oil on a walrus hide wheel, then with a fine cutting compound called ''tripoli'', then finally with rouge delicately applied on a woolen buff which gives all Kirk its distinct high luster. Kirk's was a family affair and descended uninterruptedly through generations of unfolding American history under the personal supervision of descendants of the founder.

But it was in 1979, 164 years after its founding that Samuel Kirk and Son finally merged with Stieff, another Baltimore maker, and the production of both Kirk and Stieff were consolidated in the Stieff factory. There has been no lessening of quality as the Kirk Stieff logo replaced that of Samuel Kirk and Son. The important thing for collectors to keep in mind is that all pieces made before 1980 bear the imprint of the separate companies. Samuel Kirk silver is still out there, precious and still obtainable. Sterling silver flatware made after 1980 is marked Kirk Stieff. It was in 1980 too, under the new joint name, that the company introduced a line of silverplated flatware and also a new line of jewelry designed by Douglas Legenhausen.

Kirk had an amazing record of longevity. This may be due in part to Samuel Kirk's attitude toward perfection which included his deep felt appreciation for his own rigorous training as an apprentice. Although many early craftsmen who had been apprentices themselves felt the training too harsh, Samuel Kirk subscribed to the system with enthusiasm and all of the Kirk sons were duly trained as apprentices.

The ''son'' of Samuel Kirk and Son joined the company in 1846. In 1860 two other sons became involved in the business and the name changed to Samuel Kirk and Sons. It reverted to Samuel Kirk and Son when 2 of the sons left the company.

If it is true that nothing lasts forever, Kirk can be said to have almost made it. It has a truly remarkable record. It has been a silver company which never made anything but silver and never compromised on quality, and Kirk himself, who died in 1872, felt he had achieved the goals he had set for himself that long ago day in 1815.

The silver of Samuel Kirk is in a class by itself, not only for what it is but for what the early production represents. Collectors and lovers of silver have always coveted Kirk and anyone interested can view part of Kirk's world by a visit to the Metropolitan Museum of Art in New York to see a recreation of ''The Baltimore Dining Room''. You will be transported immediately to a microcosm of the world of affluence in which Kirk himself moved and whose silver graced similar tables.

Now as our American silver industry diminishes, the elegant designs, authentic patterns, heavy weight and superior craftsmanship which characterize early Kirk represent a value which may never be equalled. The old silver of this important company becomes a national treasure to be sought after and cherished.

Fortunately for us silver is practically indestructible so that the legend that is Samuel Kirk will not be influenced by any actions of new owners whoever they may be. In 1990 Kirk Stieff was acquired by Brown-Forman of Louisville, Kentucky, a publicly held private company which sells whiskey - Jack Daniel's, Canadian Mist and the liqueur Southern Comfort.

The name Southern Comfort is apt - collectors of great silver are aware and take comfort that Samuel Kirk, this master silversmith from the American South will live as long as silver does.

KIRK PRICES

Pattern	Date of Issue	Dinner fork	Dessert knife	Dessert fork	Tea- spoon
Belle Auberge	1980	$48	$40	$50	$32

Belle Auberge

Pattern	Date of Issue	Dinner fork	Dessert knife	Dessert fork	Tea- spoon
Cheryl discontinued 6/1/1981		$35	$28	$37	$22

Cheryl

Pattern	Date of Issue	Dinner fork	Dessert knife	Dessert fork	Tea- spoon
Calvert discontinued Dec. 1979	1927	35	28	38	24

Calvert

Pattern	Date of Issue	Dinner fork	Dessert knife	Dessert fork	Tea- spoon
Cynthia discontinued Fall 1974	1957	28	22	30	19

Cynthia

Pattern	Date of Issue	Dinner fork	Dessert knife	Dessert fork	Tea- spoon
Golden Calvert, engraved	1982	37	30	38	27

Golden Calvert

Pattern	Date of Issue	Dinner fork	Dessert knife	Dessert fork	Tea- spoon
Cynthia Plain discontinued Fall 1974		25	20	28	17

Cynthia Plain

KIRK STIEFF

Pattern	Date of Issue	Dinner fork	Dessert knife	Dessert fork	Tea-spoon
Ellipse discontinued Jan. 1, 1975	1968	$28	$23	$28	$19

Pattern	Date of Issue	Dinner fork	Dessert knife	Dessert fork	Tea-spoon
Florentine discontinued Dec. 1979	1962	25	20	27	17

Florentine

Pattern	Date of Issue	Dinner fork	Dessert knife	Dessert fork	Tea-spoon
Florentine, monogrammed discontinued Dec. 1979	1962	26	21	28	18

Florentine

Pattern	Date of Issue	Dinner fork	Dessert knife	Dessert fork	Tea-spoon
Kingsley discontinued Fall, 1974	1959	26	22	28	18

Kingsley

Pattern	Date of Issue	Dinner fork	Dessert knife	Dessert fork	Tea-spoon
Kirk King	1824	45	37	48	28

Kirk King

Pattern	Date of Issue	Dinner fork	Dessert knife	Dessert fork	Tea-spoon
Mayflower	1846	45	35	47	30

Pattern	Date of Issue	Dinner fork	Dessert knife	Dessert fork	Tea-spoon
Old Maryland, plain	1850	38	30	35	26

Old Maryland

Pattern	Date of Issue	Dinner fork	Dessert knife	Dessert fork	Tea-spoon
Old Maryland, engraved	1936	$40	$32	$45	$28

Old Maryland, engraved

Pattern	Date of Issue	Dinner fork	Dessert knife	Dessert fork	Tea-spoon
Primrose discontinued Dec. 1979	1933	35	28	38	25

Primrose

Pattern	Date of Issue	Dinner fork	Dessert knife	Dessert fork	Tea-spoon
Quadrille discontinued Jan. 1977	1950	45	35	50	30

Quadrille

Pattern	Date of Issue	Dinner fork	Dessert knife	Dessert fork	Tea-spoon
Repoussé	1828	35	28	37	26

Repoussé

Pattern	Date of Issue	Dinner fork	Dessert knife	Dessert fork	Tea-spoon
Rose (Kirk Rose) discontinued, June 1, 1981	1937	45	34	47	28

Rose

Pattern	Date of Issue	Dinner fork	Dessert knife	Dessert fork	Tea-spoon
Selene	1978	30	27	31	23

Selene

Pattern	Date of Issue	Dinner fork	Dessert knife	Dessert fork	Tea-spoon
Golden Selene	1978	32	28	32	24

this pattern has a touch of 24K gold plating

Golden Selene

Pattern	Date of Issue	Dinner fork	Dessert knife	Dessert fork	Tea-spoon
Severn discontinued Fall, 1974	1940	$30	$26	$34	$25

Severn

Signet, plain	1958	26	21	28	17
Signet, monogrammed discontinued December, 1979	1958	28	22	28	19

Signet, monogrammed

Skylark discontinued Fall, 1974	1954	28	23	28	19

Skylark

Wadefield	1850	30	27	28	18

Wadefield

Winslow	1850	45	37	48	26

Winslow

Golden Winslow	1850	47	38	48	28

Golden Winslow

THE STIEFF COMPANY

In another quaintly named street in Baltimore Charles C. Stieff established his silver factory. The location was Cider Alley near Redwood Street in downtown Baltimore, the year was 1892. No longer was Baltimore the colonial bustling elegant enclave which greeted Samuel Kirk.

Company records speak of Stieff as a "born leader who left a legacy of positive actions for American silver." He also left a record of agressive advertising which made his name well known. He is remembered for being instrumental in enforcing Maryland's silver standards which demanded that all sterling silver so marked and advertised had to be at least 92.5 fine silver. The company says that as early as 1900 he was vigorously advocating the enforcement of strict silver standards by all manufacturers. His newspaper advertisements became well known. The Stieff Company placed an ad in the very first issue of the Baltimore Sunday Sun and has maintained an active advertising campaign ever since.

Stieff was a man whose principles required hard work coupled with excellent quality merchandise which would be affordable by all not merely the wealthy, and to him advertising was the best way to reach his audience. It was a very wide marketplace with many silver manufacturers and he was one of the early advocates of constant, effective newspaper ads. He was also a missionary for good quality sterling silver and as with most of the older individual entrepreneurs he insisted, even when he supplied only one retailer, that the silver he made be of the highest quality.

As the saying goes "he began as he meant to go on". He opened his first small shop, began to promote but did not feel he could advance beyond that one outlet and still keep up his standards. It was not until his son Gideon took over in 1914 that expansion began, first on the manufacturing level, then moving to a national retail campaign. In 1925 the well-known Stieff Wyman park facility was built and even in this Stieff's aesthetics are apparent. The building's landscaping, and the building itself reflected his attitude that anything as beautiful as sterling silver deserved equally beautiful surroundings. Lovers of this wonderful metal can understand that feeling.

The Wyman Park facility became a landmark and by the middle thirties Stieff began to open retail stores. Dealerships were given to other retailers in what were essentially early franchise deals. The retailers had to promise to adhere to strict quality controls set by Stieff. By the 1940s stores selling Stieff silver numbered 400 or more.

One of the greatest plums in the industry fell to Stieff in 1939 when the Stieff company was chosen to manufacture the Colonial Williamsburg reproductions. In 1951, with the cooperation of the Williamsburg staff, Stieff began to manufacture 18th century reproductions in pewter. Pewter has remained a big part of Stieff production.

The company added a stunning list of names for whom it began to make reproductions - Old Sturbridge Village, Historic Newport, Smithsonian, Monticello, and the Museum of Fine Arts in Boston. The company claims over 10 famous museums for which it makes pieces in pewter, silverplate and sterling. All of the approved reproductions are hallmarked as such.

In 1982 Stieff began making silverplated hollowware, not only approved reproductions but a new line. Advertising continues to be a big budget item, now relying heavily on women's magazines.

Stieff is another company which went its own way for a long time. The company says there were frequent offers to buy it over the years but it has remained in private hands. The company is still chock full of Stieffs all of whom run different departments. The company did begin actively seeking to buy smaller companies before the merger with Kirk. In 1967, Stieff bought the Scofield Company a local sterling manufacturer which was about to close. The Stieff company says, "We bought them mostly for their skilled craftsmen and artisans. It's hard to find skilled craftsmen anymore". In 1970, Stieff bought Colonial Miniatures, a company which made miniatures.

The American silver companies were struggling for survival and the merger of Kirk and Stieff not only united two old companies but is a good example of how accommodation to economic adversity in a cooperative spirit can save manufacturers of our great silver who could probably not have long existed independently.

The Stieff company says "the products we make are heavier than any line at a similar price, original in design and are popularly priced with a wide variety of patterns." Certainly a good enough list of reasons to collect Stieff even if they had never made the "Rose", "Forget-Me-Not", "Princess", "Carrollton", "Royal Dynasty" or "Shell Williamsburg" patterns.

Pattern	Date of Issue	Dinner fork	Dessert knife	Dessert fork	Tea-spoon
Betsy Patterson, Plain discontinued Dec. 1979		$25	$22	$28	$19

Betsy Patterson, Plain

Pattern	Date of Issue	Dinner fork	Dessert knife	Dessert fork	Tea-spoon
Betsy Patterson, engraved	1979	28	24	30	20

Betsy Patterson, engraved

Pattern	Date of Issue	Dinner fork	Dessert knife	Dessert fork	Tea-spoon
Carrollton discontinued Dec. 1979	1961	38	30	40	28

Carrollton

Pattern	Date of Issue	Dinner fork	Dessert knife	Dessert fork	Tea-spoon
Clinton discontinued Feb. 1974	1925	24	20	25	16

Clinton

Pattern	Date of Issue	Dinner fork	Dessert knife	Dessert fork	Tea-spoon
Corsage discontinued Dec. 1979	1935	48	38	42	35

Corsage

Pattern	Date of Issue	Dinner fork	Dessert knife	Dessert fork	Tea-spoon
Forget-me-not discontinued Feb. 1974	1910	40	30	42	25

Forget-me-not

Pattern	Date of Issue	Dinner fork	Dessert knife	Dessert fork	Tea-spoon
Homewood 1938 discontinued Dec. 1979		37	28	30	20

Homewood

Pattern	Date of Issue	Dinner fork	Dessert knife	Dessert fork	Tea-spoon
Lady Claire hand engraved	1925	$38	$30	$38	$25

Lady Claire

Pattern	Date of Issue	Dinner fork	Dessert knife	Dessert fork	Tea-spoon
Princess	1915	45	38	47	32

Princess

Pattern	Date of Issue	Dinner fork	Dessert knife	Dessert fork	Tea-spoon
Puritan discontinued Dec. 1979	1922	28	22	28	19

Puritan

Pattern	Date of Issue	Dinner fork	Dessert knife	Dessert fork	Tea-spoon
Rose Motif designed by Jose Barrera and Ralph W. Krusvson	1954	27	24	27	18

Rose Motif

Pattern	Date of Issue	Dinner fork	Dessert knife	Dessert fork	Tea-spoon
Rose		35	28	37	28

Rose

Pattern	Date of Issue	Dinner fork	Dessert knife	Dessert fork	Tea-spoon
Royal Dynasty	1966	45	38	50	35

Royal Dynasty

Pattern	Date of Issue	Dinner fork	Dessert knife	Dessert fork	Tea-spoon
Smithsonian	1978	45	35	45	30

Smithsonian

STIEFF

Pattern	Date of Issue	Dinner fork	Dessert knife	Dessert fork	Tea-spoon
Stieff Rose	1892	$45	$30	$35	$30

Stieff Rose

Williamsburg Queen Anne	1940	45	35	45	35

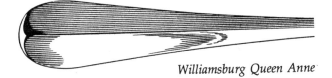

Williamsburg Queen Anne

Williamsburg Shell	1970	48	40	45	35

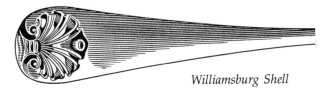

Williamsburg Shell

THE SCHOFIELD COMPANY

Consider the boast of the proud Schofield Company of Baltimore, "Our silver is made exactly as it was in the 18th century and every pattern made since 1871 is available for replacement". From its early days the company advertised that no pattern "has ever been discontinued". But in 1967 Schofield was sold to the Stieff Company and the new entity Kirk Stieff says, "None of the Schofield patterns are made. Unfortunately the tooling is not good enough to use because of our high quality standards and these patterns are permanently discontinued".

What a bonanza for collectors. All Schofield patterns permanently discontinued! It may be that the silverware is not up to Kirk or Stieff standards but many of its patterns are certainly lovely enough. In many cases surely sufficiently striking to become the goal of any collector! Lily, Mayflower, Baltimore Rose (for which Schofield is reputed to have cut the dies), Waterford and others. Most of the Schofield patterns are rarely seen, as not too much of it surfaces for resale. Imagine how scarce Schofield silver will become.

This company, which for all intents and purposes has passed into history, is considered another of the Baltimore silversmiths, although of a late vintage.

Frank M. Schofield founded the company in 1903 on Pleasant Street and like Kirk and Stieff he, too, had ancestors in the silversmithing trade. His great, great grandfather was fairly well known in London as early as 1740. All of the reports of the original production of this company speak of Schofield's "fine silverwork".

It was a rather interesting company which went through the usual series of mergers. At one point in an ingenious manner the company logo did not change basically but the "S" in its logo became an "H" to reflect a new partnership. Another intriguing aspect of this company is that the widow of Schofield ran the company from the late 1940s to 1965 when she sold the company. In a male dominated industry this was a long term tenure. Oscar Caplan, a small Baltimore manufacturer, bought the company in 1965 two years before the acquisition by Stieff.

It is easy enough to trace the progression of a company such as Schofield; what is mystifying is that what once was considered "fine silver" by knowledgeable writers is now considered inferior ware.

So little of this silver is available collectors should try for it, take it to their hearts for the waif it seems to have become. Scarcity is such a factor, many dealers have never seen examples of some of the patterns.

There are no existing company records of exact date of issue of Schofield patterns. All dates of issue are approximate.

SCHOFIELD PRICES

Pattern	Date of Issue	Dinner fork	Dessert knife	Dessert fork	Tea-spoon
Baltimore Rose	c.1900 1910	$48	$32	$40	$28
Hand Chased Rose					
Clouet	c.1905 1910	24	21	27	18

Baltimore Rose

Hand Chased Rose

Clouet

Pattern	Date of Issue	Dinner fork	Dessert knife	Dessert fork	Tea-spoon
Elizabeth Tudor both plain and hammered	c.1900	$20	$18	$22	$18
Frabee	1936	30	25	34	22
Josephine	c.1912	30	25	32	24

Elizabeth Tudor

Frabee

Josephine

SCHOFIELD

Pattern	Date of Issue	Dinner fork	Dessert knife	Dessert fork	Tea-spoon
Lady Caroline	c.1912 1913	$32	$26	$34	$24

Lady Caroline

Pattern	Date of Issue	Dinner fork	Dessert knife	Dessert fork	Tea-spoon
LaRochelle	c.1890	25	22	25	19

LaRochelle

Pattern	Date of Issue	Dinner fork	Dessert knife	Dessert fork	Tea-spoon
Lily	c.1915 1920	35	28	35	22

Lily

Pattern	Date of Issue	Dinner fork	Dessert knife	Dessert fork	Tea-spoon
Lorraine	c.1900	35	28	35	22

Lorraine

Lorraine with shield, hand engraved

Lorraine

Pattern	Date of Issue	Dinner fork	Dessert knife	Dessert fork	Tea-spoon
Mayflower	c.1915 1920	38	30	35	23

Mayflower

Pattern	Date of Issue	Dinner fork	Dessert knife	Dessert fork	Tea-spoon
Old Baltimore	c.1920	38	30	35	23

Old Baltimore

Pattern	Date of Issue	Dinner fork	Dessert knife	Dessert fork	Tea-spoon
Old English	c.before 1890	20	15	20	15

Old English

Pattern	Date of Issue	Dinner fork	Dessert knife	Dessert fork	Tea-spoon
Persian	c.1915	$26	$22	$28	$19

Persian

Pattern	Date of Issue	Dinner fork	Dessert knife	Dessert fork	Tea-spoon
Raleigh	c.1905	20	18	20	16

Raleigh

Pattern	Date of Issue	Dinner fork	Dessert knife	Dessert fork	Tea-spoon
Revere	c.1905 1910	20	18	22	18

Revere

Pattern	Date of Issue	Dinner fork	Dessert knife	Dessert fork	Tea-spoon
Scroll Edge Completely hand engraved	c.1905 1910	23	20	25	19

Scroll Edge

Pattern	Date of Issue	Dinner fork	Dessert knife	Dessert fork	Tea-spoon
Talbot	c.1912 1915	32	26	34	24

Talbot

Pattern	Date of Issue	Dinner fork	Dessert knife	Dessert fork	Tea-spoon
Virginia Dare	c.1915	34	28	36	24

Virginia Dare

Pattern	Date of Issue	Dinner fork	Dessert knife	Dessert fork	Tea-spoon
Waterford	c.1912 1915	32	26	32	24

Waterford

THE KIRK STIEFF COMPANY

All of the silverware issued after the merger of Kirk & Stieff in 1979 will be marked with the Kirk Stieff joint name. The long, admirable history of these two companies speaks well for the future.

The patterns already issued under the new corporate name - Dancing Surf and Paramount - are impressive.

The personnel of the companies seem happy with the venture and promise that the long traditions of both companies will not only be maintained, but ongoing design work and production of new patterns will strive for the same excellence.

Samuel Kirk & Son is one of the few companies to survive so long as an entrant in the American Silver Sweepstakes, Stieff has always made quality flatware so the outlook is bright for continued popularity and long life for this marriage.

Economic factors and popular appeal determine the health of any enterprise in the United States and the way of the silver industry in this country is becoming somewhat perilous. This is a fact collectors should engrave on their memories, but at the same time let us wish Kirk Stieff a glorious future.

Pattern	Date of Issue	Dinner fork	Dessert knife	Dessert fork	Tea-spoon
Paramount	1987	$32	$28	$34	$25
Dancing Surf	1986	45	35	47	28

LUNT SILVERSMITHS

  LUNT STERLING **Treasure**
(used since 1935) (used 1920-1954)

The company says the Lunt story begins in 1690 when "America was very young" and William Moulton was already considered an outstanding silversmith of his time. He began by making both table flatware and holloware which he geared to the needs and social aspirations of the sea captains and other gentry of the flourishing towns along the Massachusetts seacoast.

As with Samuel Kirk in Baltimore much later, Moulton well understood his market. So well in fact that after years of expanding business the thriving enterprise passed to his son and in succeeding generations the silversmithing Moultons carried on and became a respected family dynasty in the trade. In direct succession the business passed from son to son until the last Moulton silversmith, Joseph, was born in 1814, a somewhat unsettled time in America.

It was Joseph Moulton who took Anthony Towle as his apprentice. Today we recognize the Towle name in its own right but at that time Anthony, merely a learner, was finishing his apprenticeship with Moulton. Towle learned well and eventually began his own small business. In 1890 Anthony Towle and his son moved their business to Greenfield, Masssachusetts. The tangled skein of the early silver business cast its net over this move because among the skilled craftsmen he took with him to Greenfield was George C. Lunt. Lunt too, had been one of the well trained apprentices, he had served Anthony Towle beginning in 1882.

The removal to Greenfield did not benefit Towle and too much diversification and expansion caused the failure of his company. In 1900, A.F. Towle & Son Company allowed the ambitious George Lunt, with outside financial backing, to buy the company. In 1902 when Lunt purchased the factory, buying tools and trade marks of the A.F. Towle & Son Company, he began to create sterling silver under the Lunt name.

George Lunt was an interesting man, an artistic man and the sculptured quality of much of Lunt silverware owes its imaginative design and crisp carving to Lunt himself.

He studied design and modeling in Boston with sculptor Max Bachman and when he completed his studies he returned to his early love, silver, and became a designer for Anthony F. Towle and Son Company. Lunt's artistic bent was balanced by a wide practical streak. He became treasurer and General Manager of the new company as well as its chief designer. Many of the Rogers, Lunt and Bowlen Patterns reflect his long years of studying the craft traditions as well as the artistry of a mind well trained in the sculpture discipline. He worked well with others and it was he who was responsible for the influx of Rogers money into the enterprise. The Rogers of Rogers. Lunt and Bowlen was not of the famous silversmithing family but a resident of Greenfield who provided much of the financial backing.

The Bowlen of the Company name was William C. who arrived in Greenfield with the advent of the A.F. Towle & Son Co. and worked in the company with Lunt himself. Mr. Denham C. Lunt, Jr. says that "Bowlen was primarily factory oriented and when my grandfather George C. Lunt organized the company Mr. Bowlen put in a significant amount of money. Subsequently Bowlen ran the factory and my grandfather the office."

All of these early entrepreneurs and craftsmen seem to have been almost all things to all men. While it is true that Lunt ran the office and day to day business, both he and Bowlen were active in design and Bowlen's artistic genes were certainly passed on to his son Nord who was head designer for Rogers, Lunt and Bowlen for many years.

Their penchant for artistry in no way interfered with their penchant for business and although Lunt, as with most of the American success stories, knew prosperity and deprivation in a business sense, they did not waver from their purpose of making fine silver. Lunt always insisted on good quality and because of his own particular talents he always focused on excellent design work and his company always emphasized this facet of its work. They also claimed that every pattern was "open stock" a familiar assertion of companies of the time. Lunt utilized jewelry stores as favored outlets and even today has a line of silver designated as LUNT EXCLUSIVES which it retails only through "fine jewelry and silverware stores."

The company also felt that silver became much more personal and more loved by its owners when monogrammed and so stressed the importance of personalized silver in its advertising over a rather long period of time.

The company has heavily advertised all its patterns over the years and so the Lunt name is a familiar one. Many of their recent patterns are popular and many of the older, magnificent ones are almost forgotten. Collectors should be aware that early Lunt is affordable and beautiful. Although it made a fairly late start in the industry, Lunt is proud of the fact it can trace its direct ancestry back to the Moultons and although most people today are unaware of the Moulton name, collectors of coin silver treasure their work. Museums proudly display Moulton silver and it seems incredible that it can still be found at minimal prices. If you own any Moulton you own a piece of the silver on which the Lunt base is founded.

Recently Lunt has branched out into stainless steel and silver plated flatware in keeping with changing American tastes although Lunt patterns continue to excite silver lovers and are among the most desirable from a consistent sales aspect. Lunt is unusual not only in its direct line of succession but also in the fact that all of its sterling flatware is still made in the plant at Greenfield. One pattern, Regency Shell, is "sent out to have sections of the handles gold plated".

If you were to call the plant today and ask for Mr. Lunt, you might reach one of five Lunts currently active in the business. Lunt is controlled by Denham C. Lunt, Jr. Chairman of the Board, & CEO, James H. Lunt, President and Treasurer, George C. Hunt II, VP Sales, D. Colby Lunt III, VP Marketing, and John C. Lunt who is in sales. Very few businesses in this country have been able to succeed over so long a period of time while being privately held.

Collectors, all silver lovers, should seek the earlier Lunt patterns, they offer great potential as this long overlooked silver will rise in price. It is interesting to reflect that the 1902 formation date of Lunt is within the memory of some Americans, to others it seems a far-away world. To those to whom 1902 seems true antiquity (and isn't that what we seek?) try for patterns such as Chatelaine, Verona, Monticello, or Elaine. These early designs fit in well with our new passion for Victoriana, and can stand on their own merits as things of silver beauty.

Early Lunt should be a prime target for collectors, it is well designed, well executed, heavy and well balanced.

It is wonderful to hold a piece of this silver in your hand and to realize that in this one piece you hold the reputation and skill of the mind and hands which created it.

LUNT PRICES

Pattern	Date of Issue	Dinner fork	Dessert knife	Dessert fork	Tea-spoon
Adam	1921	$36	$30	$38	$24

Adam

Pattern	Date of Issue	Dinner fork	Dessert knife	Dessert fork	Tea-spoon
Belvedere	1972	$40	$30	$42	$32

Belvedere

Alexandra	1961	48	40	50	35

Alexandra

Bridal Lace	1973	28	24	28	22

Bridal Lace

American Victorian	1941	38	32	40	30

American Victorian

Carolina	1913	28	24	30	23

Carolina

Avondale	1978	60	48	65	35

Avondale

Carolina, engraved	1913	29	25	32	24

Carolina, engraved

Belle Chateau	1983	50	40	55	35

Belle Chateau

Carillion	1957	38	32	38	30

Carillion

Belle Meade	1967	40	30	42	32

Belle Meade

LUNT SILVERSMITHS

Pattern	Date of Issue	Dinner fork	Dessert knife	Dessert fork	Tea-spoon
Chased Classic	1936	$28	$24	$27	$19

Chased Classic

Pattern	Date of Issue	Dinner fork	Dessert knife	Dessert fork	Tea-spoon
Chateau (Chateau Thierry)	1919	26	24	28	19

Chateau

Pattern	Date of Issue	Dinner fork	Dessert knife	Dessert fork	Tea-spoon
Charles II	1934	48	42	54	30

Charles II

Pattern	Date of Issue	Dinner fork	Dessert knife	Dessert fork	Tea-spoon
Chippendale	c.1909	48	35	48	30

Chippendale

Pattern	Date of Issue	Dinner fork	Dessert knife	Dessert fork	Tea-spoon
Colonial Manor	1940	26	22	28	20

Colonial Manor

Pattern	Date of Issue	Dinner fork	Dessert knife	Dessert fork	Tea-spoon
Colonial Theme	1964	32	26	34	23

Colonial Theme

Pattern	Date of Issue	Dinner fork	Dessert knife	Dessert fork	Tea-spoon
Colony	1917	30	25	30	20

Colony

Pattern	Date of Issue	Dinner fork	Dessert knife	Dessert fork	Tea-spoon
Columbia	1982	$35	$30	$36	$22

Columbia

Pattern	Date of Issue	Dinner fork	Dessert knife	Dessert fork	Tea-spoon
Columbine	1973	48	35	55	32

Columbine

Pattern	Date of Issue	Dinner fork	Dessert knife	Dessert fork	Tea-spoon
Golden Columbine		50	38	60	35

Golden Columbine

Pattern	Date of Issue	Dinner fork	Dessert knife	Dessert fork	Tea-spoon
Coronet	1932	25	20	25	18

Coronet

Pattern	Date of Issue	Dinner fork	Dessert knife	Dessert fork	Tea-spoon
Cortland	1921	25	22	27	20

Cortland

Pattern	Date of Issue	Dinner fork	Dessert knife	Dessert fork	Tea-spoon
Counterpoint	1969	28	24	28	20

Counterpoint

Pattern	Date of Issue	Dinner fork	Dessert knife	Dessert fork	Tea-spoon
Delacourt	1966	65	45	70	40

Delacourt

LUNT SILVERSMITHS

Pattern	Date of Issue	Dinner fork	Dessert knife	Dessert fork	Tea-spoon
Delicacy	1987	$50	$37	$50	$32

Delicacy

Pattern	Date of Issue	Dinner fork	Dessert knife	Dessert fork	Tea-spoon
Dorothy Q.	c.1890	35	38	35	22

Dorothy Q

Pattern	Date of Issue	Dinner fork	Dessert knife	Dessert fork	Tea-spoon
Dresden Scroll	1971	30	25	30	23

Dresden Scroll

Pattern	Date of Issue	Dinner fork	Dessert knife	Dessert fork	Tea-spoon
Early American Plain	1926	25	23	26	18

Early American, plain

Pattern	Date of Issue	Dinner fork	Dessert knife	Dessert fork	Tea-spoon
Early American Engraved	1926	42	32	45	30

Early American, engraved

Pattern	Date of Issue	Dinner fork	Dessert knife	Dessert fork	Tea-spoon
Early Colonial	1930	27	24	28	19

Early Colonial

Pattern	Date of Issue	Dinner fork	Dessert knife	Dessert fork	Tea-spoon
Elaine	1893	$32	$28	$34	$24

Elaine

Pattern	Date of Issue	Dinner fork	Dessert knife	Dessert fork	Tea-spoon
Eloquence designed by Nord Bowlen	1953	58	40	60	37

Eloquence

Pattern	Date of Issue	Dinner fork	Dessert knife	Dessert fork	Tea-spoon
Embassy Scroll	1981	38	28	38	28

Embassy Scroll

Pattern	Date of Issue	Dinner fork	Dessert knife	Dessert fork	Tea-spoon
English Shell	1937	37	30	38	27

English Shell

Pattern	Date of Issue	Dinner fork	Dessert knife	Dessert fork	Tea-spoon
Enid (also called Chatelaine)	1894	45	32	47	30

Enid

Pattern	Date of Issue	Dinner fork	Dessert knife	Dessert fork	Tea-spoon
Festival	1936	30	26	30	18

Festival

Pattern	Date of Issue	Dinner fork	Dessert knife	Dessert fork	Tea-spoon
Fiddle	c.1885	28	24	30	20

Fiddle

LUNT SILVERSMITHS

Pattern	Date of Issue	Dinner fork	Dessert knife	Dessert fork	Tea-spoon
Floral Lace	1967	$23	$20	$23	$15

Floral Lace

Pattern	Date of Issue	Dinner fork	Dessert knife	Dessert fork	Tea-spoon
Florentine Scroll	1974	55	40	58	35

Florentine Scroll

Pattern	Date of Issue	Dinner fork	Dessert knife	Dessert fork	Tea-spoon
Georgian Manor	1958	35	25	32	25

Georgian Manor

Pattern	Date of Issue	Dinner fork	Dessert knife	Dessert fork	Tea-spoon
Golden Regency Shell	1989	50	40	55	32

Golden Regency Shell

Pattern	Date of Issue	Dinner fork	Dessert knife	Dessert fork	Tea-spoon
Granado	1929	24	20	26	20

Granado

Pattern	Date of Issue	Dinner fork	Dessert knife	Dessert fork	Tea-spoon
Greenfield	1890	28	24	30	21

Greenfield

Pattern	Date of Issue	Dinner fork	Dessert knife	Dessert fork	Tea-spoon
Jefferson	1883	24	22	25	16

Jefferson

Pattern	Date of Issue	Dinner fork	Dessert knife	Dessert fork	Tea-spoon
Jefferson, Hand hammered	1903	$25	$23	$26	$20

Jefferson, hand hammered

Pattern	Date of Issue	Dinner fork	Dessert knife	Dessert fork	Tea-spoon
John Hancock	1911	42	32	45	30

John Hancock

Pattern	Date of Issue	Dinner fork	Dessert knife	Dessert fork	Tea-spoon
Kimberley	1975	58	48	60	40

Kimberley

Pattern	Date of Issue	Dinner fork	Dessert knife	Dessert fork	Tea-spoon
Knickerbocker	c.1913	35	30	38	24

Knickerbocker

Pattern	Date of Issue	Dinner fork	Dessert knife	Dessert fork	Tea-spoon
Lace Point	1964	26	24	26	16

Lace Point

Pattern	Date of Issue	Dinner fork	Dessert knife	Dessert fork	Tea-spoon
Lasting Grace	1975	55	38	58	35

Lasting Grace

Pattern	Date of Issue	Dinner fork	Dessert knife	Dessert fork	Tea-spoon
Madrigal	1961	28	24	28	22

Madrigal

LUNT SILVERSMITHS

Pattern	Date of Issue	Dinner fork	Dessert knife	Dessert fork	Tea-spoon
Malvern	1970	$48	$32	$50	$28

Malvern

Pattern	Date of Issue	Dinner fork	Dessert knife	Dessert fork	Tea-spoon
Mary II designed by Frederick W. Koontz	1923		24	30	20

Mary II

Pattern	Date of Issue	Dinner fork	Dessert knife	Dessert fork	Tea-spoon
Memory Lane	1949	40	30	42	30

Memory Lane

Pattern	Date of Issue	Dinner fork	Dessert knife	Dessert fork	Tea-spoon
Mignonette	1960	38	30	38	26

Mignonette

Pattern	Date of Issue	Dinner fork	Dessert knife	Dessert fork	Tea-spoon
Modern Classic designed by Robert E. Locher, a well-known architect and interior designer.	1931	27	24	27	25

Modern Classic

Pattern	Date of Issue	Dinner fork	Dessert knife	Dessert fork	Tea-spoon
Modern Victorian	1941	32	28	34	23

Modern Victorian

Pattern	Date of Issue	Dinner fork	Dessert knife	Dessert fork	Tea-spoon
Monticello	1908	65	40	55	38

Monticello

Pattern	Date of Issue	Dinner fork	Dessert knife	Dessert fork	Tea-spoon
Mount Vernon	1905	35	27	32	20

Mount Vernon

Pattern	Date of Issue	Dinner fork	Dessert knife	Dessert fork	Tea-spoon
Narcissus	1903	$45	$35	$48	$30

Narcissus

Pattern	Date of Issue	Dinner fork	Dessert knife	Dessert fork	Tea-spoon
Navarre	1893	48	37	48	30

Navarre

Pattern	Date of Issue	Dinner fork	Dessert knife	Dessert fork	Tea-spoon
Nellie Custis	1915	27	24	28	18

Nellie Custis

Pattern	Date of Issue	Dinner fork	Dessert knife	Dessert fork	Tea-spoon
Old Colony	1895	48	35	48	28

Old Colony

Pattern	Date of Issue	Dinner fork	Dessert knife	Dessert fork	Tea-spoon
Old Dominion	1898	32	28	35	23

Old Dominion

Pattern	Date of Issue	Dinner fork	Dessert knife	Dessert fork	Tea-spoon
Orleans	1914	30	25	32	25

Orleans

Pattern	Date of Issue	Dinner fork	Dessert knife	Dessert fork	Tea-spoon
Priscilla	1897	29	24	30	22

Priscilla

Pattern	Date of Issue	Dinner fork	Dessert knife	Dessert fork	Tea-spoon
Provence	1896	40	32	40	26

Provence

LUNT SILVERSMITHS

Pattern	Date of Issue	Dinner fork	Dessert knife	Dessert fork	Tea-spoon
Pynchon	1908	$58	$35	$58	$32
Quintessence	1990	Prices are retail			
Raindrop	1959	27	23	28	18
Rapallo	1968	30	25	28	22
Regency	1935	28	23	25	19
Rondelay	1963	50	32	52	30
Rose Elegance	1958	40	35	42	30

Pynchon

Quintessence

Raindrop

Rapallo

Regency

Rondelay

Rose Elegance

Pattern	Date of Issue	Dinner fork	Dessert knife	Dessert fork	Tea-spoon
Shell (King's shell)	1888	$35	$29	$38	$25
Silver Poppy	1949	50	38	52	30
Spring Serenade	1957	25	21	26	17
Star Fire	1955	28	22	28	19
Summer Song designed by Nord Bowlen	1954	25	20	26	15
Sweetheart Rose	1951	25	20	26	15
Tipped	1883	32	25	32	22

Shell

Silver Poppy

Spring Serenade

Star Fire

Summer Song

Sweetheart Rose

Tipped

LUNT SILVERSMITHS

Pattern	Date of Issue	Dinner fork	Dessert knife	Dessert fork	Tea-spoon
Tudor	1900	$36	$28	$28	$25

Tudor

| Verona | 1894 | 50 | 40 | 54 | 30 |

Verona

| Virginia | 1910 | 40 | 30 | 45 | 30 |

Virginia

| Warren | 1883 | 22 | 19 | 24 | 18 |

Warren

| Wentworth | 1898 | 40 | 30 | 42 | 26 |

Wentworth

| William and Mary designed by Frederick W. Koontz | 1921 | 32 | 28 | 35 | 24 |

William and Mary

| Windsor | 1883 | 22 | 19 | 24 | 18 |

Windsor

A Modest Start — A Happy Ending

ALL Lunt patterns of Sterling are "open stock." You may start with as few pieces as you wish or can afford and add other pieces from time to time until your set is complete. It is surprising how rapidly you acquire additional pieces once you have selected your pattern and made a beginning, however modest. Friends and relatives are delighted to add to your pattern on Christmas and birthdays for they know that such gifts will please you. A penny or dime bank will help to swell your treasure. And best of all you can use and enjoy your Lunt Sterling from the acquisition of your first piece.

Your jeweler will gladly help you. He will make a record of the pieces you have and keep a copy of the marking you have chosen. Visit him soon and see the beauty of the Lunt designs in the Sterling itself. Lift and hold each piece in your hand so that you may realize its perfect proportions and balance. This visit will be a happy foretaste of the pleasure that Lunt Sterling will give you in your own home.

Lunt Silversmiths
GREENFIELD · MASSACHUSETTS

The Home of Exclusive Creations in Sterling Silver Tableware

THE TREE OF CRAFTSMANSHIP
Planted in 1690

𝕿reasure 𝕾olid 𝕾ilver
REG. U.S. PAT. OFFICE
Sterling 925/1000 *Fine*

CHATEAU-THIERRY

PRICE LIST

Prices Subject to Change Without Notice

January 1, 1924

Corrected to Sept. 22, 1924

STAPLES

	Doz.
Tea Spoons, Five O'Clock,	$15.00
Tea Spoons, Medium,	18.50
Tea Spoons, Heavy,	23.00
Tea Spoons, Ex. Heavy,	27.00
Dessert Spoons, Heavy,	37.50
Table Spoons, Heavy,	52.00
Soup Spoons, Heavy,	40.00
Dessert Forks, Heavy,	37.50
Dessert Knives, H.H.,*	40.00
Dinner Forks, Heavy,	52.00
Dinner Knives, H.H.,*	45.00
Breakfast Knives, H.H.,*	42.50

FANCY DOZENS

	Doz.
Berry Forks,	$18.00
Bouillon Spoons,	26.00
Butter Spreaders, Flat,	27.00
Butter Spreaders, H.H.,	38.00
Chocolate Spoons,	16.00
Coffee Spoons,	13.00
Fish Forks, Ind.,	50.00
Fish Knives, Ind.,	50.00
Five O'Clock Tea Spoons,	15.00
Fruit Knives, H.H.,	38.00
Grape Fruit Spoons,	29.00
Ice Cream Forks,	28.00
Ice Cream Spoons,	28.00
Iced Tea Spoons,	33.00
Lemon Knives, S.B., H.H.,	40.00
Orange Spoons,	29.00
Oyster Forks,	20.00
Ramekin Forks,	26.00
Salad Forks, Ind.,	35.00
Salt Spoons, Ind.,	6.00
Sherbet Spoons,	19.00

*Stainless Steel Blades supplied unless otherwise specified.

ROGERS, LUNT & BOWLEN CO.
Silversmiths
Makers of Distinctive Tableware
GREENFIELD, MASS.

CHATEAU-THIERRY

SETS

	Set
Baby Set, Fork & Spoon,	$3.50
Baby Set, K., F., & S.,	6.00
Child's Sets, 3 pc., H.H. Kn.,	
With Tea Spoon, Lt.,	7.50
With Tea Spoon, Med.,	7.75
Lettuce Set, F. & Sp.,	11.25
Olive Set, F. & S., Short,	4.75
Olive Set, F. & S., Long,	7.50
Salad Set, F. & S.,	16.00
Salad Set, Wood, F. & S.,	9.00

CARVING SETS, STAINLESS

Stainless Steel Blades and Forks
Carbon Steel Steels*

	Set
Meat, 2 pc., Guards,	$22.00
Meat, 3 pc., Guards,	29.00
Game, 2 pc., Guards,	22.00
Game, 3 pc., Guards,	29.00
Game, Sm., 2 pc., Guards,	20.00
Game, Sm., 3 pc., Guards,	26.00
Steak, 2 pc., Guards,	9.50
Steak, 3 pc., Guards,	14.00
Chop, 2 pc., without Guards,	8.50

*Stainless Steel is not suitable for Blade Sharpener.

CARVING SETS, CARBON†

Carbon Steel Blades,
Forks and Steels

	Set
Meat, 2 pc., Guards,	$20.00
Meat, 3 pc., Guards,	27.00
Game, 2 pc., Guards,	20.00
Game, 3 pc., Guards,	27.00
Game, Sm., 2 pc., Guards,	18.00
Game, Sm., 3 pc., Guards,	24.00
Steak, 2 pc., Guards,	9.00
Steak, 3 pc., Guards,	13.50
Chop, 2 pc., no Guards,	7.00

†If Carbon Sets are desired, kindly specify "Carbon" when ordering, for if not specified Stainless Steel will be supplied.

FANCY SINGLE PIECES

	Each
Asparagus Fork,	$14.00
Baby Food Pusher,	1.75
Baby Fork, S.H.,	1.75
Baby Knife, H.H.,	2.50
Baby Napkin Ring,	2.50
Baby Spoon, B.H., Lt.,	1.75
Baby Spoon, B.H., Med.,	2.00
Baby Spoon, S.H.,	1.75
Bacon Tongs,	4.00
Beef Fork,	3.50
Bell, Dinner Call, Lge.,	3.25
Bell, Dinner Call, Sm.,	3.00
Berry Spoon,	8.00
Bon Bon Spoon,	2.75
Bon Bon Tongs,	2.75

FANCY SINGLE PIECES
Continued

	Each
Bread Knife, H.H.,	$4.75
Butter Knife,	4.25
Butter Pick,	2.00
Cake Server, H.H.,	4.50
Carver's Assistant, H.H.,	10.00
Cheese Server, H.H.,	3.00
Cheese Scoop, Royal,	2.50
Cheese Scoop, Small,	3.75
Child's Food Pusher,	2.75
Child's Fork,	2.75
Child's Knife, H.H.,	3.20
Chocolate Muddler,	5.00
Cold Meat Fork,	5.75
Cream Ladle,	2.75
Cucumber Server,	5.75
Duck Shears, H.H.,	12.50
Egg Server, H.H.,	4.75
Fish Fork, Serving,	8.25
Fish Knife, Serving,	13.50
Grape Fruit Knife, H.H.,	3.75
Gravy Ladle,	6.25
Horse-radish Spoon,	2.75
Ice Cream Server, H.H., N.B.,	4.50
Ice Cream Server, H.H., W.B.,	4.75
Ice Spoon,	7.25
Jam Spoon,	2.25
Jelly Server, Tumbler,	2.25
Jelly Spoon,	5.00
Lemon Fork,	1.50
Lettuce Fork,	5.00
Lettuce Spoon,	6.25
Mayonnaise Ladle,	3.00
Mustard Spoon,	2.00
Nut Spoon,	9.75
Olive Fork, Long,	3.50
Olive Fork, Short,	2.00
Olive Spoon, Long,	4.00
Olive Spoon, Short,	2.75
Oyster Ladle,	19.00
Pickle Fork, Long,	3.50
Pickle Fork, Short,	2.00
Pie Server, N.B., H.H.,	4.50
Pie Server, H.H., N.B., Stainless,	5.00
Pie Server, W.B., H.H.,	4.75
Preserve Spoon,	5.75
Punch Ladle,	30.00
Salad Fork, Serving,	8.00
Salad Spoon, Serving,	8.00
Salt Spoon,	1.50
Sandwich Fork,	3.50
Sardine Fork,	2.75
Soup Ladle,	25.00
Sugar Sifter,	2.75
Sugar Spoon,	2.75
Sugar Tongs,	3.50
Teaette,	5.75
Teaette with Drip Cup,	9.75
Tea Strainer,	4.50
Tea Strainer with Drip,	9.00
Toast Fork,	7.25
Tomato Server,	7.25
Vegetable Fork,	9.00
Waffle Server, H.H.,	4.75

Prices for Gilding 10% Additional

Form 414-10-24

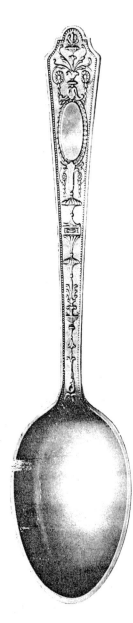

Treasure Solid Silver
REG. U.S. PAT. OFFICE
Sterling 925/1000 Fine

ADAM
PRICE LIST

Prices Subject to Change Without Notice

January 1, 1924
Corrected to Sept. 22, 1924

STAPLES

	Doz.
Tea Spoons, Five O'Clock,	$17.00
Tea Spoons, Medium,	20.00
Tea Spoons, Heavy,	25.00
Tea Spoons, Ex. Heavy,	30.00
Dessert Spoons, Heavy,	45.00
Table Spoons, Heavy,	60.00
Soup Spoons, Heavy,	47.00
Dessert Forks, Heavy,	42.50
Dessert Knives, H.H.,*	41.00
Dinner Forks, Heavy,	60.00
Dinner Knives, H.H.,*	45.00
Breakfast Knives, H.H.,*	43.00

FANCY DOZENS

	Doz.
Berry Forks,	$19.00
Bouillon Spoons,	29.00
Butter Spreaders, Flat,	29.00
Butter Spreaders, H.H.,	39.00
Coffee Spoons,	12.50
Fish Forks, Individual (*See Salad Forks, Ind.*),	40.00
Five O'Clock Tea Spoons,	17.50
Fruit Knives, H.H.,	39.00
Grape Fruit Spoons (*See Orange Spoons*),	29.00
Ice Cream Forks,	28.00
Iced Tea Spoons,	37.50
Orange Spoons (*Also appropriate for Grape Fruit*),	29.00
Oyster Forks,	21.00
Salad Forks, Ind. (*Also appropriate for Fish*),	40.00
Salt Spoons, Individual,	9.00

*Stainless Steel Blades supplied unless otherwise specified.

ROGERS. LUNT & BOWLEN CO.
Silversmiths
Makers of Distinctive Tableware
GREENFIELD. MASS.

ADAM

SETS

	Set
Baby Set, F. & S.,	$4.00
Baby Set, K. F. & S.,	6.75
Child's Sets, 3 pc., H.H., Kn.	
With Tea Spoon, Lt.,	8.00
With Tea Spoon, Med.,	8.25
Salad Set, F. & S.,	18.00

CARVING SETS, STAINLESS

Stainless Steel Blades and Forks, Carbon Steel Steels*

	Set
Meat, 2 pc., Guards,	$22.00
Meat, 3 pc., Guards,	30.00
Game, 2 pc., Guards,	22.00
Game, 3 pc., Guards,	30.00
Steak, 2 pc., Guards,	9.50
Steak, 3 pc., Guards,	14.00

*Stainless Steel is not suitable for Blade Sharpener.

FANCY SINGLE PIECES

	Each
Baby Fork, Short Handle,	$2.00
Baby Knife, H.H.,	2.75
Baby Spoon, Short Handle,	2.00
Berry Spoon (*See Serving Spoon, Large*),	9.00
Bread Knife, H.H.,	5.00
Butter Knife,	4.50
Cake Server, H.H., P.B.,	4.50
Cheese Server, H.H., P.B.,	3.25
Child's Fork,	3.10
Child's Knife, H.H.,	3.25
Cold Meat Fork (*Serving Fork, Small*),	6.50
Cream Ladle (*Also appropriate for Salad Dressing and Whipped Cream*),	3.00
Cucumber Server (*Server, Flat, Small*),	6.50
Duck Shears, H.H.,	12.50
Egg Server, H.H., P.B.,	5.00
Fish Fork, Serving (*See Serving Fork, Large*),	9.00
Fish Knife, Serving (*See Server, Flat, Large*),	9.00
Gravy Ladle,	6.00
Ice Cream Server, H.H., N.B.,	4.50

FANCY SINGLE PIECES
Continued

	Each
Ice Cream Server, H.H., W.B.,	$4.75
Jelly Server, Tumbler (*Also appropriate for Cream Cheese. Honey, etc.*),	2.75
Jelly Spoon (*See Serving Spoon, Small*),	6.50
Lemon Fork,	1.75
Mayonnaise Ladle (*See Cream Ladle*),	3.00
Olive Fork, Short,	2.00
Pickle Fork, Short,	2.00
Pie Server, H.H., N.B.,	4.50
Pie Server, H.H., N.B., Stainless,	5.00
Pie Server, H.H., W.B.,	4.75
Preserve Spoon (*See Serving Spoon, Small*),	6.50
Salad Fork, Serving (*See Serving Fork, Large*),	9.00
Salad Spoon, Serving (*See Serving Spoon, Large*),	9.00
Salt Spoon,	1.75
Server, Flat, Large (*Desirable for Fish. Fried Eggs, Sliced Tomatoes, etc.*),	9.00
Server, Flat, Small (*Used for Sliced Cucumbers, Croquettes, etc.*),	6.50
Serving Fork, Large (*Correct Service for Salads; appropriate for Serving Fish*),	9.00
Serving Fork, Small (*Correct Fork for Cold Meat. Also used as Small Salad Fork, Serving*),	6.50
Serving Spoon, Large (*Correct Service for Salads, Berries, etc.*),	9.00
Serving Spoon, Small (*Appropriate for Serving Preserves, Jelly. Also used as a Small Salad Spoon*),	6.50
Sugar Spoon,	3.00
Sugar Tongs,	3.75
Tomato Server (*See Server, Flat, Large*),	9.00
Waffle Server, H.H., P.B.,	5.00

Prices for Gilding 10% Additional

Form 490-10-24

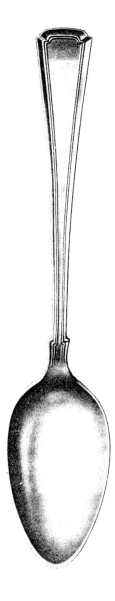

𝔗𝔯𝔢𝔞𝔰𝔲𝔯𝔢 𝔖𝔬𝔩𝔦𝔡 𝔖𝔦𝔩𝔳𝔢𝔯
REG. U.S. PAT. OFFICE
Sterling 925/1000 *Fine*

CORTLAND
PRICE LIST

Prices Subject to Change Without Notice

January 1, 1924
Corrected to Oct. 17, 1924

STAPLES

	Doz.
Tea Spoons, Five O'Clock,	$15.00
Tea Spoons, Medium,	17.50
Tea Spoons, Heavy,	21.00
Tea Spoons, Ex. Heavy,	26.00
Dessert Spoons, Heavy,	35.50
Table Spoons, Heavy,	48.00
Soup Spoons, Heavy,	38.00
Dessert Forks, Heavy,	35.50
Dessert Knives, H.H.,*	39.50
Dinner Forks, Heavy,	48.00
Dinner Knives, H.H.,*	44.00

FANCY DOZENS

	Doz.
Berry Forks,	$15.00
Bouillon Spoons,	24.00
Butter Spreaders, Flat,	26.00
Butter Spreaders, H.H.,	37.00
Chocolate Spoons,	14.00
Coffee Spoons,	10.00
Fish Forks, Ind.,	46.00
Fish Knives, Ind.,	46.00
Five O'Clock Tea Spoons,	15.00
Fruit Knives, H.H.,	37.00
Grape Fruit Spoons,	29.00
Ice Cream Forks,	28.00
Ice Cream Spoons,	28.00
Iced Tea Spoons,	32.00
Lemon Knives, H.H.,	39.00
Orange Spoons,	29.00
Oyster Forks,	19.00
Ramekin Forks,	26.00
Salad Forks, Ind.,	33.00
Salt Spoons, Ind.,	5.75
Sherbet Spoons,	19.00

*Stainless Steel Blades supplied unless otherwise specified.

ROGERS, LUNT & BOWLEN CO.
Silversmiths
Makers of Distinctive Tableware
GREENFIELD, MASS.

CORTLAND

SETS

	Set
Baby Set, Fork & Spoon,	$3.50
Baby Set, K., F., & S.,	6.00
Child's Set, 3 pc., H.H., Kn.,	
With Tea Spoon, Light,	7.50
With Tea Spoon, Med.,	7.75
Lettuce Set, F. & S.,	11.00
Olive Set, F. & S., Long,	7.00
Olive Set, F. & S., Short,	4.00
Salad Set, Fork & Spoon,	15.50
Salad Set, Wood, F. & S.,	9.00

CARVING SETS, STAINLESS

Stainless Steel Blades and Forks
Carbon Steel Steels*

	Set
Meat, 2 pc., Guards,	$20.00
Meat, 3 pc., Guards,	26.00
Game, 2 pc., Guards,	20.00
Game, 3 pc., Guards,	26.00
Game, Sm., 2 pc., Guards,	18.00
Game, Sm., 3 pc., Guards,	23.00
Steak, 2 pc., Guards,	9.00
Steak, 3 pc., Guards,	13.50
Chop, 2 pc., no Guards,	8.00

*Stainless Steel is not suitable for Blade sharpener.

CARVING SETS, CARBON†

Carbon Steel Blades,
Forks and Steels

	Set
Meat, 2 pc., Guards,	$18.00
Meat, 3 pc., Guards,	24.00
Game, 2 pc., Guards,	18.00
Game, 3 pc., Guards,	24.00
Game, Sm., 2 pc., Guards,	16.00
Game, Sm., 3 pc., Guards,	21.00
Steak, 2 pc., Guards,	7.50
Steak, 3 pc., Guards,	11.50
Chop, 2 pc., no Guards,	6.50

†If Carbon Sets are desired, kindly specify "Carbon" when ordering, for if not specified Stainless Steel will be supplied.

FANCY SINGLE PIECES

	Each
Asparagus Fork,	$13.50
Baby Food Pusher, S.H.,	1.75
Baby Fork, Short Hdle.,	1.75
Baby Knife, H.H.,	2.50
Baby Napkin Ring,	2.50
Baby Spoon, B., Light,	1.75
Baby Spoon, B., Med.,	2.00
Baby Spoon, S. Hdle.,	1.75
Bacon Tongs,	4.00
Beef Fork,	3.25
Bell, Dinner Call, Large,	3.25

FANCY SINGLE PIECES
Continued

	Each
Bell, Dinner Call, Small,	$3.00
Berry Spoon,	7.75
Bon Bon Spoon,	2.25
Bon Bon Tongs,	2.75
Bread Knife, H.H.,	4.75
Butter Knife,	3.75
Butter Pick,	2.00
Cake Server, H.H.,	4.50
Carver's Assistant, H.H.,	9.00
Cheese Scoop, Royal,	2.25
Cheese Server, H.H.,	2.75
Child's Food Pusher,	2.75
Child's Fork,	2.75
Child's Knife, H.H.,	3.20
Chocolate Muddler,	4.50
Cold Meat Fork,	5.50
Cream Ladle,	2.50
Cucumber Server,	5.50
Duck Shears, H.H.,	12.50
Egg Server, H.H.,	4.75
Fish Fork, Serving,	7.75
Fish Knife, Serving,	13.00
Grape Fruit Knife, H.H.,	3.75
Gravy Ladle,	5.50
Horse-radish Spoon,	2.50
Ice Cream Server, H.H., N.B.,	4.50
Ice Cream Server, H.H., W.B.,	4.75
Ice Spoon,	7.25
Jam Spoon,	2.25
Jelly Server, Tumbler,	2.25
Jelly Spoon,	4.75
Lemon Fork,	1.30
Lettuce Fork,	4.75
Lettuce Spoon,	6.25
Mayonnaise Ladle,	2.75
Mustard Spoon, Large,	2.00
Nut Spoon,	9.00
Olive Fork, Long,	3.25
Olive Fork, Short,	1.75
Olive Spoon, Long,	3.75
Olive Spoon, Short,	2.25
Pickle Fork, Long,	3.25
Pickle Fork, Short,	1.75
Pie Server, H.H., N.B.,	4.50
Pie Server, H.H., N.B., Stainless	5.00
Pie Server, H.H., W.B.,	4.75
Preserve Spoon,	5.50
Salad Fork, Serving,	7.75
Salad Spoon, Serving,	7.75
Salad Fork, Serv., Wood,	4.50
Salad Spoon, Serv., Wood,	4.50
Salt Spoon, Serving,	1.25
Sandwich Fork,	3.25
Sardine Fork,	2.75
Sugar Sifter,	2.75
Sugar Spoon,	2.50
Sugar Tongs,	3.50
Teaette,	5.75
Teaette, with Drip Cup,	9.75
Tea Strainer, Short Hdle.,	4.50
Tea Strainer, with Drip,	9.00
Tomato Server,	7.00
Waffle Server, H.H.,	4.75

Prices for Gilding 10% Additional

Form 427-10-24

MOUNT VERNON
PRICE LIST

Prices Subject to Change Without Notice

April 9, 1931

Treasure Solid Silver
REG. U.S. PAT. OFFICE
Sterling 925/1000 Fine

ROGERS. LUNT & BOWLEN Co.
Silversmiths
Makers of Distinctive Tableware
GREENFIELD. MASS.

MOUNT VERNON

STAPLES

	Twelve	Eight	Six	*One
Tea Spoons, Five O'Clock,	$11.00	$7.33	$5.50	$1.10
Tea Spoons, Medium,	14.00	9.33	7.00	1.35
Tea Spoons, Heavy,	16.00	10.67	8.00	1.50
Tea Spoons, Extra Heavy,	19.00	12.67	9.50	1.75
Dessert Spoons, Heavy,	30.00	20.00	15.00	2.65
Soup Spoons, Heavy,	31.00	20.67	15.50	2.75
Dessert Forks, Heavy,	30.00	20.00	15.00	2.65
Dessert Knives, H.H.,	36.00	24.00	18.00	3.15
Dinner Forks, Heavy,	40.00	26.67	20.00	3.50
Dinner Knives, H.H.,	40.00	26.67	20.00	3.50
Tea Knives, H.H.,	34.00	22.67	17.00	3.00

*The "One" price rate applies on purchases in lots of less than six.

FANCY DOZENS

	Twelve	Eight	Six	*One
Bouillon Spoons,	$23.00	$15.33	$11.50	2.10
Butter Spreaders, Flat,	22.00	14.67	11.00	2.00
Butter Spreaders, H.H.,	34.00	22.67	17.00	3.00
Coffee Spoons,	11.00	7.33	5.50	1.10
Fish Forks, Individual,	40.00	26.67	20.00	3.50
Fish Knives, Individual, H.H.,	45.00	30.00	22.50	3.90
Five O'Clock Tea Spoons,	11.00	7.33	5.50	1.10
Fruit Knives, H.H.,	34.00	22.67	17.00	3.00
Grape Fruit Spoons (See Orange Spoons),	24.00	16.00	12.00	2.15
Ice Cream Forks,	26.00	17.33	13.00	2.35
Iced Tea Spoons,	28.00	18.67	14.00	2.50
Orange Spoons (Also appropriate for Grape Fruit),	24.00	16.00	12.00	2.15
Oyster Forks,	17.00	11.33	8.50	1.60
Salad Forks, Individual,	24.00	16.00	12.00	2.15
Salt Spoons, Individual,	6.00	4.00	3.00	.65

*The "One" price rate applies on purchases in lots of less than six.

Stainless Steel Blades supplied on all cutlery and hollow handle serving pieces unless otherwise specified.

MOUNT VERNON

SETS

	Set
Baby Set, F. & S.,	$2.50
Baby Set, K., F. & S.,	4.50
Child's Set, 3 pc., H.H. Kn.,	
With Tea Spoon, Lt.,	6.75
With Tea Spoon, Med.,	7.00
Salad Set, Wood, F. & S.,	8.00

CARVING SETS
STAINLESS

Stainless Steel Blades and Forks
Carbon Steel Steels*

	Set
Meat, 2 pc., Guards,	$18.00
Meat 3 pc., Guards,	25.00
Game, 2 pc., Guards,	18.00
Game, 3 pc., Guards,	25.00
Steak, 2 pc., Guards,	8.00
Steak, 3 pc., Guards,	12.00
Chop, 2 pc., without Guards,	7.50

*Stainless Steel is not suitable or Blade Sharpener.

FANCY SINGLE PIECES

	Each
Baby Food Pusher,	$1.25
Baby Fork, S. Hdle.,	1.25
Baby Knife, H.H.,	2.00
Baby Napkin Ring,	2.50
Baby Spoon, B.H., M.,	1.75
Baby Spoon, S. Hdle.,	1.25
Berry Spoon,	8.25
Bon Bon Spoon,	2.25
Bon Bon Tongs,	2.25
Bread Knife, H.H.,	4.75
Butter Knife,	3.50

FANCY SINGLE PIECES
Continued

	Each
Butter Pick, H.H.,	$1.75
Cake Server, H.H., Stainless,	4.25
Cheese Server, H.H.,	2.75
Child's Fork,	2.65
Child's Knife, H.H.,	3.00
Cold Meat Fork,	5.00
Cream Ladle,	2.50
Cucumber Server,	5.00
Duck Shears, H.H., Plated Bl.,	12.00
Egg Server, H.H., S.S.,	4.50
Fish Fork, Serving,	8.25
Fish Knife, Serving,	13.50
Gravy Ladle,	5.00
Ice Cream Server, H.H., Stainless, Narrow	4.25
Ice Cream Server, H.H., Stainless, Wide,	4.50
Jam Spoon,	2.00
Jelly Server, Tumbler,	1.75
Jelly Spoon,	4.50
Lemon Fork,	1.25
Mayonnaise Ladle,	2.50
Olive Fork, Short,	1.50
Olive Spoon, Short,	2.25
Pickle Fork, Short,	1.50
Pie Server, H.H., Stainless, Narrow,	4.25
Pie Server, H.H., Stainless, Wide,	4.50
Preserve Spoon,	5.00
Salad Fork, Serving,	8.25
Salad Spoon, Serving,	8.25
Salt Spoon, Serving,	1.25
Sugar Spoon,	2.25
Sugar Tongs, Large,	3.00
Sugar Tongs, Small,	2.25
TABLE SPOON,	3.50
Tomato Server,	7.25
Waffle Server, H.H., S.S.,	4.50

Prices for Gilding 10% Additional

Form 120-7-31

WILLIAM & MARY
PRICE LIST

Prices Subject to Change Without Notice

April 9, 1931

Corrected to May 27, 1931

Treasure Solid Silver
REG. U.S. PAT. OFFICE
Sterling 925/1000 *Fine*

Rogers, Lunt & Bowlen Co.
Silversmiths
Makers of Distinctive Tableware
GREENFIELD, MASS.

WILLIAM and MARY

STAPLES

	Twelve	Eight	Six	*One
Tea Spoons, Five O'Clock,	$12.00	$8.00	$6.00	$1.15
Tea Spoons, Medium,	14.00	9.33	7.00	1.35
Tea Spoons, Heavy,	17.00	11.33	8.50	1.60
Tea Spoons, Extra Heavy,	21.00	14.00	10.50	1.90
Dessert Spoons, Heavy,	35.00	23.33	17.50	3.10
Soup Spoons, Heavy,	36.00	24.00	18.00	3.15
Dessert Forks, Heavy,	32.00	21.33	16.00	2.85
Dessert Knives, H.H.,	38.00	25.33	19.00	3.35
Dinner Knives, H.H.,	42.00	28.00	21.00	3.65
Dinner Forks, Heavy,	44.00	29.33	22.00	3.85
Tea Knives, H.H.,	34.00	22.67	17.00	3.00

*The "One" price rate applies on purchases in lots of less than six.

FANCY DOZENS

	Twelve	Eight	Six	*One
Bouillon Spoons,	$22.00	$14.67	$11.00	2.00
Bread and Butter Knives, H.H.,	34.00	22.67	17.00	3.00
Butter Spreaders, Flat,	24.00	16.00	12.00	2.15
Butter Spreaders, H.H.,	34.00	22.67	17.00	3.00
Coffee Spoons,	11.00	7.33	5.50	1.10
Cream Soup Spoons,	26.00	17.33	13.00	2.35
Fish Forks, Individual,	45.00	30.00	22.50	3.90
Fish Knives, Individual, H.H.	45.00	30.00	22.50	3.90
Five O'Clock Tea Spoons,	12.00	8.00	6.00	1.15
Fruit Knives, H.H.,	34.00	22.67	17.00	3.00
Grape Fruit Spoons (*See Orange Spoons*),	24.00	16.00	12.00	2.15
Ice Cream Forks,	26.00	17.33	13.00	2.35
Iced Tea Spoons,	30.00	20.00	15.00	2.65
Orange Spoons (*Also appropriate for Grape Fruit*),	24.00	16.00	12.00	2.15
Oyster Forks,	17.00	11.33	8.50	1.60
Salad Forks, Individual,	24.00	16.00	12.00	2.15
Salad Knives, H.H. (Tea Knives),	34.00	22.67	17.00	3.00
Salt Spoons, Individual,	7.00	4.67	3.50	.75

*The "One" price rate applies on purchases in lots of less than six.

Stainless Steel Blades supplied on all cutlery and hollow handle serving pieces unless otherwise specified.

WILLIAM and MARY

SETS

	Set
Baby Set, F. & S.,	$3.00
Baby Set, K., F. & S.,	5.00
Child's Sets, 3 pc., H.H. Kn.	
With Tea Spoon, Lt.,	6.75
With Tea Spoon, Med.,	7.00
Salad Set, Wood, F. & S.,	8.00

CARVING SETS STAINLESS

Stainless Steel Blades and Forks Carbon Steel Steels*

	Set
Meat, 2 pc., Guards,	$18.00
Meat, 3 pc., Guards,	25.00
Game, 2 pc., Guards,	18.00
Game, 3 pc., Guards,	25.00
Steak, 2 pc., Guards,	8.00
Steak, 3 pc., Guards,	12.00
Chop, 2 pc., without Guards,	7.50

*Stainless Steel is not suitable for Blade Sharpener.

FANCY SINGLE PIECES

	Each
Baby Food Pusher,	$1.50
Baby Fork, S. Hdle.,	1.50
Baby Knife, H.H., S.S.,	2.00
Baby Napkin Ring,	2.50
Baby Spoon, B.H., L.,	1.50
Baby Spoon, B.H., M.,	2.00
Baby Spoon, S.H.,	1.50
Berry Spoon (*Serving Spoon, Large*),	8.00
Bon Bon Spoon,	2.25
Bon Bon Tongs,	1.50
Bread Knife, H.H., S.S.,	4.75
Butter Knife,	3.75
Butter Pick,	1.75
Cake Server, H.H., Stainless Steel Blade,	4.25
Cheese Server, H.H., S.S.,	2.75
Child's Fork,	2.60
Child's Knife, H.H., S.S.,	3.00
Cold Meat Fork (*Serving Fork, Small*),	5.00
Cream Ladle (*Also appropriate for Salad Dressing and Whipped Cream*),	2.50
Cucumber Server (*Server, Flat, Small*),	6.00
Duck Shears, H.H., Plated Bl.,	12.00
Egg Server, H.H., S.S.,	4.50
Fish Fork, Serving (*See Serving Fork, Large*),	8.00

Continued

	Each
Fish Knife, Serving (*See Server, Flat, Large*),	$8.00
Gravy Ladle,	5.00
Ice Cream Server, H.H., Stainless, Narrow Blade,	4.25
Ice Cream Server, H.H., Stainless, Wide Blade	4.50
Jam Spoon,	2.00
Jelly Server, Tumbler (*Also appropriate for Cream Cheese, Honey, etc.*),	2.00
Jelly Spoon (*See Serving Spoon, Small*),	5.00
Lemon Fork,	1.25
Mayonnaise Ladle (*See Cream Ladle*),	2.50
Mayonnaise Ladle, Small,	1.75
Olive Fork, Short,	1.50
Olive Spoon, Short,	2.25
Pickle Fork, Short,	1.50
Pie Server, H.H., Stainless, Narrow Blade,	4.25
Pie Server, H.H., Stainless, Wide Blade,	4.50
Preserve Spoon (*See Serving Spoon, Small*),	5.00
Salad Fork, Serving (*See Serving Fork, Large*),	8.00
Salad Spoon, Serving (*See Serving Spoon, Large*),	8.00
Salt Spoon,	1.25
Server, Flat, Large (*Desirable for Fish, Fried Eggs, Sliced Tomatoes, etc.*),	8.00
Server, Flat, Small (*Used for Sliced Cucumbers, Croquettes, etc.*),	6.00
Serving Fork, Large (*Correct Service for Salads; appropriate for Serving Fish*),	8.00
Serving Fork, Small (*Correct Fork for Cold Meats; also used as Small Salad Fork, Serving*),	5.00
Serving Spoon, Large (*Correct Service for Salads, Berries, etc.*),	8.00
Serving Spoon, Small (*Appropriate for Serving Preserves, Jelly; also used as a Small Salad Spoon*),	5.00
Sugar Spoon,	2.25
Sugar Tongs, Large	3.00
Sugar Tongs, Small,	1.50
TABLE SPOON,	3.75
Tomato Server (*See Server, Flat, Large,*	8.00
Waffle Server, H.H., S.S.,	4.50

Prices for Gilding 10% Additional

WILLIAM and MARY HOLLOW WARE

768 Almond Dish, Diameter 5½ inches,	$10.00
769 Almond Dishes, Ind., doz.	35.00
713 Berry or Fruit Bowl, Diameter 8 inches,	40.00
747 Berry or Fruit Bowl, Diameter 9 inches,	50.00
749 Bouillon Cups, Lenox China Linings, doz.	150.00
714 Bread and Butter Plates, Diameter 6 inches, doz.	90.00
715 Bread Tray, Length 12 in.,	32.00
716 Candle Sticks, Height 10 inches, pair	66.00
714 Card Tray, Diameter 6 inches,	7.50
747/773/774 Centerpiece,	150.00
747/774 Centerpiece, without flange,	100.00
745 Child's Bowl, Diameter 5 inches,	10.00
714 Child's Plate, Diameter 6 inches,	7.50
754 Child's Cup, Height 2½ inches,	8.75
711 Chop Dish, Diameter 11¾ inches,	50.00
748 Coffee Cups, China Lining, with Saucers, doz.	150.00
708 Coffee Pot, capacity 1½ pints,	95.00
709 Sugar,	42.00
710 Creamer,	38.00
Coffee Set, 3 piece,	175.00
711 Coffee Set Tray, Round	50.00
766 Coffee Set Tray, Well 7 x 10 inches,	100.00
719 Compotier, Height 7 in.,	35.00
720 Compotier, Height 5 in.,	15.00
747 Fruit or Berry Bowl, Diameter 9 inches,	50.00
767 Goblets, Height 6 in., doz.	225.00
724 Gravy Boat, Length 7¾ inches,	$60.00
725 Gravy Boat Tray, Length 9¼ inches,	30.00
742 Mayonnaise or Sauce Bowl, Diameter 5 inches,	19.00
746 Mayonnaise or Sauce Bowl, Diameter 4½ inches,	10.00
753 Parfait Cups, Glass Lined, Height 5⅞ inches, doz.	125.00
713 Salad Bowl, Diameter 8 in.,	40.00
734 Salt, Open, Diameter 2½ inches,	4.50
743 Salt Shaker or Pepper (744), Height 4¼ inches, each	10.00
756 Salt Shaker or Pepper, Ind., Height 1 $\frac{9}{16}$ inches, each	2.50
735 Sandwich or Cake Plate, Diameter 9¾ inches,	25.00
771 Service or Place Plates, Diameter 10½ in., doz.	420.00
751 Sherbet or Fruit Cocktail Cups, doz.	150.00
700 Coffee Pot, capacity 2½ pints,	105.00
701 Tea Pot, capacity 2¼ pts.,	100.00
702 Sugar, Height 5¾ inches,	60.00
703 Creamer, Height 5½ in.,	50.00
704 Waste, Height 3⅛ inches,	35.00
Tea Set, 5 piece,	350.00
705 Kettle, capacity 2¾ pints,	325.00
706 Tray, Well 11 x 16½ in.,	275.00
707 Tray, Well 14 x 20¼ in.,	375.00
737-8 Vegetable Dish, Double, Length 11½ inches,	125.00
737 Vegetable Dish, Open, Length 11½ inches,	45.00
740 Water Pitcher, capacity 4 pints,	85.00
711 Water Pitcher Tray, Diameter 11¾ inches,	50.00

William and Mary 5-Piece Tea Set and Tray

Form 491-11-31

THE MOUNT VERNON COMPANY
Mt. Vernon, New York

The Mount Vernon Silver Company took its name from its location, Mt. Vernon, New York, on the edge of Westchester County. Its distinctive trademark reflects both its founder's orientation and its amalgamation with its predecessor Mauser Company, also of Mt. Vernon.

Although the Mauser name is almost never mentioned today by silver collectors the company was making fine sterling silver in the latter part of the 19th century. By the time the company had moved to Mt. Vernon and consolidated with other small manufacturers, Hays and McFarland, also of Mt. Vernon and the Roger Williams Silver Co., they presented an enticing target to the aggressive managers of Gorham which was ever expanding. By 1913, Mauser, as well as Hayes and McFarland, were part of a holding company controlled by Gorham. This holding company still exists and is known as the Sterling Silversmiths Guild. In effect, the company was no longer completely autonomous but actual purchase by Gorham did not take place until 1923.

Mt. Vernon was relatively short-lived as an independent - the mergers of Mauser, Hays and McFarland with Mt. Vernon did not lead to greater prosperity; in fact only made it more desirable for what we would call today a 'takeover'.

The production of Mt. Vernon was uneven. Some of the patterns are quite traditional, many are utterly simple but the design work on some of the patterns is exceptional. This small company produced L'Art Nouveau, for example, which while relatively plain manages by excellent artistic execution to embody the essence of the style. This one pattern rivals any of the pieces of that period issued by larger and better known companies. But even as early as 1922 this pattern was no longer being produced. A tremendous challenge to collectors.

The silver flatware of this company is not well known and not widely sought after as yet, but patterns such as Yetive, Queen, Sheraton, Louis XVI, Adolphus, Florence, Fontenay and Mexico and all of the florals are highly innovative and could easily satisfy today's burgeoning taste for the ornate in old silver.

The quality is good, the patterns often beautiful and obviously someone in the company was forward-looking and willing to experiment with design. Companies such as this produced much that is stunning. The Mexico pattern is a good example and can be compared with much that is supposedly new and modern. This company does not receive the recognition it deserves. No doubt this is so because Mt. Vernon was a shooting star in the industry. It came, it dazzled for awhile, it was absorbed and has almost disappeared. Collectors should seek out this mark embedded on some of the really exquisite silver the Mt. Vernon company made.

MOUNT VERNON PRICES

Pattern	Date of Issue	Dinner fork	Dessert knife	Dessert fork	Tea-spoon
Adolphus	c.1901	$42	$30	$45	$30

Adolphus

Pattern	Date of Issue	Dinner fork	Dessert knife	Dessert fork	Tea-spoon
Alden	c.1910	$20	$17	$22	$15

Alden

| Alamo | c.1905 | 30 | 25 | 34 | 25 |

Alamo

| Angelo | c.1909 1915 | 40 | 35 | 42 | 28 |

Angelo

MOUNT VERNON

Pattern	Date of Issue	Dinner fork	Dessert knife	Dessert fork	Tea-spoon
Apollo	1892	$38	$30	$40	$27

Apollo

Pattern	Date of Issue	Dinner fork	Dessert knife	Dessert fork	Tea-spoon
Chelsea	c.1916 1920	28	23	30	33

Chelsea

Corinthian	1902	40	32	45	28

Corinthian

Dahlia	c.1900 1908	40	30	48	32

Dahlia

Empire	c.1908	28	24	30	23

Empire

Florence	1905	45	32	45	28

Florence

Fontenay	c.1905 1912	38	30	38	27

Fontenay

Pattern	Date of Issue	Dinner fork	Dessert knife	Dessert fork	Tea-spoon
George II	c.1912	$28	$24	$28	$21

George II

George Washington	c.1910	37	32	40	27

George Washington

Harewood	c.1915	24	21	25	20
Harewood, engraved		25	22	26	22

Harewood, engraved

Harvard	c.1913 1915	38	32	40	28

Harvard

Hope	1899	35	30	40	25

Hope

Josephine	1899	35	28	39	25

Josephine

Kenwood	c.1916	28	24	30	24

Kenwood

148

MOUNT VERNON

Pattern	Date of Issue	Dinner fork	Dessert knife	Dessert fork	Tea-spoon
Lady Wynn	c.1913	$35	$30	$38	$24

Lady Wynn

Pattern	Date of Issue	Dinner fork	Dessert knife	Dessert fork	Tea-spoon
L'Art Nouveau	c.1910	40	30	45	30

L'Art Nouveau

Pattern	Date of Issue	Dinner fork	Dessert knife	Dessert fork	Tea-spoon
Laurel	c.1905	32	27	30	22

Laurel

Pattern	Date of Issue	Dinner fork	Dessert knife	Dessert fork	Tea-spoon
Lexington	c.1900	30	24	35	25

Lexington

Pattern	Date of Issue	Dinner fork	Dessert knife	Dessert fork	Tea-spoon
Louis XVI	c.1912	42	32	47	30

Louis XVI

Pattern	Date of Issue	Dinner fork	Dessert knife	Dessert fork	Tea-spoon
Louise	c.1904	40	35	45	30

Louise

Pattern	Date of Issue	Dinner fork	Dessert knife	Dessert fork	Tea-spoon
Mauser Warren	c.1900 1916	$28	$24	$30	$26

Mauser Warren

Pattern	Date of Issue	Dinner fork	Dessert knife	Dessert fork	Tea-spoon
Medford	c.1905 1906	30	26	32	25

Medford

Pattern	Date of Issue	Dinner fork	Dessert knife	Dessert fork	Tea-spoon
Mexico	c.1912 1915	40	35	45	30

Mexico

Pattern	Date of Issue	Dinner fork	Dessert knife	Dessert fork	Tea-spoon
Mount Vernon	c.1911	24	19	26	17

Mount Vernon

Pattern	Date of Issue	Dinner fork	Dessert knife	Dessert fork	Tea-spoon
Old South	c.1907	23	19	25	19

Old South

Pattern	Date of Issue	Dinner fork	Dessert knife	Dessert fork	Tea-spoon
Old South, engraved	c.1907	25	20	26	20

Old South, engraved

Pattern	Date of Issue	Dinner fork	Dessert knife	Dessert fork	Tea-spoon
Paul Revere	c.1913	$35	$28	$35	$25

Paul Revere

Pattern	Date of Issue	Dinner fork	Dessert knife	Dessert fork	Tea-spoon
Plymouth	c.1907	28	23	30	24

Plymouth

Pattern	Date of Issue	Dinner fork	Dessert knife	Dessert fork	Tea-spoon
Pointed Antique	before 1900	25	22	27	19

Pointed Antique

Pattern	Date of Issue	Dinner fork	Dessert knife	Dessert fork	Tea-spoon
Pomona	c.1905	32	26	35	24

Pomona

Pattern	Date of Issue	Dinner fork	Dessert knife	Dessert fork	Tea-spoon
Pompeiian	c.1910	30	25	30	23

Pompeiian

Pattern	Date of Issue	Dinner fork	Dessert knife	Dessert fork	Tea-spoon
Poppy	c.1900 1906	38	28	38	27

Poppy

Pattern	Date of Issue	Dinner fork	Dessert knife	Dessert fork	Tea-spoon
Princeton	c.1915	$27	$23	$28	$18

Princeton

Pattern	Date of Issue	Dinner fork	Dessert knife	Dessert fork	Tea-spoon
Queen	1898	45	32	47	30

Queen

Pattern	Date of Issue	Dinner fork	Dessert knife	Dessert fork	Tea-spoon
Queen Anne	c.1915	26	22	28	18

Queen Anne

Pattern	Date of Issue	Dinner fork	Dessert knife	Dessert fork	Tea-spoon
Queen Elizabeth	c.1900 1908	25	21	27	19

Queen Elizabeth

Pattern	Date of Issue	Dinner fork	Dessert knife	Dessert fork	Tea-spoon
R.W. Empire	c.1895 1905	30	26	35	25

R.W. Empire

Pattern	Date of Issue	Dinner fork	Dessert knife	Dessert fork	Tea-spoon
Ribbed Antique	before 1900	25	22	27	15

Ribbed Antique

MOUNT VERNON

Pattern	Date of Issue	Dinner fork	Dessert knife	Dessert fork	Tea-spoon
Round Antique	before 1900	$25	$22	$27	$15

Round Antique

Pattern	Date of Issue	Dinner fork	Dessert knife	Dessert fork	Tea-spoon
Rose	c.1909 1915	50	38	55	35

Rose

Pattern	Date of Issue	Dinner fork	Dessert knife	Dessert fork	Tea-spoon
Salem	c.1912	25	22	28	20

Salem

Pattern	Date of Issue	Dinner fork	Dessert knife	Dessert fork	Tea-spoon
Sedgwick	c.1908	23	18	25	15

Sedgwick

Pattern	Date of Issue	Dinner fork	Dessert knife	Dessert fork	Tea-spoon
Sheraton	c.1910 1915	40	30	42	28

Sheraton

Pattern	Date of Issue	Dinner fork	Dessert knife	Dessert fork	Tea-spoon
Strapped Antique	c.1910	23	19	25	18

Strapped Antique

Pattern	Date of Issue	Dinner fork	Dessert knife	Dessert fork	Tea-spoon
Sulgrave	c.1912	$24	$20	$25	$17

Sulgrave

Pattern	Date of Issue	Dinner fork	Dessert knife	Dessert fork	Tea-spoon
Tropea	c.1905 1910	35	27	38	26

Tropea

Pattern	Date of Issue	Dinner fork	Dessert knife	Dessert fork	Tea-spoon
Twentieth Century	c.1901	38	28	38	25

Twentieth Century

Pattern	Date of Issue	Dinner fork	Dessert knife	Dessert fork	Tea-spoon
Warren	c.1911	22	18	24	15

Warren

Pattern	Date of Issue	Dinner fork	Dessert knife	Dessert fork	Tea-spoon
Warwick	c.1905	30	25	34	23

Warwick

Pattern	Date of Issue	Dinner fork	Dessert knife	Dessert fork	Tea-spoon
Wentworth	c.1900 1908	25	21	27	20

Wentworth

MOUNT VERNON

Pattern	Date of Issue	Dinner fork	Dessert knife	Dessert fork	Tea-spoon
Westchester	c.1906 1915	$26	$22	$26	$19

Westchester

| West Point | c.1916 1920 | 23 | 20 | 25 | 17 |

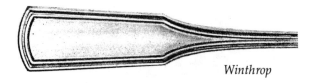

West Point

| Winthrop | c.1909 | 25 | 20 | 27 | 20 |

Winthrop

| Yetive | 1898 | 45 | 30 | 48 | 26 |

Yetive

COMMUNITY
STERLING

ONEIDA® *Heirloom*® STERLING

𝕳𝖊𝖎𝖗𝖑𝖔𝖔𝖒 𝕾𝖙𝖊𝖗𝖑𝖎𝖓𝖌
FROM GENERATION TO GENERATION

Oneida Community ⓄⒸ *Sterling*
(used since 1952)

◨ONEIDA®
The silver cube. Our silversmiths' mark of excellence.
(used since 1965)

In the year 1975 I bought two sterling silver spoons in a small shop in rural Wales. They were made by the Oneida Silversmiths and the progression of those spoons to such an isolated place is almost as unusual as the beginnings of the company which made them.

Upper New York State is a place of great pastoral beauty, a place which in the year 1848 attracted John Humphrey Noyes, a controversial religious leader. He saw Oneida, New York on the banks of the bubbling Oneida Creek as the panacea, where he and his followers could reach total equality which in the religious sense, means Utopia. A haven where he and his cult could settle in peace and harmony with their neighbors, unlike the hostility they had encountered in their previous home in Vermont. Noyes oversaw a true commune, all was sacrificed for the common good, and in keeping with his philosophy he called the place ONEIDA COMMUNITY. His vision encompassed work certainly, but he could never have imagined that the Oneida name would survive not because of its religious tenets but because of the great prestige it would achieve in the American silver industry.

All his followers were committed to the work ethic and in the early years almost exclusively farmed the land. This was not a commune looking only inward, indeed they worked actively with those outside their own group and as the need for money to support their life style increased so did their willingness to explore new financial fields. They began to produce for sale much that was useful and is now collectible but what has made them memorable to lovers of American silver was their foray in the year 1880 into the manufacture of silver plated flatware. Appropriately, they named their new enterprise ONEIDA COMMUNITY PLATE. Today we recognize it instantly and appreciate its quality.

Oneida still commands a large segment of the silverplate market but eventually it branched out to realize the profits to be made in sterling flatware. From 1933 to 1982 thirty one patterns had been manufactured. Most of them were so in tune with the times of production that they clearly and accurately mirror changing tastes. Some of the work produced by Oneida in the 1960s which seems so dated to us now represents the best of that particular period made by any manufacturer.

Oneida patterns continued popular. Life continued placid but the company's methods and the almost somnolent attitude of the hierarchy was about to receive a rude awakening.

As with most of the older American silver companies the workers in the factories were often second and third generations of the same families. It was comfortable and the system generally operated successfully but the machines were the same old models, life was predictable and safe for the community as well as the company.

In the 1970s the Asian giant stirred and the American flatware market for stainless particularly, became a target for low priced imports. As yet the sterling flatware seems safe, there have been no great inroads. Oneida was forced to change its ways. It upgraded its plant, sold off its Northern Ireland foctory, acquired Webster-Wilcox from International and computerized its technology among other things. It was the passing of the old order at Oneida except for its emphasis on taste and quality, always among its major priorities.

The future looks as bright as its silver. Oneida is a grand old name in American annals. October, 1981, in fact saw the first chief executive of the company who had been chosen from outside the founding Noyes family, a telling statistic.

Flatware is the key to success at Oneida. The company makes stainless, silverplate, gold electroplate as well as its sterling. The days of the hand-made silver have pretty well disappeared almost everywhere, at Oneida the company has installed a CAD/CAM system for the design and manufacture of flatware. Only a few of the old time skilled artisans are still hammering out designs by hand, so it behooves collectors to buy the older patterns as the supply lasts.

In recent years Oneida by dint of stringent economic management has moved from a low share of the silver flatware business to a strong, energetic position within that marketplace. The company is 110 years old, has only lately moved away from active management by a descendant of John Humphrey Noyes himself and is becoming of deep interest to collectors of older patterns. Oneida's newer patterns are ornate for the most part and quite stunning. The older sterling patterns while not exactly steeped in antiquity are part of the American silver legend - a company founded by an independent, zealous religious cult leader looking for an earthly Utopia but not too unworldly to see the need for profits to fuel his dream. The success of his pragmatism is evident and he probably would be pleased to note that 15 percent of the company's stock is now owned by the employees. This story of Oneida Silversmiths is a fascinating one, all the key elements of high drama are present.

Oneida has made some beautiful patterns, it is still fairly easy to fill out sets, prices on the secondary markets are overly reasonable and as a collectible it is unbeatable. If you've ever seen a full table setting of the King Cedric pattern, for example, you would be impressed. The company designs seem to have anticipated fashion in many cases and the silver, even the plain patterns, are always stylish.

Most of the sterling flatware was made after 1933, and these earlier patterns are waiting for collectors to realize their potential. Remember new developments have made obsolete much handwork on silver. Collectors surely realize such American silver at this price may never again be possible in this plastic world.

Pattern	Date of Issue	Dinner fork	Dessert knife	Dessert fork	Tea-spoon
American Colonial Heirloom sterling	1975	$27	$24	$28	$23

American Colonial

Pattern	Date of Issue	Dinner fork	Dessert knife	Dessert fork	Tea-spoon
Damask Rose designed by Grosvernor N. Allen and Mary Parker Fleming	1946	$35	$30	$38	$26

Damask Rose

Afterglow Oneida Heirloom Sterling	1956	40	32	45	28

Afterglow

Dover Oneida Heirloom sterling	1968	32	28	35	25

Dover

Belle Rose designed by Frank R. Perry	1963	28	22	25	20

Belle Rose

DuMaurier Oneida Community Sterling	1967	45	32	48	30

DuMaurier

Botticelli Oneida Heirloom Sterling	1972	45	36	48	30

Botticelli

Engagement Oneida Community Sterling designed by Mary Parker Fleming	1952	32	28	35	25

Engagement

Bountiful	1967	32	28	35	25

Bountiful

First Frost (discontinued) designed by Frank R. Perry Heirloom Sterling	1965	28	24	28	23

First Frost

Casa Grande Oneida Community Sterling	1967	35	28	38	25

Casa Grande

Flower Lane	1957	32	25	32	23

Flower Lane

ONEIDA

Pattern	Date of Issue	Dinner fork	Dessert knife	Dessert fork	Tea-spoon
Glenrose Designed by Ellen B. Manderfield	1959	$32	$26	$32	$24

Glenrose

Pattern	Date of Issue	Dinner fork	Dessert knife	Dessert fork	Tea-spoon
Grandeur Oneida Heirloom Sterling Designed by Frank R. Perry	1960	35	28	35	25

Grandeur

Pattern	Date of Issue	Dinner fork	Dessert knife	Dessert fork	Tea-spoon
Grand Majesty Oneida Heirloom Sterling	1976	48	35	48	32

Grand Majesty

Pattern	Date of Issue	Dinner fork	Dessert knife	Dessert fork	Tea-spoon
Guinevere	1967	35	28	35	25

Guinevere

Pattern	Date of Issue	Dinner fork	Dessert knife	Dessert fork	Tea-spoon
Heiress	1942	28	22	28	17

Heiress

Pattern	Date of Issue	Dinner fork	Dessert knife	Dessert fork	Tea-spoon
Impressario Oneida Heirloom St.	1974	35	25	35	26

Impressario

Pattern	Date of Issue	Dinner fork	Dessert knife	Dessert fork	Tea-spoon
King Cedric	1949	$40	$35	$45	$30

King Cedric

Pattern	Date of Issue	Dinner fork	Dessert knife	Dessert fork	Tea-spoon
Lasting Spring Oneida Heirloom Sterling Designed by Grosvenor N. Allen & Mary Parker Fleming & Lloyd	1949	30	25	35	21

Lasting Spring

Pattern	Date of Issue	Dinner fork	Dessert knife	Dessert fork	Tea-spoon
Mansion House (Casa Grande)	1948	37	27	35	24

Mansion House

Pattern	Date of Issue	Dinner fork	Dessert knife	Dessert fork	Tea-spoon
Martinique Oneida Heirloom Sterling	1967	34	28	35	24

Martinique

Pattern	Date of Issue	Dinner fork	Dessert knife	Dessert fork	Tea-spoon
Mediterranea (discontinued) Oneida Community Sterling	1967	45	32	45	28

Mediterranea

Pattern	Date of Issue	Dinner fork	Dessert knife	Dessert fork	Tea-spoon
Melbourne (discontinued) Oneida Community Sterling	1952	35	28	37	26

Melbourne

Pattern	Date of Issue	Dinner fork	Dessert knife	Dessert fork	Tea-spoon
Michaelangelo Designed by Frank R. Perry	1970	48	38	50	35

Michaelangelo

ONEIDA

Pattern	Date of Issue	Dinner fork	Dessert knife	Dessert fork	Tea-spoon
Patrician Community Sterling	1914	$25	$22	$28	$22

Patrician

Pattern	Date of Issue	Dinner fork	Dessert knife	Dessert fork	Tea-spoon
Reigning Beauty	1953	32	26	35	24

Reigning Beauty

Pattern	Date of Issue	Dinner fork	Dessert knife	Dessert fork	Tea-spoon
Rubaiyat discontinued	1969	28	24	30	23

Rubaiyat

Pattern	Date of Issue	Dinner fork	Dessert knife	Dessert fork	Tea-spoon
Satin Beauty (discontinued) Oneida Community Sterling	1966	32	26	35	24

Satin Beauty

Pattern	Date of Issue	Dinner fork	Dessert knife	Dessert fork	Tea-spoon
Sentimental Designed by Ellen G. Manderfield	1960	30	26	32	20

Sentimental

Pattern	Date of Issue	Dinner fork	Dessert knife	Dessert fork	Tea-spoon
Silver Rose (discontinued) Oneida Community Sterling	1956	27	24	27	20

Silver Rose

Pattern	Date of Issue	Dinner fork	Dessert knife	Dessert fork	Tea-spoon
Stanton Hall Oneida Heirloom Sterling	1949	45	37	48	30

Stanton Hall

Pattern	Date of Issue	Dinner fork	Dessert knife	Dessert fork	Tea-spoon
Teramo	1967	$25	$20	$25	$16

Teramo

Pattern	Date of Issue	Dinner fork	Dessert knife	Dessert fork	Tea-spoon
Twilight	1942	25	22	28	22

Twilight

Pattern	Date of Issue	Dinner fork	Dessert knife	Dessert fork	Tea-spoon
Venetian Scroll (discontinued) Oneida Heirloom Sterling	1970	32	26	32	24

Venetian Scroll

Pattern	Date of Issue	Dinner fork	Dessert knife	Dessert fork	Tea-spoon
Virginian Oneida Heirloom Sterling	1942	30	26	32	24

Virginian

Pattern	Date of Issue	Dinner fork	Dessert knife	Dessert fork	Tea-spoon
Vivant	1963	30	24	30	23

Vivant

Pattern	Date of Issue	Dinner fork	Dessert knife	Dessert fork	Tea-spoon
Will O' Wisp	1968	25	20	25	19

Will O' Wisp

Pattern	Date of Issue	Dinner fork	Dessert knife	Dessert fork	Tea-spoon
Young Love (discontinued) by Frank R. Perry	1958	28	24	28	21

Young Love

REED & BARTON

In 1984 Reed & Barton celebrated its 160th birthday. It evolved into this prestigious company out of the background of a small shop run by one man who was not only a skilled pewterer but a watch repairman as well. A man, like most others of his time and condition, who was insatiably curious about mechanical things, a general tinkerer who seemed to have been born with an instinctive feel for what was about to happen to his world.

What was happening in his time, 1824, was a changing domestic scene; pewter was beginning to lose popularity and as Isaac Babbitt discovered after a series of experiments in his little shed, the new and shiny durable metal alloy called Brittania was the coming thing. It had all the attributes necessary for hard use while keeping its luster. Britannia, simply a high grade of pewter, was far superior to the everyday pewter then in use. Britannia was the way to success, reasoned Babbitt - and so it proved. He began to expand his workspace, hired craftsmen to help him in his little building and business began to boom.

Among those workmen he hired were Henry G. Reed and Charles Barton. The year was 1826 and as with all new companies periods of hardship and distress hit Babbitt's enterprise. Henry Reed and Charles Barton, who had little money themselves, bought him out, and began to produce the wares under the name of Reed and Barton. This is an over simplification of the vagaries of the times and the gamut of emotions which must have beset them all, particularly Babbitt, but it is a tribute to all these men that they put aside personal differences and got on with it. To all of them, industry and hard work as well as innate taste and obvious intelligence were common factors. Above all though, was the willingness to work hard. All reports talk of the long hours and a "Willingness to work hard" which was true of all of them.

All contemporary articles speak of Reed's devotion not only to the workbench but to his absolute passion for "quality". It was almost an obsession and even when he became president of the growing company he still spent those long hours "at the bench". Reed actually spent 73 years with the company from 1828 to 1901. All these facts lead us to suspect that these men considered their work part of their being rather than just a way to make a living.

Originally Charles E. Barton and Henry Reed were just two of the workmen but they were jacks of all trades. They designed, crafted, administered, sold; anything that needed doing they were willing to do. Company titles meant little, in those days before the advent of sophisticated machinery clever hands meant the difference between success and failure.

But it was Henry Reed who masterminded the company through times of great troubles, through all the early peaks and valleys, and it is to him that the success of Reed and Barton is directly attributed. He was a master at production and when the Victorian age began to dawn he was willing to adjust to the new day. It is incredible to reflect on the fact that the highly successful and beautifully simple Britannia that was turned out by the company was, in reality, pretty much designed at the "bench" by the men making it. There were no committees, no consultants, no artists. What would they make of today's over-specialized world? The most interesting aspect of all this is that these men were basically technicians, they had great mechanical ability but for the most part, no formal artistic background. True, in the early days, they imitated designs, many of them English. They did it so well that eventually they surpassed their sources in line and quality. When practical electroplating of nickel silver became possible and enabled the Rogers Brothers to become the first American platers in 1830, Reed & Barton became aware but did not immediately act.

It was not until the mid 1850s that plating came to Reed and Barton. With the discoveries of large deposits of silver the price of the metal came down and many manufacturers seized the opportunity to branch out. Reed and Barton, with great vision, hired a skilled chaser and this handwork permitted them to abandon the very plain surfaces to decorate the handles with intricate carvings - in the early days mostly florals which we marvel at today.

Plated silver is almost unique in American business. It barely appeared on the scene when it became an instant success. Very few but the wealthy could afford solid silver and since plate silver mimicked the real thing so well it filled a great void for those who could not afford the real thing. It was a step up though and led the way to opening vast markets for sterling silver flatware, which became affordable for many rather than just the few.

The Civil War brought great changes to the country and the silver industry. A great depression set in, railroads were dispersing populations, silver prices were in decline and competition for both Britannia ware and silver plated wares was almost cut-throat. It was administrator George Brabrook who decided in the midst of the upheaval that marketing was the key. He knew sales and he was determined to sell Reed & Barton products.

By the 1870s he had pretty well captured the lucrative hotel market and this sustained the company through some very hard times. Brabrook realized the necessity and practicality of the well illustrated catalogue and today these catalogues sometimes are more costly than the silver they picture.

By the 1880s all companies were finding silverplated flatware harder to sell while many companies had jumped on the bandwagon. Earlier Reed & Barton, moving cautiously, finally made the decision to manufacture sterling silver flatware. Sterling flatware production began in 1889. This decision was not a creative one, but an entirely practical one. The company was forced to react to the fact of the huge merger of silver companies which became International. Competition was keen, but from the very beginning of the new venture when profits were not high, Henry Reed insisted, in the words of one report, "demanded" that every piece turned out to be of the highest quality. It is still a truism, if now a chiché, "that quality will tell" and it is probably that insistence on highest quality which brought prosperity to the company and accounts for its reputation today.

In the hard times to come with the death of Henry Reed in 1901 there was turmoil within the company. The man who took over, Reed's son-in-law, was a very different type but eventually he came to the same conclusion which had seen so much success for the company - "quality and more quality". He took the company into other lines as well but the sterling products became a mainstay. William Dowse, the son-in-law also realized the value of advertising and these promotions really paid off. Dowse also took over design and brought in others to help. When Dowse retired in 1923, control passed to another family member, Sinclair Weeks. He was married to Beatrice Dowse.

Under Mr. Weeks, Reed & Barton purchased Dominic and Haff in 1928. Dominic & Haff was in reality merged into Reed & Barton with co-mingling of personnel and patterns as well as the dies. One of the reasons Dominic & Haff is so difficult to find today is that some of the less profitable patterns of this very old company were soon abandoned and only the more popular patterns maintained. Reed & Barton tried other buyouts. The company says ''From 1949 until the mid 1960s we owned a company called the Webster Company in Attleboro. After we sold this company the patterns came under the control of the Towle Co''. Reed & Barton currently owns Eureka Manufacturing Co. which makes silverware chests and Sheffield Silver Co. which makes silver plated wares.

Reed & Barton is remarkable. Mr. Sinclair Weeks, Jr. continues the line which began with Isaac Babbitt in 1824. Reed & Barton has never lost sight to the two important functions of any good business - quality and design work suited to the needs and desires of the customer - not art for art's sake alone.

This privately held company has existed for so long because of its response to public demand and good management. It was indeed fortunate in Henry Reed but it also has had some talented designers - always the forgotten men and women. In the early days of sterling manufacture in this country most of the designers were foreign-trained but around the turn of the century many good art schools were established and almost all designers, except for exceptional reasons, were trained in this country.

Whenever a company has been privately held for so long they have obviously been doing many things right, besides turning out a superior product. In the case of Reed & Barton the company seems to have a long history of caring for its people. Anecdotes abound concerning benevolent treatment of retirees and those reluctant to retire. The feeling persists and today management seems unusually gracious for such a large business.

The company has produced approximately 110 patterns under the Reed & Barton name and 70 under the Dominic & Haff label. The company says many of these have never been pictured in recent literature. Some of these patterns are so spectacular they stand alone as pure art. Francis I which took three years to complete has a design so intricate and detailed it has to be studied to be truly appreciated. No wonder it has survived for more than 80 years as one of the favored patterns made in American silver. Marlborough is another classic. Interestingly enough, at one time this pattern was withdrawn and then reissued in the 1930s to capture the more subdued taste of that period. It is difficult to single out preference in the Reed & Barton design work because so much of it is wonderful. Love Disarmed which has a French Gray finish (which gives it a soft effect of light and shade) is so magnificent it has been recast. Les cinq Fleurs was enormously popular and continues to attract collectors. Les Six Fleurs, La Parisienne, the new Florentine Lace and Burgundy from the 1950s are quite beautiful. Serenade and Jubilee from the 1930s are masterful in their interpretation of the era. Pointed Antique, originally a Dominic & Haff pattern, is so well proportioned in its exquisite simplicity it continues very popular although first made in 1895.

Reed & Barton is not only a premier silver maker whose patterns should certainly command collector attention, it is a company which has mirrored our society almost precisely in its designs and advertising. Collectors should look, not only for their superb old catalogues but should buy the patterns of this company at current prices for prices can only go up on this fine collectible silver.

The company manufactures not only sterling flatware and holloware but stainless flatware, pewter holloware, Damascene as well as jewelry. Their annual Christmas ornaments are a marvelously inexpensive way to build an heirloom collection. There is also a line called Sterling II ''a new kind of flatware designed for the way we live today''. The pieces have stainless steel blades, bowls and tines ''and are practically care free''. The handles are sterling and the flatware costs about half the price of full sterling. This was introduced in 1989 and the company says ''it is the best of both worlds''.

You might say that of Reed & Barton itself. It has straddled both the 19th and 20th centuries with grace, it has made some truly splendid silverware. Among some grand, even noble designs which are now beginning to be avidly sought after, it has made its share of the mundane as well but even in these the quality of the workmanship is obvious.

Reed & Barton, the men and the company have been in a unique position in American life, when men wore silver buckled shoes and breeches and carriages could be heard moving over the cobbles the company recorded its own history of the times, during wares, depression, periods of great opulance and prosperity and periods of equally stark and severe economic distress Reed & Barton has been there; from pewter, to Britannia to silver plate to sterling, Reed & Barton has done it all. It is an amazing record.

Pattern	Date of Issue	Dinner fork	Dessert knife	Dessert fork	Tea-spoon
American Federal	1982	$35	$28	$34	$25

American Federal

Pattern	Date of Issue	Dinner fork	Dessert knife	Dessert fork	Tea-spoon
Antique	c.1912	25	22	28	20

Antique

Athenian	1891	30	26	35	23

Athenian

Athenian, engraved	1891	32	28	35	24

Athenian engraved

Betty Alden	1921	27	23	28	22

Betty Alden

Burgundy	1949	42	30	48	30

Burgundy

Cameo	1959	38	30	40	30

Cameo

Pattern	Date of Issue	Dinner fork	Dessert knife	Dessert fork	Tea-spoon
Chambord	1909	$35	$32	$38	$24

Chambord

Classic Rose designed by Theodore E. Cayer	1954	32	26	32	24

Classic Rose

Clovelly	1912	25	20	26	19

Clovelly

Colonial Classic	1937	38	30	40	30

Colonial Classic

Columbia	1912	25	22	27	20

Columbia

Copley	c.1912	25	23	27	21

Copley

Cotillion	1938	30	25	30	22

Cotillion

Pattern	Date of Issue	Dinner fork	Dessert knife	Dessert fork	Tea-spoon
Devon	c.1910	$32	$26	$32	$24

Devon

Pattern	Date of Issue	Dinner fork	Dessert knife	Dessert fork	Tea-spoon
Empire	1892	$42	$32	$45	$30

Empire

| Diadem | 1967 | 32 | 26 | 32 | 24 |

Diadem

| English Chippendale | 1984 | 37 | 30 | 40 | 28 |

English Chippendale

| Diamond | 1958 | 28 | 24 | 28 | 23 |

Diamond

| English Provincial | 1965 | 30 | 24 | 30 | 25 |

English Provincial

| Dimension | 1961 | 25 | 22 | 28 | 22 |

Dimension

| Flora | 1890 | 50 | 40 | 55 | 37 |

Flora

| Dorothy Quincy | 1912 | 28 | 24 | 28 | 24 |

Dorothy Quincy

| Florentine Lace | 1951 | 60 | 45 | 62 | 38 |

Florentine Lace

| Eighteenth Century | 1971 | 38 | 32 | 40 | 28 |

Eighteenth Century

| Four Georges | c.1920 | 24 | 18 | 25 | 19 |

Four Georges

| El Greco | 1972 | 55 | 45 | 58 | 38 |

El Greco

| Four Georges, engraved | c.1920 | 25 | 19 | 26 | 20 |

Four Georges, engraved

| Fragrance | 1941 | 40 | 35 | 45 | 30 |

Fragrance

REED & BARTON

Pattern	Date of Issue	Dinner fork	Dessert knife	Dessert fork	Tea-spoon
Francis I designed by Ernest Meyer	1906	$65	$48	$55	$38

Francis I

Pattern	Date of Issue	Dinner fork	Dessert knife	Dessert fork	Tea-spoon
French Antique	1901	24	20	25	17

French Antique

Pattern	Date of Issue	Dinner fork	Dessert knife	Dessert fork	Tea-spoon
French Antique, engraved	1901	25	22	25	18

French Antique, engraved

Pattern	Date of Issue	Dinner fork	Dessert knife	Dessert fork	Tea-spoon
French Antique-Watteau, engraved	1901	28	24	28	23

French Antique-Watteau, engraved

Pattern	Date of Issue	Dinner fork	Dessert knife	Dessert fork	Tea-spoon
French Renaissance	1941	50	40	55	37

French Renaissance

Pattern	Date of Issue	Dinner fork	Dessert knife	Dessert fork	Tea-spoon
Georgian Rose	1941	40	35	45	28

Georgian Rose

Pattern	Date of Issue	Dinner fork	Dessert knife	Dessert fork	Tea-spoon
Grand Renaissance	1967	48	35	48	30

Grand Renaissance

Pattern	Date of Issue	Dinner fork	Dessert knife	Dessert fork	Tea-spoon
Guildhall	1941	38	30	40	28

Guildhall

Pattern	Date of Issue	Dinner fork	Dessert knife	Dessert fork	Tea-spoon
Hampton Court	1964	35	30	35	24

Hampton Court

Pattern	Date of Issue	Dinner fork	Dessert knife	Dessert fork	Tea-spoon
Hawthorn	1934	28	24	28	21

Hawthorn

Pattern	Date of Issue	Dinner fork	Dessert knife	Dessert fork	Tea-spoon
Hepplewhite	1907	26	22	28	20

Hepplewhite

Pattern	Date of Issue	Dinner fork	Dessert knife	Dessert fork	Tea-spoon
Hepplewhite Chased	1907	28	26	28	26

Hepplewhite Chased

Pattern	Date of Issue	Dinner fork	Dessert knife	Dessert fork	Tea-spoon
Hepplewhite, engraved	1907	27	23	28	20

Hepplewhite, engraved

Pattern	Date of Issue	Dinner fork	Dessert knife	Dessert fork	Tea-spoon
Heritage	1924	30	25	34	22

Heritage

Pattern	Date of Issue	Dinner fork	Dessert knife	Dessert fork	Tea-spoon
Intaglio	1905	45	35	48	30

Intaglio

Pattern	Date of Issue	Dinner fork	Dessert knife	Dessert fork	Tea-spoon
Jacobean	1911	$35	$26	$36	$26

Jacobean

Pattern	Date of Issue	Dinner fork	Dessert knife	Dessert fork	Tea-spoon
Jacobean, engraved	1911	36	28	38	28

Jacobean, engraved

Pattern	Date of Issue	Dinner fork	Dessert knife	Dessert fork	Tea-spoon
Jubilee	1936	28	22	30	20

Jubilee

Pattern	Date of Issue	Dinner fork	Dessert knife	Dessert fork	Tea-spoon
Kings	c.1888 1890	45	35	48	30

Kings

Pattern	Date of Issue	Dinner fork	Dessert knife	Dessert fork	Tea-spoon
LaComtesse	1897	32	28	35	27

LaComtesse

Pattern	Date of Issue	Dinner fork	Dessert knife	Dessert fork	Tea-spoon
L'Elegante	1900	40	30	35	28

L'Elegante

Pattern	Date of Issue	Dinner fork	Dessert knife	Dessert fork	Tea-spoon
LaMarquise	1895	38	30	42	28

LaMarquise

Pattern	Date of Issue	Dinner fork	Dessert knife	Dessert fork	Tea-spoon
La Parisienne	1902	$55	$38	$55	$32

La Parisienne

Pattern	Date of Issue	Dinner fork	Dessert knife	Dessert fork	Tea-spoon
La Perle	1902	35	28	37	28

La Perle

Pattern	Date of Issue	Dinner fork	Dessert knife	Dessert fork	Tea-spoon
La Perle, engraved	1902	38	30	40	30

La Perle, engraved

Pattern	Date of Issue	Dinner fork	Dessert knife	Dessert fork	Tea-spoon
La Reine	1893	52	40	55	37

LaReine

Pattern	Date of Issue	Dinner fork	Dessert knife	Dessert fork	Tea-spoon
Lark	1960	28	23	28	24

Lark

Pattern	Date of Issue	Dinner fork	Dessert knife	Dessert fork	Tea-spoon
La Rocaille Later called Rocaille	1890	40	30	40	27

La Rocaille

REED & BARTON

Pattern	Date of Issue	Dinner fork	Dessert knife	Dessert fork	Tea-spoon
La Splendide	1902	$55	$38	$58	$35

La Splendide

Pattern	Date of Issue	Dinner fork	Dessert knife	Dessert fork	Tea-spoon
La Touraine	1895	38	30	40	28

La Touraine

Les Cinq Fleurs	1900	48	40	50	35

Les Cinq Fleurs

Les Six Fleurs	1901	95	60	100	60

Les Six Fleurs

Liberty	1917	25	22	27	20

Liberty

Love Disarmed	1899	165	125	165	85

Love Disarmed

Luxembourg	1890	32	28	35	26

Luxembourg

Pattern	Date of Issue	Dinner fork	Dessert knife	Dessert fork	Tea-spoon
Majestic	1894	$32	$26	$35	$26

Majestic

Marlborough	1906	38	30	38	27

Marlboro

Nancy Lee	1939	30	24	30	22

Nancy Lee

Old English Antique	c.1891 1895	25	22	25	19

Old English Antique

Old English Antique, etched	c.1891 1895	28	24	28	23

Old English Antique, etched

Old Virginia	1973	50	40	56	37

Old Virginia

Oval Thread	c.1890	28	22	28	19

Oval Thread

REED & BARTON

Pattern	Date of Issue	Dinner fork	Dessert knife	Dessert fork	Tea-spoon
Oxford	1928	$28	$22	$28	$20

Oxford

Pattern	Date of Issue	Dinner fork	Dessert knife	Dessert fork	Tea-spoon
Petite Fleur	1961	30	26	34	23

Petite Fleur

Pattern	Date of Issue	Dinner fork	Dessert knife	Dessert fork	Tea-spoon
Pointed Antique	1895	32	27	32	22

Pointed Antique

Pattern	Date of Issue	Dinner fork	Dessert knife	Dessert fork	Tea-spoon
Rembrandt	1915	38	28	38	27

Rembrandt

Pattern	Date of Issue	Dinner fork	Dessert knife	Dessert fork	Tea-spoon
Renaissance Scroll	1969	28	24	28	22

Renaissance Scroll

Pattern	Date of Issue	Dinner fork	Dessert knife	Dessert fork	Tea-spoon
Riviera	c.1911	26	22	26	19

Riviera

Pattern	Date of Issue	Dinner fork	Dessert knife	Dessert fork	Tea-spoon
Romaine	1933	40	30	45	28

Romaine

Pattern	Date of Issue	Dinner fork	Dessert knife	Dessert fork	Tea-spoon
Rose Cascade	1957	30	25	30	23

Rose Cascade

Pattern	Date of Issue	Dinner fork	Dessert knife	Dessert fork	Tea-spoon
Saint George	1918	$27	$23	$28	$23

Saint George

Pattern	Date of Issue	Dinner fork	Dessert knife	Dessert fork	Tea-spoon
Saint George, chased	1918	32	26	30	27

Saint George Chased

Pattern	Date of Issue	Dinner fork	Dessert knife	Dessert fork	Tea-spoon
Savannah	1962	40	30	42	27

Savannah

Pattern	Date of Issue	Dinner fork	Dessert knife	Dessert fork	Tea-spoon
17th Century	1941	32	26	35	25

17th Century

Pattern	Date of Issue	Dinner fork	Dessert knife	Dessert fork	Tea-spoon
Shell	c.1900	36	30	34	25

Shell

Pattern	Date of Issue	Dinner fork	Dessert knife	Dessert fork	Tea-spoon
Silver Sculpture	1954	28	23	28	20

Silver Sculpture

Pattern	Date of Issue	Dinner fork	Dessert knife	Dessert fork	Tea-spoon
Silver Wheat	1952	25	20	25	18

Silver Wheat

Pattern	Date of Issue	Dinner fork	Dessert knife	Dessert fork	Tea-spoon
Spanish Baroque	1965	40	32	45	30

Spanish Baroque

REED & BARTON

Pattern	Date of Issue	Dinner fork	Dessert knife	Dessert fork	Tea-spoon
Tapestry	1964	$28	$24	$30	$24

Tapestry

Tara	1955	35	27	35	26

Tara

Trajan	1892	50	40	55	32

Trajan

Tree of Life	1974	38	30	40	28

Tree of Life

Golden Tree Life 24K gold electroplate	1974	40	32	44	30

Golden Tree of Life

Vienna	1970	58	48	60	40

Vienna

Wakefield	1925	23	19	25	18

Wakefield

Woodwind	1986	48	40	48	32

Woodwind

165

Reed & Barton issued these price lists to their dealers for each pattern.

BETTY ALDEN

STAPLES	Per Dozen
Tea Spoons	
Five O'Clock	$16.00
Full Size, Trade	18.50
Full Size, Regular	23.00
Full Size, Heavy	30.00
Dessert Forks	
Trade	37.00
Regular	42.00
Heavy	50.00
Dessert Spoons	
Regular	42.00
Heavy	50.00
Table Spoons or Dinner Forks	
Regular	57.00
Heavy	68.00
Dessert Knives, stainless	39.00
Breakfast Knives, stainless	42.00
Dinner Knives, stainless	47.00

DOZENS	
Berry Forks	$16.00
Bouillon Spoons, small	26.00
Butter Spreaders	26.00
Chocolate Spoons, small	17.50
Coffee Spoons	12.00
Fish Forks, small, ind	36.00
Fish Knives, small, ind	50.00
Fruit Knives, stainless	38.00
Grape Fruit Spoons	25.00
Ice Cream Forks, small	23.00
Ice Cream Spoons, small	26.00
Iced Tea Spoons	26.00
Orange Knives, stainless	38.00
Orange Spoons	32.00
Oyster Forks	20.00
Oyster Cocktail Forks	16.00
Pastry Forks	37.00
Ramequin Forks, small	23.00
Salad Forks, small, ind	36.00
Sherbet Spoons, small	17.50
Soup Spoons	46.00

BETTY ALDEN

CARVERS	Each
Roast Knife, Fork or Steel	$9.50
Roast Knife, stainless steel	10.50
Roast Fork, plated tines	11.00
Game Knife, Fork or Steel	9.00
Game Knife, stainless steel	10.00
Steak Knife, Fork or Steel	4.75
Steak Knife stainless steel	5.50
Steak Set, small, two pieces	7.50
Steak Knife, small, stainless	4.50
Joint Fork, large	8.50

MISCELLANEOUS	Each
Almond Spoon	$3.00
Asparagus Fork	15.00
Asparagus Server	15.00
Beef Fork, small	5.50
Berry Spoon, large	11.00
Bon Bon Spoon	3.00
Butter Knife	4.25
Butter Pick, Gimlet	2.25
Butter Pick, Two Tines	2.25
Cake Server, h. h., p. b.	4.75
Cheese Server, h. h., p. b.	3.25
Child's Fork	3.50
Child's Knife h. h., p. b.	3.50
Child's Spoon	3.50
Cold Meat Fork, large	11.00
Cold Meat Fork, small	7.00
Cream Dipper	3.00
Cucumber Server	5.50
Egg Server, h. h., p. b.	5.50
Fish Fork, large	15.00
Fish Knife, large	17.50
Food Pusher, large	3.00
Food Pusher small	2.50
Gravy Spoon	15.00
Griddle Cake Server	13.00
Ice Cream Server	15.00
Ice Cream Slicer, h. h., p. b.	7.50
Ice Spoon	12.50
Ice Tongs, large	12.00
Jelly Server, extra small	3.00
Jelly Spoon, small	5.00
Ladle, Cream	3.50
Ladle, Gravy	7.00
Ladle, Oyster	18.00
Lemon Fork, three tines	2.75

	Each
Lemon Fork, two tines	$2.25
Lemon Server	5.50
Lettuce Fork	5.50
Lettuce Spoon	5.50
Mustard Spoon	1.75
Olive Fork	2.75
Olive Fork, long	2.75
Olive Spoon	2.75
Olive Spoon, long	2.75
Pastry Server, h. h., p. b.	4.75
Pea Spoon	12.00
Pie Knife, large	12.00
Pie Server, h. h., p. b.	4.75
Platter Spoon	15.00
Preserve Spoon	7.00
Salad Fork, large	13.50
Salad Fork, small	8.50
Salad Set, Olive wood	8.00
Salad Spoon, large	12.00
Salad Spoon, small	7.00
Salt Spoon	1.75
Serving Fork, plain tines	12.00
Serving Spoon, plain bowl	12.00
Sugar Spoon	3.50
Sugar Tongs, small	3.25
Toast Server	13.00
Tomato Server, large	12.00
Tomato Server, small	8.50
Waffle Server	13.00

For gilt bowls or tines add 10%

Retail Price List

Betty Alden

Bright or Oxidized Finish

Sterling Silver Flatware

TRADE MARK · STERLING

...effect Sept. 15, 1923. Subject to change without notice.

REED & BARTON

Established 1824

TAUNTON, MASSACHUSETTS

REPRESENTED AT

578 FIFTH AVENUE	- - -	NEW YORK
4 MAIDEN LANE	- - -	NEW YORK
5 NORTH WABASH AVENUE	- -	CHICAGO
150 POST STREET	- - -	SAN FRANCISCO
1005 COMMERCE STREET	- -	DALLAS
59 TEMPLE PLACE	- - -	BOSTON

CHAMBORD   FRENCH ANTIQUE   JACOBEAN
SAINT GEORGE   LIBERTY

Retail Price List

CHAMBORD
Oxidized Finish

FRENCH ANTIQUE
JACOBEAN
Bright Finish

ST. GEORGE
Bright or Oxidized Finish

LIBERTY
Oxidized Finish

Sterling Silver Flatware

TRADE MARK

STERLING

In effect Sept. 15, 1923.   Subject to change without notice.

REED & BARTON
Established 1824

TAUNTON, MASSACHUSETTS

REPRESENTED AT

578 FIFTH AVENUE	- - -	NEW YORK
4 MAIDEN LANE	- - -	NEW YORK
5 NORTH WABASH AVENUE	-	CHICAGO
150 POST STREET	- -	SAN FRANCISCO
1005 COMMERCE STREET	-	DALLAS
59 TEMPLE PLACE	- -	BOSTON

STAPLES

	Per Dozen
Tea Spoons	
Five O'Clock	$16.00
Full Size, Trade	18.50
Full Size, Regular	23.00
Full Size, Heavy	30.00
Dessert Spoons or Forks	
Regular	42.00
Heavy	50.00
Table Spoons or Dinner Forks	
Regular	57.00
Heavy	68.00
Dessert Knives, stainless	39.00
Breakfast Knives, stainless	42.00
Dinner Knives, stainless	47.00

DOZENS

Berry Forks	$16.00
Bouillon Spoons, small	26.00
Butter Spreaders	26.00
Chocolate Spoons, small	17.50
Coffee Spoons	12.00
Fish Forks, small, ind.	36.00
Fish Knives small, ind.	50.00
Fruit Knives, stainless	38.00
Grape Fruit Spoons	33.00
Ice Cream Forks, small	25.00
Ice Cream Spoons, small	23.00
Iced Tea Spoons	26.00
Orange Knives, stainless	38.00
Orange Spoons	32.00
Oyster Forks	20.00
Oyster Cocktail Forks	16.00
Pastry Forks	37.00
Ramequin Forks, small	23.00
Salad Forks, small, ind.	36.00
Sherbet Spoons, small	17.50
Soup Spoons	46.00

CARVERS

	Each
Roast Knife, Fork or Steel	$9.50
Roast Knife, stainless steel	10.50
Roast Fork, plated tines	11.00
Game Knife, Fork or Steel	9.00
Game Knife, stainless steel	10.00
Steak Knife, Fork or Steel	4.75
Steak Knife, stainless steel	5.50

	Each
Steak Set, small, two pieces	7.50
Steak Knife, small, stainless	4.50
Joint Fork, large	8.50

MISCELLANEOUS

	Each
Almond Spoon	$3.00
Asparagus Fork	15.00
Asparagus Server	15.00
Beef Fork, small	5.50
Berry Spoon, large	11.00
Bon Bon Spoon	3.00
Butter Knife	4.25
Butter Pick, Gimlet	2.25
Butter Pick, Two Tines	2.25
Cake Server, h. h., p. b.	4.75
Cheese Server, h. h., p. b.	3.25
Child's Fork	3.50
Child's Knife, h. h., p. b.	3.50
Child's Spoon	3.50
Cold Meat Fork, large	11.00
Cold Meat Fork, small	7.00
Cream Dipper	3.00
Cucumber Server	5.50
Egg Server, h. h., p. b.	5.50
Fish Fork, large	15.00
Fish Knife, large	17.50
Food Pusher, large	3.00
Food Pusher, small	2.50
Gravy Spoon	15.00
Griddle Cake Server	13.00
Ice Cream Server	15.00
Ice Cream Slicer, h. h., p. b.	7.50
Ice Spoon	12.50
Ice Tongs, large	12.00
Jelly Server, extra small	3.00
Jelly Spoon, small	5.00
Ladle, Cream	3.50
Ladle, Gravy	7.00
Ladle, Oyster	18.00
Lemon Fork, three tines	2.75
Lemon Fork, two tines	2.25
Lemon Server	5.50
Lettuce Fork	5.50
Lettuce Spoon	5.50
Mustard Spoon	1.75
Olive Fork	2.75
Olive Fork, long	2.75
Olive Spoon	2.75
Olive Spoon, long	2.75
Pastry Server, h. h., p. b.	4.75
Pea Spoon	12.00
Pie Knife, large	12.00
Pie Server, h. h., p. b.	4.75
Platter Spoon	15.00
Preserve Spoon	7.00
Salad Fork, large	13.50
Salad Fork, small	8.50
Salad Set, Olive wood	8.00
Salad Spoon, large	12.00
Salad Spoon, small	7.00
Salt Spoon	1.75
Serving Fork, plain tines	12.00
Serving Spoon, plain bowl	12.00
Sugar Spoon	3.50
Sugar Tongs, small	3.25
Toast Server	13.00
Tomato Server, large	12.00
Tomato Server, small	8.50
Waffle Server	13.00

For gilt bowls or tines add 10%.

CLOVELLY AND COLUMBIA

MISCELLANEOUS	Each
Almond Spoon	$2.75
Asparagus Fork	11.00
Asparagus Server	13.00
Baby Food Pusher	3.25
Baby Fork	2.75
Baby Knife, h. h., p. b.	2.75
Baby Spoon	2.75
Beef Fork, small	4.75
Berry Spoon, large	10.00
Bon Bon Spoon	2.75
Butter Knife	4.00
Butter Pick, Gimlet	1.75
Butter Pick, two tines	1.75
Cake Server, h. h., p. b.	4.50
Cheese Server, h. h., p. b.	3.00
Child's Fork	3.25
Child's Knife, h. h., p. b.	3.25
Child's Spoon	3.25
Cold Meat Fork, large	10.00
Cold Meat Fork, small	6.50
Cream Dipper	2.75
Cucumber Server	4.75
Egg Server, h. h., p. b.	4.75
Fish Fork, large	13.00
Fish Knife, large	16.00
Food Pusher, large	2.75
Food Pusher, small	2.25
Gravy Spoon	13.50
Griddle Cake Server	11.00
Ice Cream Server	13.00
Ice Cream Slicer, h. h., p. b.	6.50
Ice Spoon	11.00
Ice Tongs, large	11.00
Jelly Server, extra small	2.75
Jelly Spoon, small	4.50
Ladle, Cream	3.25
Ladle, Gravy	6.50
Ladle, Oyster	16.50
Lemon Fork, three tines	2.25
Lemon Fork, two tines	1.75
Lemon Server	4.75
Lettuce Fork	4.75
Lettuce Spoon	4.75
Mustard Spoon	1.75
Olive Fork	2.50
Olive Fork, long	2.50
Olive Spoon	2.50
Olive Spoon, long	2.50
Pastry Server, h. h., p. b.	4.50
Pea Spoon	11.00
Pie Knife, large	11.00
Pie Server, h. h., p. b.	4.50
Platter Spoon	13.50
Preserve Spoon	6.50
Salad Fork, large	12.50
Salad Fork, small	8.00
Salad Set, Olive wood	7.50
Salad Spoon, large	11.00
Salad Spoon, small	6.50
Salt Spoon	1.75
Serving Fork	11.00
Serving Spoon	11.00
Sugar Spoon	3.25
Sugar Tongs, small	3.00
Toast Server	11.00
Tomato Server, large	11.00
Tomato Server, small	8.00
Waffle Server	11.00

CLOVELLY
Bright Finish

COLUMBIA
Bright Finish

STAPLES	Per Dozen
Tea Spoons	
Five O'Clock	14.00
Full Size, Trade	17.00
Full Size, Regular	21.00
Full Size, Heavy	25.00
Dessert Spoons or Forks	
Regular	34.00
Heavy	42.00
Table Spoons or Dinner Forks	
Regular	44.00
Heavy	55.00
Dessert Knives, stainless	37.00
Breakfast Knives, stainless	40.00
Dinner Knives, stainless	45.00

DOZENS	
Berry Forks	$14.00
Bouillon Spoons, small	23.00
Butter Spreaders	23.00
Chocolate Spoons	15.00
Coffee Spoons	11.00
Fish Forks, small, ind.	32.00
Fish Knives, small, ind.	45.00
Fruit Knives, stainless	36.00
Grape Fruit Spoons	28.00
Ice Cream Forks, small	22.00
Ice Cream Spoons, small	21.00
Iced Tea Spoons	24.00
Orange Knives, stainless	36.00
Orange Spoons	28.00
Oyster Forks	15.00
Oyster Cocktail Forks	14.00
Pastry Forks	33.00
Ramequin Forks	21.00
Salad Forks, small, ind.	32.00
*Salt Spoons, ind.	6.50
Sherbet Spoons	15.00
Soup Spoons	38.00
*Made only in Clovelly.	

CARVERS	Each
Roast Knife, Fork or Steel	$8.50
Roast Knife, stainless steel	9.50
Roast Fork, plated tines	9.50
Game Knife, Fork or Steel	8.00
Game Knife, stainless steel	9.00
Steak Knife, Fork or Steel	4.50
Steak Knife, stainless steel	5.50
Steak Set, small, two pieces	7.00
Steak Knife, small, stainless	4.25
Joint Fork, large	7.50

For gilt bowls or tines add 10%.

DOROTHY QUINCY

STAPLES	Per Dozen
Tea Spoons	
Five O'Clock	$19.00
Full Size, Trade	21.00
Full Size, Regular	24.00
Full Size, Heavy	30.00
Dessert Spoons or Forks	
Regular	40.00
Heavy	48.00
Table Spoons or Dinner Forks	
Regular	53.00
Heavy	63.00
Dessert Knives, stainless	43.00
Breakfast Knives, stainless	46.00
Dinner Knives, stainless	51.00

DOZENS	
Berry Forks	$17.50
Bouillon Spoons, small	26.00
Butter Spreaders	26.00
Chocolate Spoons	13.50
Coffee Spoons	13.50
Fish Forks, small, ind	36.00
Fish Knives, small, ind	51.00
Fruit Knives, stainless	40.00
Grape Fruit Spoons	33.00
Ice Cream Forks, small	28.00
Ice Cream Spoons, small	25.00
Iced Tea Spoons	28.00
Orange Knives, stainless	40.00
Orange Spoons	33.00
Oyster Forks	20.00
Oyster Cocktail Forks	18.50
Pastry Forks	37.00
Ramequin Forks	25.00
Salad Forks, small, ind	36.00
Sherbet Spoons	18.50
Soup Spoons	44.00

CARVERS	Each
Roast Knife, Fork or Steel	$9.50
Roast Knife, stainless steel	10.50
Roast Fork, plated tines	11.00
Game Knife, Fork or Steel	9.00
Game Knife, stainless steel	10.00
Steak Knife, Fork or Steel	5.50
Steak Knife, stainless steel	6.00
Steak Set, small, two pieces	8.50
Steak Knife, small, stainless	5.00
Joint Fork, large	9.00

DOROTHY QUINCY

MISCELLANEOUS	Each
Almond Spoon	$3.00
Asparagus Fork	14.00
Asparagus Server	14.00
Baby Food Pusher	3.50
Baby Fork	3.00
Baby Knife, h. h., p. b.	3.00
Baby Spoon	3.00
Beef Fork, small	5.50
Berry Spoon, large	11.00
Bon Bon Spoon	3.00
Butter Knife	4.50
Butter Pick, Gimlet	2.25
Butter Pick, Two Tines	2.25
Cake Server, h. h., p. b.	5.50
Cheese Server, h. h., p. b.	4.00
Child's Fork	3.75
Child's Knife, h. h., p. b.	3.75
Child's Spoon	3.75
Cold Meat Fork, large	11.00
Cold Meat Fork, small	7.50
Cream Dipper	3.25
Cucumber Server	5.50
Egg Server, h. h., p. b.	6.00
Fish Fork, large	14.00
Fish Knife, large	17.00
Food Pusher, large	3.25
Food Pusher, small	2.50
Gravy Spoon	15.00
Griddle Cake Server	13.00
Ice Cream Server	14.00
Ice Cream Slicer, h. h., p. b.	7.50
Ice Spoon	12.00
Ice Tongs, large	12.00
Jelly Server, extra small	3.25
Jelly Spoon, small	5.50
Ladle, Cream	4.00
Ladle, Gravy	7.50
Ladle, Oyster	18.00
Lemon Fork, three tines	2.75
Lemon Fork two tines	2.25
Lemon Server	5.50
Lettuce Fork	6.00
Lettuce Spoon	6.00
Mustard Spoon	2.25
Olive Fork, small	3.00
Olive Fork, long	3.00
Olive Spoon	3.00

	Each
Olive Spoon, long	3.00
Pastry Server, h. h., p. b.	5.50
Pea Spoon	12.50
Pie Knife, large	12.50
Pie Server, h. h., p. b	5.50
Platter Spoon	15.00
Preserve Spoon	7.50
Salad Fork, large	13.50
Salad Fork, small	8.50
Salad Set, Olive wood	9.00
Salad Spoon, large	12.50
Salad Spoon, small	7.50
Salt Spoon	2.25
Serving Fork	12.50
Serving Spoon	12.50
Sugar Spoon	4.00
Sugar Tongs, small	3.75
Toast Server	13.00
Tomato Server, large	12.50
Tomato Server, small	8.50
Waffle Server	13.00

For gilt bowls or tines add 10%.

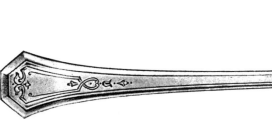

Retail Price List

Dorothy Quincy

Oxidized Finish

Sterling Silver Flatware

TRADE MARK [R] STERLING

In effect Sept. 15, 1923. Subject to change without notice

REED & BARTON

Established 1824

TAUNTON, MASSACHUSETTS

REPRESENTED AT

578 FIFTH AVENUE	NEW YORK
4 MAIDEN LANE	NEW YORK
5 NORTH WABASH AVENUE	CHICAGO
150 POST STREET	SAN FRANCISCO
1005 COMMERCE STREET	DALLAS
59 TEMPLE PLACE	BOSTON

Retail Price List

Francis I.

Oxidized Finish

Sterling Silver Flatware

TRADE MARK

R STERLING

In effect Sept. 15, 1923.   Subject to change without notice.

REED & BARTON

Established 1824

TAUNTON, MASSACHUSETTS

REPRESENTED AT

578 FIFTH AVENUE	- - NEW YORK
4 MAIDEN LANE	- - NEW YORK
5 NORTH WABASH AVENUE	- - CHICAGO
150 POST STREET	- - SAN FRANCISCO
1005 COMMERCE STREET	- - DALLAS
59 TEMPLE PLACE	- - BOSTON

FRANCIS I.

STAPLES	Per Dozen
Tea Spoons	
Five O'Clock	$21.00
Full Size, Heavy	33.00
Full Size, Massive	41.00
Dessert Spoons or Forks	
Heavy	58.00
Massive	66.00
Table Spoons or Dinner Forks	
Heavy	73.00
Massive	82.00
Dessert Knives, stainless	43.00
Breakfast Knives, stainless	46.00
Dinner Knives, stainless	51.00

DOZENS	
Berry Forks	$17.50
Bouillon Spoons, small	30.00
Butter Spreaders	35.00
Chocolate Spoons	19.00
Coffee Spoons	13.00
Fish Forks, small, ind.	40.00
Fish Knives, small, ind.	55.00
Fruit Knives, stainless	42.00
Grape Fruit Spoons	36.00
Ice Cream Forks, small	28.00
Ice Cream Spoons, small	25.00
Iced Tea Spoons	30.00
Orange Knives, stainless	42.00
Orange Spoons	34.00
Oyster Forks	24.00
Oyster Cocktail Forks	17.50
Pastry Forks	42.00
Ramequin Forks	25.00
Salad Forks, small, ind.	40.00
Sherbet Spoons	19.00
Soup Spoons	55.00

CARVERS	Each
Roast Knife, Fork or Steel	$11.00
Roast Knife, stainless steel	12.00
Roast Fork, plated tines	12.00
Game Knife, Fork or Steel	10.00
Game Knife, stainless steel	11.00
Steak Knife, Fork or Steel	6.00
Steak Knife, stainless steel	6.50
Steak Set, small, two pieces	8.50
Steak Knife, small, stainless	9.00
Joint Fork, large	9.50

MISCELLANEOUS	Each
Almond Spoon	$3.25
Asparagus Fork	17.00
Asparagus Server	17.00
Beef Fork, small	6.00
Berry Spoon, large	12.50
Bon Bon Spoon	3.25
Butter Knife	4.75
Butter Pick, Gimlet	2.50
Butter Pick, Two Tines	2.50
Cake Server, h. h., p. b.	5.50
Cheese Server, h. h., p. b.	4.00
Child's Fork	4.00
Child's Knife, h. h., p. b.	4.00
Child's Spoon	4.00
Cold Meat Fork, large	12.00
Cold Meat Fork, small	8.00
Cream Dipper	3.25
Cucumber Server	6.00
Egg Server, h. h., p. b.	6.00
Fish Fork, large	17.00
Fish Knife, large	19.00
Food Pusher, large	3.25
Food Pusher, small	2.75
Gravy Spoon	19.50
Griddle Cake Server	14.00
Ice Cream Server	17.00
Ice Cream Slicer, h. h., p. b.	8.50
Ice Spoon	13.50
Ice Tongs, large	13.00
Jelly Server, extra small	3.25
Jelly Spoon, small	6.00
Ladle, Cream	4.00
Ladle, Gravy	8.00
Ladle, Oyster	19.00
Lemon Fork, three tines	3.25
Lemon Fork, two tines	2.75
Lemon Server	6.00
Lettuce Fork	6.00
Lettuce Spoon	6.00
Mustard Spoon	2.25
Olive Fork	3.25
Olive Fork, long	3.25
Olive Spoon	3.25
Olive Spoon. long	3.25
Pastry Server, h. h., p. b.	5.50
Pea Spoon	13.50

FRANCIS I.

	Each
Pie Knife, large	$13.50
Pie Server, h. h., p. b.	5.50
Platter Spoon	19.50
Preserve Spoon	8.00
Salad Fork, large	19.00
Salad Fork, small	9.50
Salad Set, Olive wood	9.50
Salad Spoon, large	17.00
Salad Spoon, small	8.00
Salt Spoon	2.25
Serving Fork	13.50
Serving Spoon	13.50
Sugar Spoon	4.00
Sugar Tongs, large	6.00
Toast Server	14.00
Tomato Server, large	13.00
Tomato Server, small	9.50
Waffle Server	14.00

For gilt bowls or tines add 10%.

FRENCH ANTIQUE ENGRAVED
JACOBEAN ENGRAVED
SAINT GEORGE CHASED

STAPLES

	Per Dozen
Tea Spoons	
Five O'Clock	$21.00
Full Size, Trade	24.00
Full Size, Regular	30.00
Full Size, Heavy	36.00
Dessert Spoons or Forks	
Regular	50.00
Heavy	59.00
Table Spoons or Dinner Forks	
Regular	68.00
Heavy	80.00
Dessert Knives, stainless	47.00
Breakfast Knives, stainless	50.00
Dinner Knives, stainless	59.00

DOZENS

Berry Forks	$20.00
Bouillon Spoons, small	32.00
Butter Spreaders	32.00
Chocolate Spoons	22.00
Coffee Spoons	16.50
Fish Forks, small, ind	42.00
Fish Knives, small, ind	59.00
Fruit Knives, stainless	44.00
Grape Fruit Spoons	39.00
Ice Cream Forks, small	30.00
Ice Cream Spoons, small	28.00
Iced Tea Spoons	32.00
Orange Knives, stainless	44.00
Orange Spoons	38.00
Oyster Forks	26.00
Oyster Cocktail Forks	20.00
Pastry Forks	43.00
Ramequin Forks	28.00
Salad Forks, small, ind	43.00
Sherbet Spoons	22.00
Soup Spoons	55.00

CARVERS

	Each
Roast Knife, Fork or Steel	$11.50
Roast Knife, stainless steel	12.50
Roast Fork, plated tines	13.00
Game Knife, Fork or Steel	10.50
Game Knife, stainless steel blade	11.50
Steak Knife, Fork or Steel	6.50
Steak Knife, stainless steel	7.50
Steak Set, small, two pieces	10.00
Steak Knife, small, stainless	6.00
Joint Fork, large	10.00

MISCELLANEOUS

	Each
Almond Spoon	$3.50
Asparagus Fork	16.50
Asparagus Server	16.50
Beef Fork, small	6.50
Berry Spoon, large	12.50
Bon Bon Spoon	3.50
Butter Knife	5.50
Butter Pick, Gimlet	2.75
Butter Pick, Two Tines	2.75
Cake Server, h. h., p. b.	6.00
Cheese Server, h. h., p. b.	4.00
Child's Fork	4.25
Child's Knife, h. h., p. b.	4.25
Child's Spoon	4.25
Cold Meat Fork, large	12.50
Cold Meat Fork, small	8.00
Cream Dipper	3.50
Cucumber Server	6.50
Egg Server, h. h., p. b.	6.50
Fish Fork, large	16.50
Fish Knife, large	19.00
Food Pusher, large	3.75
Food Pusher, small	3.00
Gravy Spoon	17.00
Griddle Cake Server	15.00
Ice Cream Server	16.50
Ice Cream Slicer, h. h., p. b.	8.50
Ice Spoon	13.50
Ice Tongs, large	13.50
Jelly Server, extra small	3.50
Jelly Spoon, small	6.00
Ladle, Cream	4.25
Ladle, Gravy	8.00
Ladle, Oyster	19.50
Lemon Fork, three tines	3.25
Lemon Fork, two tines	2.75
Lemon Server	6.50
Lettuce Fork	6.50
Lettuce Spoon	6.50
Mustard Spoon	2.50
Olive Fork	3.50
Olive Fork, long	3.50
Olive Spoon	3.50
Olive Spoon, long	3.50
Pastry Server, h. h., p. b.	6.00
Pea Spoon	13.50
Pie Knife, large	13.50
Pie Server, h. h., p. b.	$6.00
Platter Spoon	17.00
Preserve Spoon	8.00
Salad Fork, large	15.00
Salad Fork, small	10.00
Salad Set, Olive wood	10.50
Salad Spoon, large	13.50
Salad Spoon, small	8.00
Salt Spoon	2.50
Serving Fork, plain tines	13.50
Serving Spoon, plain bowl	13.50
Sugar Spoon	4.25
Sugar Tongs, small	4.25
Toast Server	15.00
Tomato Server, large	13.50
Tomato Server, small	10.00
Waffle Server	15.00

For gilt bowls or tines add 10%.

Retail Price List

French Antique Engraved
Bright Finish

Jacobean Engraved
Bright Finish

Saint George Chased
Oxidized Finish

Sterling Silver Flatware

TRADE MARK

STERLING

In effect Sept. 15, 1923. Subject to change without notice

REED & BARTON

Established 1824

TAUNTON, MASSACHUSETTS

REPRESENTED AT

578 FIFTH AVENUE	- - -	NEW YORK
4 MAIDEN LANE	- - -	NEW YORK
5 NORTH WABASH AVENUE	- -	CHICAGO
150 POST STREET	- -	SAN FRANCISCO
1005 COMMERCE STREET	- -	DALLAS
59 TEMPLE PLACE	- -	BOSTON

FRENCH ANTIQUE ENGRAVED
Bright Finish

JACOBEAN ENGRAVED
Bright Finish

SAINT GEORGE CHASED
Oxidized Finish

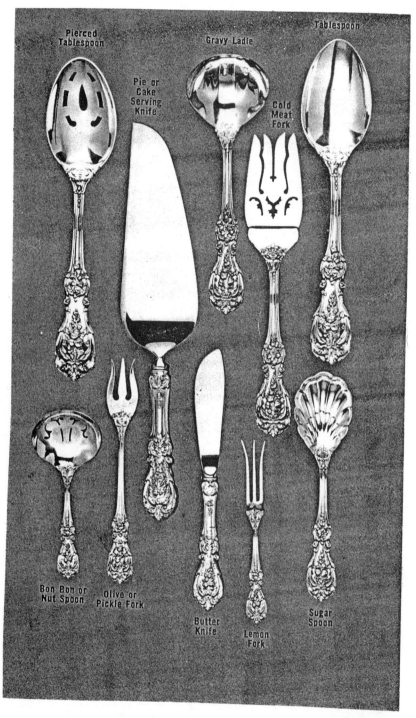

Dessert Spoon

Tea Spoon

HEPPELWHITE

STAPLES	Per Dozen
Tea Spoons	
Five O'Clock	$16.00
Full Size, Trade	18.50
Full Size, Regular	23.00
Full Size, Heavy	30.00
Full Size, Massive	37.00
Dessert Spoons or Forks	
Regular	42.00
Heavy	50.00
Massive	58.00
Table Spoons or Dinner Forks	
Regular	57.00
Heavy	68.00
Massive	75.00
Dessert Knives, stainless	39.00
Breakfast Knives, stainless	42.00
Dinner Knives, stainless	47.00

DOZENS	
Berry Forks	$16.00
Bouillon Spoons, large	33.00
Bouillon Spoons, small	26.00
Butter Spreaders	26.00
Butter Spreaders, Heavy	32.00
Chocolate Spoons, small	17.50
Coffee Spoons	12.00
Egg Spoons	21.00
Fish Forks, small, ind	36.00
Fish Knives, small, ind	50.00
Fish Knives, h. h., ind	42.00
Fruit Forks, h. h.	38.00
Fruit Knives, stainless	38.00
Grape Fruit Spoons	33.00
Ice Cream Forks, large	34.00
Ice Cream Forks, small	25.00
Ice Cream Spoons, large	32.00
Ice Cream Spoons, small	23.00
Iced Tea Spoons	26.00
Orange Knives, stainless	32.00
Orange Spoons	20.00
Oyster Forks	16.00
Oyster Cocktail Forks	37.00
Pastry Forks	23.00
Ramequin Forks, small	51.00
Salad Forks, large, ind	36.00
Salad Forks, small, ind	7.00
Salt Spoons, ind	17.50
Sherbet Spoons, small	46.00
Soup Spoons	

CARVERS	Each
Roast Knife, Fork or Steel	$9.50
Roast Knife, stainless steel	10.50
Roast Fork, plated tines	11.00
Game Knife, Fork or Steel	9.00
Game Knife, stainless steel	10.00
Steak Knife, Fork or Steel	4.75
Steak Knife, stainless steel	5.50
Steak Set, small, two pieces	7.50
Steak Knife, small stainless	4.50
Joint Fork, large	8.50
Poultry Shears	16.00

MISCELLANEOUS	Each
Almond Spoon	$3.00
Asparagus Fork	15.00
Asparagus Server	15.00
Baby Food Pusher	3.50
Baby Fork	3.00
Baby Knife, h. h., p. b.	3.00
Baby Spoon	3.00
Beef Fork, small	5.50
Berry Spoon, large	11.00
Bon Bon Spoon	3.00
Butter Knife	4.25
Butter Pick, Gimlet	2.25
Butter Pick, One Tine	2.25
Butter Pick, Two Tines	2.25
Cake Server, h. h., p. b.	4.75
Cheese Server, h. h., p. b.	3.25
Child's Fork	3.50
Child's Knife, h. h., p. b.	3.50
Child's Spoon	3.50
Cold Meat Fork, large	11.00
Cold Meat Fork, small	7.00
Cream Dipper	3.00
Cucumber Server	5.50
Egg Server, h. h., p. b.	5.50
Fish Fork, large	15.00
Fish Fork, small	9.50
Fish Knife, large	17.50
Fish Knife, small	11.00
Food Pusher, large	3.00
Food Pusher, small	2.50
Gravy Spoon	15.00
Griddle Cake Server	13.00
Ice Cream Server	15.00
Ice Cream Slicer, h. h., p. b.	7.50
Ice Spoon	12.50
Ice Tongs, large	12.00

HEPPELWHITE	Each
Ice Tongs, small	$7.00
Jelly Server, extra small	3.00
Jelly Spoon, small	5.00
Ladle, Cream	3.50
Ladle, Gravy	7.00
Ladle, Oyster	18.00
Ladle, Soup	25.00
Lemon Fork, three tines	2.75
Lemon Fork, two tines	2.25
Lemon Server	5.50
Lettuce Fork	5.50
Lettuce Spoon	5.50
Mustard Spoon	1.75
Olive Fork	2.75
Olive Fork, long	2.75
Olive Spoon	2.75
Olive Spoon, long	2.75
Pastry Server, h. h., p. b.	4.75
Pea Spoon	12.00
Pickle Fork	4.00
Pie Knife, large	12.00
Pie Knife, small	8.50
Pie Server, h. h., p. b.	4.75
Platter Spoon	15.00
Preserve Spoon	13.50
Salad Fork, large	8.50
Salad Fork, small	8.00
Salad Set, Olive wood	8.00
Salad Spoon, large	7.00
Salad Spoon, small	1.75
Salt Spoon	12.00
Serving Fork, plain tines	12.00
Serving Spoon, plain bowl	3.50
Sugar Spoon	5.50
Sugar Tongs, large	3.25
Sugar Tongs, small	13.00
Tomato Server, large	12.00
Tomato Server, small	8.50
Waffle Server	13.00

For gilt bowls or tines add 10%.

Retail Price List

Heppelwhite

Bright Finish

Sterling Silver Flatware

TRADE MARK [R logo] STERLING

In effect Sept. 15, 1923. Subject to change without notice

REED & BARTON

Established 1824

TAUNTON, MASSACHUSETTS

REPRESENTED AT

578 FIFTH AVENUE	NEW YORK
4 MAIDEN LANE	NEW YORK
5 NORTH WABASH AVENUE	CHICAGO
150 POST STREET	SAN FRANCISCO
1005 COMMERCE STREET	DALLAS
59 TEMPLE PLACE	BOSTON

STAPLES — Per Dozen

Tea Spoons	
Five O'Clock	$21.00
Full Size, Trade	24.00
Full Size, Regular	30.00
Full Size, Heavy	36.00
Full Size, Massive	43.00
Dessert Spoons or Forks	
Regular	50.00
Heavy	59.00
Massive	64.00
Table Spoons or Dinner Forks	
Regular	68.00
Heavy	80.00
Massive	87.00
Dessert Knives, stainless	47.00
Breakfast Knives, stainless	50.00
Dinner Knives, stainless	59.00

DOZENS

Berry Forks	20.00
Bouillon Spoons, large	39.00
Bouillon Spoons, small	32.00
Butter Spreaders, Heavy	39.00
Chocolate Spoons	22.00
Coffee Spoons	16.50
Egg Spoons	26.00
Fish Forks, small, ind	42.00
Fish Knives, small, ind	59.00
Fish Knives, h. h., ind	48.00
Fruit Forks, h. h.	44.00
Fruit Knives, stainless	44.00
Grape Fruit Spoons	39.00
Ice Cream Forks, large	40.00
Ice Cream Forks, small	30.00
Ice Cream Spoons, large	38.00
Ice Cream Spoons, small	28.00
Iced Tea Spoons	32.00
Orange Knives, stainless	44.00
Orange Spoons	38.00
Oyster Forks	26.00
Oyster Cocktail Forks	20.00
Pastry Forks	43.00
Ramequin Forks	28.00
Salad Forks, large, ind	60.00
Salad Forks, small, ind	42.00

STAPLES — Per Dozen

Salt Spoons, ind	$11.00
Sherbet Spoons	22.00
Soup Spoons	55.00

CARVERS — Each

Roast Knife, Fork or Steel	$11.50
Roast Knife, stainless steel	12.50
Roast Fork, plated tines	13.00
Game Knife, Fork or Steel	10.50
Game Knife, stainless steel	11.50
Steak Knife, Fork or Steel	6.50
Steak Knife, stainless steel	7.50
Steak Set, small, two pieces	10.00
Steak Knife, small, stainless	6.00
Joint Fork, large	10.00
Poultry Shears	20.00

MISCELLANEOUS — Each

Almond Spoon	$3.50
Asparagus Fork	16.50
Asparagus Server	16.50
Baby Food Pusher	4.25
Baby Fork	3.50
Baby Knife, h. h., p. b.	3.50
Baby Spoon	3.50
Beef Fork, small	6.50
Berry Spoon, large	12.50
Bon Bon Spoon	3.50
Butter Knife	5.50
Butter Pick, Gimlet	2.75
Butter Pick, One Tine	2.75
Butter Pick, Two Tines	2.75
Cake Server, h. h., p. b.	6.00
Cheese Server, h. h., p. b.	4.00
Child's Fork	4.25
Child's Knife, h. h., p. b.	4.25
Child's Spoon	4.25
Cold Meat Fork, large	12.50
Cold Meat Fork, small	8.00
Cream Dipper	3.50
Cucumber Server	6.50
Egg Server, h. h., p. b.	6.50
Fish Fork, large	16.50
Fish Fork, small	10.50
Fish Knife, large	19.00
Fish Knife, small, ind	12.50
Food Pusher, large	3.75

Food Pusher, small	$3.00
Gravy Spoon	17.00
Griddle Cake Server	15.00
Ice Cream Server	16.50
Ice Cream Slicer, h. h., p. b.	8.50
Ice Spoon	13.50
Ice Tongs, large	13.50
Ice Tongs, small	8.50
Jelly Server, extra small	3.50
Jelly Spoon, small	6.00
Ladle, Cream	4.25
Ladle, Gravy	8.00
Ladle, Oyster	19.50
Ladle, Soup	28.00
Lemon Fork, three tines	3.25
Lemon Fork, two tines	2.75
Lemon Server	6.50
Lettuce Fork	6.50
Lettuce Spoon	6.50
Mustard Spoon	2.50
Olive Fork	3.50
Olive Fork, long	3.50
Olive Spoon	3.50
Olive Spoon, long	3.50
Pastry Server, h. h., p. b.	6.00
Pea Spoon	13.50
Pickle Fork	4.75
Pie Knife, large	13.50
Pie Knife, small	10.00
Pie Server, h. h., p. b.	6.00
Platter Spoon	17.00
Preserve Spoon	8.00
Salad Fork, large	15.00
Salad Fork, small	10.00
Salad Set, Olive wood	10.50
Salad Spoon, large	13.50
Salad Spoon, small	8.00
Salt Spoon	2.50
Serving Fork, plain tines	13.50
Serving Spoon, plain bowl	13.50
Sugar Spoon	4.25
Sugar Tongs, large	7.50
Sugar Tongs, small	4.25
Toast Server	15.00
Tomato Server, large	13.50
Tomato Server, small	10.00
Waffle Server	15.00

For gilt bowls or tines add 10%.

SIMPSON, HALL, MILLER & CO.
Wallingford, Connecticut

The basic ways of the business world have not changed appreciably since the first small Britannia shops saw the wisdom of bowing to the bigger and better silverplaters. Today a successful small company sells its name and assets to a large company for many reasons, usually because the smaller company sees an opportunity for immediate cash or because competition from a larger entity makes their position difficult. This is somewhat the situation Samuel Simpson found himself in in the year 1852.

For many years he was a well-established businessman in Wallingford, CT. His Britannia ware was considered very fine and when he decided to sell his company to the larger Meriden Britannia Company his reason seems to have been a tapering off of personal interest rather than any financial necessity. One account mentions his need to meet "a new challenge". With his own thriving business now in other hands, he tried retirement, or what he termed a period of inactivity. He found this retired state intolerable. Today we can relate to the fact that this lack of action did not suit the personality of the man who had begun in such a small way and had achieved such a big success. He decided to form another company which he called Simpson, Hall, Miller & Co.

Simpson was not a passive person, he sought opportunity and scope. He looked about him, saw the emergence of silver plated flatware as the newest phenomenon and a potential big money maker.

Simpson was considered by contemporaries to be a restless doer, never content with present success. When he organized Simpson Hall and Miller he saw that the way to good fortune was to align himself with William Rogers Jr. whose mark on silverware had brought Rogers to the forefront of the industry. Simpson was an intelligent man, awake to all opportunities and he realized in the year 1878 that Rogers contract with the Meriden Britannia Company was about to expire. One of Simpson's great skills was the ability to sell not only merchandise but himself, so he had no difficulty in bringing Rogers into his orbit. Rogers also was impressed with the fact that Simpson was another old-time Britannia metal man who had always insisted on quality. Simpson prospered under the imprint SIMPSON, HALL, MILLER & CO. and Rogers' EAGLE BRAND, as he seemed to know it would. This blending of Rogers' great popularity and Simpson's particular attributes worked very well, so well that in 1895 the factory expanded into the manufacture of sterling flatware which again, not surprisingly, sold in "great quantities". Simpson was another of those who knew his markets and gave the public what it wanted. One difference between Simpson and some of his contemporaries was his attitude - he was essentially a businessman who made great silver but who dealt in silver as a commodity.

The sterling silver aspect of Simpson's endeavors achieved major success. It was one of the early companies to be absorbed into the new giant International Silver Company when it was formed in 1898. It is difficult to assess the thinking of Samuel Simpson from this vantage point; he had a highly successful operation (so successful that International made his factory at Wallingford the center of its sterling production); money was no problem, he was President and Chief Officer of the company bearing his name but he was above all a realist and he was surely aware of the threat that an entity the size of International posed to smaller companies. It may be that the philosophy of "if you can't beat them, join them" prevailed. International continued to use the separate mark of Simpson, Hall, Miller & Co. but apparently did not issue any new patterns under this name after the late 1920s. Simpson was a master of diversification. The Simpson Nickel Co. was formed simply to make nickel silver blanks which were sold to Simpson, Hall, Miller & Co. He had other interests as well but these are not clearly delineated in old records.

Simpson, Hall, Miller & Co. is one of those enterprises which hold an excitement for true collectors not always generated by bigger and better known silver manufacturers. As with other companies of their time the patterns vary from ornate to plain with everything in between, although many of them reflect the influence of the experiences the leader had had in the Britannia field. The company issued more than its share of undecorated patterns; the very beautiful and well done florals (Oak is an absolute standout) their one venture into the pierced in Whitehall; the typical shapes and rather mundane patterns of the 1920s. The thing that sets Simpson, Hall & Miller apart is their great craftsmanship, in many cases, and their essential good taste. Somehow even the totally plain handles have a life not found in similar patterns put out by other companies. It probably has to do with Mr. Samuel Simpson and his aggressive pursuit of the markets with wares made well and geared exactly to those markets. He was an agressive man, one can almost feel him breathing life into the silver produced in the factory. Collectors have a wide choice here. Although it is not a particularly easy mark to find, Simpson Hall and Miller silver is available and patterns such as Leicester, Frontenac, Mille Fleurs, Duchesse and Jeanne D'Arc border on the magnificent; Vandyke, with its hammered surface, has great vibrancy and Trianon is a masterpiece of elegance.

Simpson, Hall, Miller & Co. was considered a company of importance in its day. Its workmanship was careful and Simpson himself had great merchandising ability so today we recognize the name even though the company phased out for all practical purposes in 1898. This is the story of Samuel Miller as much as that of a leading 19th century American silver company. His ties with the monumental International Silver Company now seem ironic. Simpson, Hall and Miller long ago passed into oblivion. International which was responsible for the fact has now itself been taken over by another company.

Collectors should be vying for Simpson, Hall & Miller's silverware - the company was a star in its day and it has left behind a legacy of excellence which fits well into our living scheme today. All of this would have delighted Samuel Simpson who ever had an eye for investment potential. If somehow he could return he'd be the very best customer for his old silverware.

175

Pattern	Date of Issue	Dinner fork	Dessert knife	Dessert fork	Tea-spoon	Pattern	Date of Issue	Dinner fork	Dessert knife	Dessert fork	Tea-spoon
Branford	1920	$25	$23	$27	$22	Milford	c.1919	$28	$23	$28	$22
Guilford	1915	26	24	28	29	Stamford	c.1915	28	23	28	22
Lambeth	1915	32	27	35	25	Westover	1913	26	23	28	22

Simpson, Hall, Miller & Co. deserves recognition for its many beautiful patterns which International Silver adopted as its own. The following patterns made by Simpson, Hall & Miller Co. are listed under International Silver Co.

Abbottsford
Andover
Berkeley
Brandon
Cambridge
Copley
Coventry
Devonshire
Duchesse
Edgewood
Frontenac
Jeanne D'Arc
Kenilworth
Lady Betty
Leicester
Luzon
Marathon
Margaret
Mille Fleurs
New Marathon
New Margaret
Old English

Patria
Rosalind
Sedan
Shirley
Stratford
Stuyvesant
Tipped
Trianon
Trumbull
Van Dyke and
Van Dyke with
Initial Applied
Wakefield
Waterford
Wellesley
Westfield
Westminster
Whitehall
Wickfield
Wickford
Winchester
Wingfield

FRANK W. SMITH SILVER COMPANY, INC.
Gardner, MA
(since 1891)

TRADE MARK.
STERLING $\frac{925}{}$

In 1952 it was the Frank Smith Silver Company. In 1941 it was Frank W. Smith, Inc., "Silversmiths for nearly half a century", in the early 1940s it was also STERLING BY SMITH and in the early 1920s and beyond it was the Frank W. Smith Co. Through it all the name Frank Smith prevailed and for many years it was indeed Smith himself who sustained the business.

This was a typical 19th century American company. It was founded in 1886 and powered by a talented silversmith with a long background in the craft. He had been born into a family related to William B. Durgin and with him he served his apprenticeship in Concord, Massachusetts. Since Durgin produced some of the most beautiful silver ever made, it follows that his dedicated pupil Smith would also make some exquisite patterns in a superior way.

When Smith began his own business after his family moved to Gardner, Massachusetts, sterling flatware was already an accomplished fact of life; to succeed in such a competitive field it was necessary to produce exactly what the public wanted and at that time tastes were eclectic. Victoriana with all its attendant elaboration was in vogue but the influential Arts and Crafts movement was hovering. The English born and trained silver artisan Arthur Stone worked for Smith after employment in various other factories in Concord, Massachusetts. He organized and oversaw his department with Smith but felt that his powers of self expression were being wasted in the factory methods and routine and left to open his own shop in Gardner. Stone is now considered a premier exponent of silver of the Arts and Crafts period, his work is sought after, museum quality, scarce and expensive and it is reasonably certain that he designed and executed some of the early patterns. Collectors of this period ware can have a field day tracking down Stone's factory made silver, even though he himself deplored this method of creating silver and to vary his experiences decided to work in as many shops as possible before setting up on his own.

Smith & Co. survived this and other defections and accommodated to the Art Nouveau style which was already having an impact - Frank Smith's silver reflects with great precision every style period which assailed the United States as it grew. At first Smith was the traditionalist, his very early patterns mirror his own beginnings and training. Antique, Fiddle, Tipt and Windsor, are typical and even when the plain patterns began to have decorative handles in the Britannia manner the silver patterns were somewhat subdued and not unusual.

By 1900 tradition bowed to demand, and florals and other beautifully chased patterns appeared in his line. Consider the Lion pattern made in 1905, possibly one of the most spectacular patterns ever made by anyone and in the future sure to rival some of today's super favorites such as the Medallions among advanced collectors. Federal Cotillion was avant garde in 1901 and quite similar patterns have been made in recent years by some large manufacturers. Oak, Ivy, Century and Kensington are ornate and masterfully crafted. Woodlily and Golden Age are unusual and pretty. Most of Smith's patterns were exceptionally well made and although today's preferences have swung back to the heavily decorated silver, even Smith's simple flatware fits comfortably into any table decor. It is heavy and, for the most part, well designed. We collectors should be concerned with Frank Smith silver, some excellent period examples would be an attractive collection of American silver.

Smith's factory in Gardner was a successful operation. One of his sons entered the business and judging by the heavy and consistent advertising over the years, the silverware was popular. It is not an easy thing today to find this silverware, although the production period was long; However, if you are a lover of the earlier silver made in this country remember that in Frank Smith silver you have the product of a man who had been through the rigorous training of the early apprentice system and made the first pieces pretty much by hand. For a long time business flourished, but for a period of many years production seems almost to have stopped, certainly there were few patterns issued during the early 1920s and the early 1930s. 1933 saw a return to production with the striking Tulipan pattern but until 1958 when the company was sold to the Webster Company and moved to North Attleboro, Massachusetts, output continued sporadic. The Webster Company, in turn, was owned by Reed and Barton until the 1960s when Reed and Barton says it came under the control of Towle.

Frank W. Smith Co. is a good example of how the design work of the early companies was generally inconsistent. These inconsistencies point up the scarcity of truly inspired designers and the temptation to copy from other companies to make up for this lack. It is fascinating to track the patterns to see how the companies would use the slightest variations on a design to avoid patent infringements and so be able to issue a new silver flatware piece.

The Smith Company passed into silver heaven with little notice and today there are not many collectors of the ware. This is unfortunate since the silver is of excellent quality even if the patterns were not always responsive to public fancy. Times have changed, tastes have changed but everyone still loves a bargain - the silver made by Frank Smith Co. is just that.

Pattern	Date of Issue	Dinner fork	Dessert knife	Dessert fork	Tea-spoon	Pattern	Date of Issue	Dinner fork	Dessert knife	Dessert fork	Tea-spoon
Adrienne	1919	$25	$23	$27	$19	Cambodia	c.1916	$32	$30	$36	$28

Adrienne

Cambodia

Alden (Fiddle Shell)	1914	38	30	40	28	Century	1900	45	32	48	28

Alden

Century

Antique	1886	28	23	28	20	Chippendale (American Chippendale)	1917	28	24	30	24

Antique

Chippendale

Baronial	1920	38	28	38	22	Colbert	1921	40	30	42	28

Baronial

Colbert

Bead	1917	27	22	28	19	Countess	c.1920	35	30	38	26

Bead

Countess

Beverly	c.1917	27	23	28	21

Beverly

Bostonia	1914	26	22	28	21

Bostonia

FRANK W. SMITH

Pattern	Date of Issue	Dinner fork	Dessert knife	Dessert fork	Tea-spoon
Crystal	c.1921	$35	$30	$38	$25

Crystal

Pattern	Date of Issue	Dinner fork	Dessert knife	Dessert fork	Tea-spoon
Islesworth (Georgian Garland)	1914	$25	$20	$25	$19

Islesworth

| Edward VII | 1889 | 40 | 30 | 45 | 28 |

Edward VII

| Ivanhoe | 1915 | 32 | 27 | 35 | 22 |

Ivanhoe

| Fiddle | 1886 | 30 | 25 | 32 | 26 |

Fiddle

| Ivy | 1915 | 55 | 38 | 60 | 40 |

Ivy

| Fiddle Shell originally Alden | 1914 | 38 | 30 | 40 | 30 |

Fiddle Shell

| Jac Rose | c.1900 | 35 | 28 | 35 | 24 |

Jac Rose

| French Thread (Fiddle Thread) | 1902 | 30 | 25 | 30 | 23 |

French Thread

| Kensington | c.1900 | 65 | 40 | 70 | 40 |

Kensington

| French Antique | 1887 | 28 | 23 | 28 | 22 |

French Antique

| L. Kraft | 1910 | 35 | 28 | 38 | 28 |

L. Kraft

| George VI | 1912 | 40 | 30 | 45 | 28 |

George VI

| Laurel | c.1919 | 24 | 20 | 25 | 18 |

Laurel

FRANK W. SMITH

Pattern	Date of Issue	Dinner fork	Dessert knife	Dessert fork	Tea-spoon
Lincoln	1905	$35	$26	$35	$25

Lincoln

Pattern	Date of Issue	Dinner fork	Dessert knife	Dessert fork	Tea-spoon
Lincoln, engraved	c.1912	35	28	32	26

Lincoln, engraved

Pattern	Date of Issue	Dinner fork	Dessert knife	Dessert fork	Tea-spoon
Lincoln, K engraved	c.1915	35	28	32	26

Lincoln K. engraved

Pattern	Date of Issue	Dinner fork	Dessert knife	Dessert fork	Tea-spoon
Lion	1905	75	50	75	40

Lion

Pattern	Date of Issue	Dinner fork	Dessert knife	Dessert fork	Tea-spoon
M.W. Lily	c.1915	25	21	25	18

M.W. Lily

Pattern	Date of Issue	Dinner fork	Dessert knife	Dessert fork	Tea-spoon
M.W. Star	c.1916	25	21	25	18

M.W. Star

Pattern	Date of Issue	Dinner fork	Dessert knife	Dessert fork	Tea-spoon
Marie Louise	1907	25	20	28	19

Marie Louise

Pattern	Date of Issue	Dinner fork	Dessert knife	Dessert fork	Tea-spoon
Marie Louise	1939	35	32	38	27

Marie Louise

Pattern	Date of Issue	Dinner fork	Dessert knife	Dessert fork	Tea-spoon
Martha Randolph	1921	$28	$23	$28	$23

Martha Randolph

Pattern	Date of Issue	Dinner fork	Dessert knife	Dessert fork	Tea-spoon
Martha Washington	c.1916	24	19	25	19

Martha Washington

Pattern	Date of Issue	Dinner fork	Dessert knife	Dessert fork	Tea-spoon
Mayfair	1951	38	20	40	27
Mayflower	1918	26	22	28	18

Mayflower

Pattern	Date of Issue	Dinner fork	Dessert knife	Dessert fork	Tea-spoon
Mayflower hand chased	1918	28	24	28	19

Mayflower hand chased

Pattern	Date of Issue	Dinner fork	Dessert knife	Dessert fork	Tea-spoon
Newport Shell (Puritan)	1910	38	28	38	28

Newport Shell

Pattern	Date of Issue	Dinner fork	Dessert knife	Dessert fork	Tea-spoon
No. 2	1918	35	30	40	27

No. 2

Pattern	Date of Issue	Dinner fork	Dessert knife	Dessert fork	Tea-spoon
No. 4	1918	42	30	45	28

No. 4

FRANK W. SMITH

Pattern	Date of Issue	Dinner fork	Dessert knife	Dessert fork	Tea-spoon
No. 9, engraved	1891	$28	$23	$28	$22

No. 9 engraved

Pattern	Date of Issue	Dinner fork	Dessert knife	Dessert fork	Tea-spoon
No. 10	1917	55	38	55	30

No. 10

No. 12	1919	35	30	38	27

No. 12

No. 14	1918	28	23	28	23

No. 14

No. 15	1919	35	28	35	25

No. 15

Oak	1912	55	40	58	40

Oak

Paul Revere, engraved	c.1916	25	21	25	18

Paul Revere

Pattern	Date of Issue	Dinner fork	Dessert knife	Dessert fork	Tea-spoon
Pilgrim	1909	$25	$20	$28	$19

Pilgrim

Priscilla	c.1918	30	25	32	24

Priscilla

Richfield	c.1900	40	30	45	27

Richfield

Salem	c.1917	25	22	25	20

Salem

Shell	1890	30	26	32	24

Shell

Silver Age	c.1945	45	32	45	27

Silver Age

Tipt	1887	30	25	32	26

Tipt

Pattern	Date of Issue	Dinner fork	Dessert knife	Dessert fork	Tea-spoon
Tokay	1952	$28	$24	$28	$20
Tulipan	1933	35	30	37	27

Tulipan

V. Kraft	1921	30	25	35	25

V. Kraft

Vergennes	1913	25	22	28	22

Vergennes

Windsor	1895	26	23	28	20

Windsor

Winslow	1922	28	24	28	24

Winslow

Woodlily	1945	55	40	58	35

Woodlily

TOWLE SILVERSMITHS
Newburyport, Massachusetts

Towle is one of the oldest silver manufacturers in America with a distinguished history of long and discriminating production. The Towle name can safely rest on its past but as of the year 1990, Towle Silversmiths are in serious financial trouble and have filed for protection under the U.S. Bankruptcy laws. The troubled history of the company in recent years, particularly the 1980s, is a saga of poor management, too much diversification, less emphasis on fine quality and uncontrollable disasters such as the 43 containers of Towle merchandise left undelivered on Boston Harbor when the Port fired half its clerical workers. A serious loss of credibility ocurred when the company's newly consolidated shipping operations became victim of a computer shutdown with attendant loss of business due to inability to deliver goods. Although these problems were transient and were corrected, they have, together with the general turmoil which has existed in the silver industry for the last ten years or more, made complete recovery impossible. Syratech Corp. of Boston, Mass., now also owns Towle.

This is Towle's second resort to Bankruptcy. In 1986 Towle first filed for protection. It sold many of the companies it had acquired, restructed the business and became more focused on its sterling line, and emerged from chapter 11 in 1987. It was then promptly bought by First Republic Corporation of America, New York based and primarily concerned with sea food, textiles, and real estate. Towle again seems to be in disarray. After the 1987 plan did not work, the company again was forced to file for bankruptcy and says now it can probably return to a profitable company status.

All of this is a far cry from A.F. Towle and his venture into silversmithing. The company derives from the same roots as Lunt and has been one of the six largest silversmiths in the United States. It is also one of the most prestigious. While Lunt traces its roots to the well known early American silversmithing family of Moultons, it is primarily through Anthony F. Towle that the connection exists. The tree which Lunt sometimes used to delineate its beginnings to Moulton really depicts the lineage of Towle, who was apprenticed to Moulton and eventually bought the business from Moulton in 1873. As with most early silver entrepreneurs, Anthony Towle formed other companies with other partners usually as finances dictated, before organizing A.F. Towle & Son Co., Inc. in 1880. The early saga of Towle is largely the tale of temperament and business acumen. Towle's proficiency at his craft has never been in question. Anthony Towle was a clever, even masterful silversmith and when he retired in 1892 he was 76 years old and was probably happy to yield the solution of his business problems to someone else.

The modern factory in Newburyport shows a corporate regard for history not always evident in American business. The company has preserved and displays a copy of every sterling pattern it has made. Some of these patterns have long been among the most wanted by buyers of American Silver - Georgian, Old Master and Benjamin Franklin - but most of the Towle patterns are things of beauty. Even their patterns of the 1950s, when many companies were certainly making the mundane reflect good design work and fairly traditional forms. So the current problems of Towle certainly can be blamed on the usual causes but there is an overriding intangible - a falling off of popularity in the general area of sterling silver flatware which forced management to cut back on slow selling and duplicating patterns to reduce inventory (after all, buying 14 businesses in five years would be a challenge to any business). Think what a bonanza this situation presents for silver collectors.

This latest financial maneuver through the courts, gives this great company time to reorganize in a telling way - it also should give collectors incentive as well as other buyers of our superlative American silver.

Since many of the Towle patterns were made well before many collectors were born, they are relatively unknown and these should be a logical target since they have not yet achieved enormous popularity with attendant price rises. Just think, not only all this beauty, but utility as well.

Towle is the only publicly traded company of the big six and whether or not it survives both the chaos within its own business as well as the chaos in the silver industry generally, it will always be a treasured part of the American silver picture. It made magnificent flatware and all collectors should realize prices will escalate if the pieces became scarce.

Benjamin Franklin, Colonial and William and Mary have become increasingly popular among lovers of our old silver and Orchid is truly outstanding not only in execution of design but the shapes of the pieces themselves, KING RICHARD and PRINCESS are equally lovely, and as with the Orchids and Pomona they are so intricate and complex, they require a second or third look to appreciate the art. The later patterns such as Spanish Provincial, Danish Baroque, Grand Duchess are impressive and Celtic Weave is a masterpiece. The 1690 pattern shows a return to simplicity which is part of the szichophrenia of the taste in this country, a basic yearning for all that is uncluttered and simple while being mesmerized by the ornate.

Towle is a classic case history of American business lore in the way it began, developed, grew and grew and eventually became part of a conglomerate which obviously was not able to deal with the problems of an unrelated business. Towle has been a colossus, hopefully it will rise and shine again, meantime Towle is a sleeping giant of a collectible.

TOWLE PRICES

Pattern	Date of Issue	Dinner fork	Dessert knife	Dessert fork	Tea-spoon
Albany	1890	$48	$32	$45	$28

Albany

| Antique | c.1880 | 30 | 25 | 30 | 20 |

Antique

| Arcadian | 1916 | 30 | 25 | 32 | 23 |

Arcadian

| Aquilla | c.1885 | 35 | 27 | 37 | 25 |

Aquilla

| Aristocrat | 1934 | 28 | 24 | 28 | 21 |

Aristocrat

| Arlington | 1884 | 48 | 30 | 50 | 28 |

Arlington

| Auvergne | 1905 | 38 | 28 | 35 | 25 |

Auvergne

Pattern	Date of Issue	Dinner fork	Dessert knife	Dessert fork	Tea-spoon
Awakening designed by Clifton Barr, Rowley and Robert J. King	1958	$30	$26	$34	$24

Awakening

| Benjamin Franklin | 1904 | 50 | 35 | 55 | 30 |

Benjamin Franklin

| Cambridge | c.1902 | 45 | 32 | 48 | 28 |

Cambridge

| Candlelight | 1934 | 35 | 30 | 37 | 27 |

Candlelight

| Canterbury | 1893 | 38 | 28 | 32 | 25 |

Canterbury

| Carpenter Hall | 1975 | 50 | 40 | 55 | 32 |

Carpenter Hall

| Cascade | 1933 | 28 | 24 | 28 | 22 |

Cascade

TOWLE

Pattern	Date of Issue	Dinner fork	Dessert knife	Dessert fork	Tea-spoon
Celtic Weave	1979	$60	$45	$65	$38

Celtic Weave

Celtic Weave Gold	1979	65	50	68	38

Celtic Weave Gold

Charlemagne	1963	50	40	52	32

Charlemagne

Chippendale	1937	28	25	25	18

Chippendale

Clifton, hand engraved	1891	30	27	32	24

this is another variant of the plain WARREN patern

Clifton, hand engraved

Clover	1887	30	27	32	24

Clover

Colonial (Old Colonial)	1895	56	50	68	40

Colonial

Pattern	Date of Issue	Dinner fork	Dessert knife	Dessert fork	Tea-spoon
Contessina	1965	$30	$25	$34	$23

Contessina

Contour	1950	28	25	30	23

Contour

Cordova	1902	28	24	30	22

Cordova

Country Manor	1966	35	28	38	25

Country Manor

Craftsman	1932	40	34	45	28

Designed by Harold E. Nock

Craftsman

Daisy	1883	30	27	32	25

Daisy

Danish Baroque	1970	55	40	60	35

Danish Baroque

Pattern	Date of Issue	Dinner fork	Dessert knife	Dessert fork	Tea-spoon
Debussy	1959	$48	$35	$50	$32

Debussy

Pattern	Date of Issue	Dinner fork	Dessert knife	Dessert fork	Tea-spoon
D'Orleans Designed by Harold E. Nock	1923	32	28	35	23

D'Orleans

Dorothy Bradford	1913	35	28	35	24

Dorothy Bradford

Dorothy Manners	1919	30	25	32	23

Dorothy Manners

Dover	c.1900	25	22	25	18

Dover

Du Barry	1900	35	27	38	24

Du Barry

El Grandee	1964	55	45	60	35

El Grandee

Pattern	Date of Issue	Dinner fork	Dessert knife	Dessert fork	Tea-spoon
Empire	1894	$40	$30	$42	$25

Empire

Esplanade	1953	40	30	42	28

Elplande

Essex	1890	35	26	38	24

Essex

Fiddle	c.1880	30	25	30	23

Fiddle

Fontana designed by Robert J. King	1956	32	27	30	22

Fontana

French Provincial	1948	38	30	40	26

French Provincial

Georgian (Grecian)	1889	65	45	70	35

Georgian

TOWLE

Pattern	Date of Issue	Dinner fork	Dessert knife	Dessert fork	Tea-spoon
Georgian, H.H.	c.1889 1900	$40	$30	$42	$26

Georgian H.H.

Pattern	Date of Issue	Dinner fork	Dessert knife	Dessert fork	Tea-spoon
Lady Constance	1922	$25	$20	$25	$19

Lady Constance

Glenmore	c.1890	35	25	35	25

Glenmore

Lady Diana	1929	32	28	35	25

Lady Diana

Godroon	1907	32	26	30	22

Godroon

Lady Diana, Chased Designed by Harold E. Nock	1930	35	30	38	26

Lady Diana, Chased

Grand Duchess	1973	55	45	65	38

Grand Duchess

LaFayette	1905	23	18	23	18

LaFayette

Hampton	1892	38	28	40	27

Hampton

LaFayette, engraved	1905	25	20	25	19

LaFayette, engraved

King Richard	1932	50	38	50	30

King Richard

Laureate	1968	40	35	42	27

Laureate

Kings	1904	48	35	50	30

Kings

Legato	1962	40	35	42	27

Legato

Pattern	Date of Issue	Dinner fork	Dessert knife	Dessert fork	Tea-spoon
Lenox	1890	$30	$25	$30	$23

Lenox

Louis XIV	1924	30	26	32	24

Designed by Harold E. Nock

Louis XIV

Madame LaFayette	1905	28	23	28	23

Madame LaFayette

Madeira	1948	35	26	32	25

Madeira

Mandarin	1972	35	30	38	27

Mandarin

Mary Chilton	1912	35	30	35	25

Designed by Henry Charles Quincy

Mary Chilton

Mary Chilton, engraved	1912	37	32	38	26

Mary Chilton, engraved

Pattern	Date of Issue	Dinner fork	Dessert knife	Dessert fork	Tea-spoon
Mary Chilton No. 10, engraved	1912	$37	$32	$38	$26

The engraved and No. 10 are variations of the basic shape. These are extra heavyweight.

Mary Chilton No. 10, engraved

Margaux	1982	55	42	60	35

Margaux

Meadow Song	1967	28	23	28	20

Meadow Song

Merrimac	1916	32	25	30	23

Merrimac

Monte Cristo	1971	38	30	38	28

Monte Cristo

Novantique	1969	27	23	28	23

Novantique

Number 38	1880	35	27	35	25

This is a variant of the plain WINDSOR pattern but heavily hand engraved

Number 38

TOWLE

Pattern	Date of Issue	Dinner fork	Dessert knife	Dessert fork	Tea- spoon
No. 43	1882	$35	$27	$35	$25

Pattern	Date of Issue	Dinner fork	Dessert knife	Dessert fork	Tea- spoon
Number 128	1880 probably never made in full sets				$28

Number 128

Old Brocade	1932	38	28	40	28

Old Brocade

Old English	1892	45	20	38	30

Old English

Old Lace	1939	28	23	28	23

Old Lace

Old Master	1942	40	30	45	30

Designed by Harold E. Nock

Old Master

Old Mirror	1940	45	55	48	30

Designed by Arim R. Kalashian

Old Mirror

Old Newbury (Newbury)	1900	28	23	28	22

Old Newbury

Orchids	1887	$48	$35	$55	$30

Orchids

Orleans	1890	45	32	48	30

Orleans

Paul Revere	1906	35	27	35	24

Paul Revere

Peachtree Manor	1957	38	30	40	26

Peachtree Manor

Petit Point	1957	30	23	28	22

Petite Point

Pomona	1887	48	32	48	30

Pomona

Princess	1892	55	35	50	32

Princess

189

Pattern	Date of Issue	Dinner fork	Dessert knife	Dessert fork	Tea-spoon
Queen Elizabeth I	1970	$38	$28	$40	$28

Queen Elizabeth I

Pattern	Date of Issue	Dinner fork	Dessert knife	Dessert fork	Tea-spoon
Rambler Rose	1937	28	24	30	24

Rambler Rose

Richmond	1901	35	26	32	25

Richmond

Rose Solitaire	1954	28	24	30	23

Rose Solitaire

Royal Windsor	1936	38	30	40	28

Royal Windsor

R.S.V.P.	1965	25	21	27	18

R.S.V.P.

Rustic	1895	30	25	30	23

Rustic

Sculptured Rose	1961	28	24	28	23

Sculptured Rose

Pattern	Date of Issue	Dinner fork	Dessert knife	Dessert fork	Tea-spoon
Seville Designed by Harold E. Nock	1926	$30	$26	$32	$24

Seville

Shell	1889	30	25	30	25

Shell

Silver Flutes	1941	28	24	28	20

Silver Flutes

Silver Plumes	1939	40	36	45	30

Silver Plumes

Silver Spray Designed by Robert J. King	1955	25	21	28	21

Silver Spray

Southwind Designed by John O. Van Koert	1952	25	21	28	21

Southwind

Spanish Provincial	1967	48	35	50	32

Spanish Provincial

Stuart	c.1893	40	30	40	27

Stuart

190

TOWLE

Pattern	Date of Issue	Dinner fork	Dessert knife	Dessert fork	Tea-spoon
Symphony	1931	$28	$22	$28	$22

Symphony

Pattern	Date of Issue	Dinner fork	Dessert knife	Dessert fork	Tea-spoon
Symphony, chased	1934	30	23	20	23

Symphony, chased

Pattern	Date of Issue	Dinner fork	Dessert knife	Dessert fork	Tea-spoon
Tipped	c.1880-1890	25	22	25	20

Tipped

Pattern	Date of Issue	Dinner fork	Dessert knife	Dessert fork	Tea-spoon
Vespera	1961	$25	$22	$28	$22

Vespera

Pattern	Date of Issue	Dinner fork	Dessert knife	Dessert fork	Tea-spoon
Virginia Carvel	1919	28	24	28	20

Virginia Carvel

Pattern	Date of Issue	Dinner fork	Dessert knife	Dessert fork	Tea-spoon
Virginia Lee	1920	30	25	30	22

Virginia Lee

The following patterns were all out of production by 1921: Albany, Antique, Aquilla, Cambridge, Daisy, Dover, Du Barry, Essex, Fiddle, Glenmore, Georgian H.H., Lenox, No. 128, Orlean, Hampton, Princess, Stuart, Tipped.

The Tuttle name has been a rather shadowy one to American Silver lovers. Company records are sketchy as to complete pattern production and Wallace which owns the company cannot supply a full accounting of the inventory of Tuttle. In fact, it is only since 1955 when Wallace silversmiths bought the company and began to heavily advertise some of the patterns that the name has become familiar. The company is not particularly historic. It was founded in 1890 by Timothy Tuttle, but it has one claim to fame which is unusual in American silver; its method of marking each piece of its sterling. Every piece made bears a crescent and the initials of the incumbent President of the United States on the date of manufacture. This practice began about 1923 and still exists. All pieces also carry a pine tree in a circle, a copy of the early American coin the Pine Tree shilling.

Although Wallace seems not to have complete records of Tuttle patterns certainly the company never produced in great quantities. Tuttle reorganized in 1909 which speaks to some difficulties and may account for low production. Some of the patterns are highly individualistic and imaginative - the Paul Laremie and its slightly more elaborate reincarnation as Crest of Arden was stylized and ahead of its time. It is as different in feeling from Hannah Hull as two patterns made by the same company could ever be. The patterns of the 1920s are typical and mundane but in 1967 under the aegis of Wallace the company made BEAUVOIR, a still grossly underappreciated silver pattern. As the company advertised it boasts "masterful sculpting" which is entirely true, "massive weight" also true. It is a magnificent pattern, all swags and florals, quite dramatic and beautiful. Another truth about Tuttle production is that most patterns are very heavyweight silver. The company made only sterling, never plated ware, and as with all specialists they did it very well.

The recent trend toward Georgian silver patterns proves that Tuttle was covering all bases when it released its Onslow pattern, a beautifully balanced example. This pattern completely embodies Tuttle's original philosophy. Timothy Tuttle was essentially a copyist. Unlike most American silversmiths who eventually outgrew their roots and moved toward their own styles - and in most cases surpassed the originals - Tuttle always returned to his early inspiration, and so much of the company's silver is traditional.

There is research to be done on Tuttle, a company which started late, and which has many gaps in its recorded history. Wallace which owns it is in difficulties itself but it has done very well by Tuttle. In recent years it has efficiently promoted Onslow, Hannah Hull and Beauvoir. Collectors should gear up for Tuttle - it's one of those companies little noticed but which will be long remembered, if not for its imagination at least for its quality.

TUTTLE PRICES

Pattern	Date of Issue	Dinner fork	Dessert knife	Dessert fork	Tea-spoon	Pattern	Date of Issue	Dinner fork	Dessert knife	Dessert fork	Tea-spoon
Aberdeen (Classic Antique)	c.1926	$27	$23	$28	$20	Beauvoir	1967	$60	$40	$65	$38
Basket of Flowers	c.1928	25	20	25	19	Charles II	c.1915	28	24	30	25

Aberdeen

Beauvoir

Basket of Flowers

Charles II

TUTTLE

Pattern	Date of Issue	Dinner fork	Dessert knife	Dessert fork	Tea-spoon
Crest of Arden	1954	$55	$40	$58	$36

Crest of Arden

| Feather Edge | 1938 | 27 | 23 | 28 | 22 |

Feather Edge

| Georgian | 1929 | 30 | 25 | 35 | 25 |

Georgian

| Hannah Hull | 1928 | 32 | 27 | 35 | 25 |

Hannah Hull

| Onslow | 1929-1930 | 42 | 32 | 45 | 30 |

Onslow

| Paul Laremie | c.1925 | 48 | 36 | 50 | 30 |

Paul Laremie

| Queen Anne | 1928 | 25 | 21 | 25 | 21 |

Queen Anne

| Windsor Castle | 1929 | 25 | 20 | 25 | 19 |

Windsor Castle

 Used since 1890

R·WALLACE
Used since 1918

Used since 1910

WALLACE SILVERSMITHS
Watson and Tuttle

Used since 1956 but this has been
a Wallace mark in a different form
since 1895.

WALLACE   SILVERSMITHS
Used since 1956

WALLACE STERLING

Used since 1910

WALLACE ⚜ STERLING
Used since 1923

WALLACE SILVERSMITHS
Used since 1930

TRADE
R₩ 🦌 & S
STERLING

When Wallace Silversmiths says Grand they mean really Grande. Grande Baroque, Grand Victorian are examples of the truly splendid works of art produced by the company. Some of the most elaborate patterns ever made are from this factory and some of them stemmed from the imagination and skill of William S. Warren who designed them. It is a tribute not only to Warren's great ability but ability but also to the sensibility of Wallace itself that Warren's name is so well known - until recently it was unusual for the silver companies to promote their designers as a selling point. Others who designed for the company but who are not equally well known are Richard C. Gavette, Amedie J. Germain, William Toth, Irving F. Wahl and David B. Hoover. Warren's name stands out not only because the company heavily advertised his designs but because of the designs themselves, "Three dimensional" was the slogan and it meant the design was highly delineated and could be appreciated viewed from the front, back and side. This sort of attention to detail has always been one of the outstanding facets of Wallace silver even from its earliest days.

The company's beginnings are typical and have been described in much of the company literature over the years. Robert Wallace, they say, son of a Scottish immigrant, made the first nickel spoon in America. In 1835, Wallace, at the age of 18, was already in business for himself making the pewter spoons so in demand at the time when he heard about the new nickel silver from Germany. The story goes that he bought the formula from a German chemist in New York for $20, which was high stakes in those years, but nevertheless the buy put it on a par with the purchase of Manhattan Island for all-time bargains.

The whole intricately woven history of early silversmiths in this country reads like the personna in a novel and the plot thickens with the introduction of each new character. Robert Wallace, for example, supplied Horace Wilcox of International silver fame with spoons to sell from his well stocked wagon. Wallace and David Stevens were operating at Quinnie, Connecticut on the edge of Wallingford and benefiting from Stevens' skill with the buff wheel to give the metal its unique sheen. It was 1848 and Wallace Stevens had combined to run a flatware plant and grist mill. A few years later Robert Wallace took himself into Wallingford proper to run his own business leaving to Stevens the lucrative trade of supplying great quantities of silverware to Hall & Elton, then a very large dealer in flatware. Wallace obviously anticipated his success, for he built his first plant in Wallingford and designated it "Building No. 1". Although the Wallace name had remained bright, the Stevens name is less well known although David Stevens' grandson carried on the tradition when he became President of International Silver.

The Robert Wallace works stayed at this location in Wallingford for 113 years. With all the others in those early days, he watched the rise of silverplate and in 1875 his company issued its first three sterling silver patterns - Hawthorne, The Crown and St. Leon. Holloware was added to the line and the entire production was unbelievably eclectic - ornamental silver ornaments for horses' saddles and harnesses, ladies' dresser sets and many other small decorative silver pieces.

The early lines were successful and led to the majestic, impressive patterns. The St. Leon, for instance has an intricate carved sculptural handle which required care and great skill. It was the nature of these early silversmiths to do things that were both imaginative, even daring, all the while keeping the public taste in mind, for they all seemed to know that love silver as they did, profit made it possible. When Robert Wallace died in 1892 his son Frank succeeded to the business. Again it was typical that the son was more open to new production methods and busily encouraged the use of the new machines. In the question of quality it was definitely like father like son. Wallace quality has been a byword. It was son Frank who encouraged William Warren to create his many beautiful patterns and many now consider (along with the company) that Warren was perhaps the greatest designer of silver flatware of the 20th century. Collectors should always keep this in mind; when the time comes that these great designers of our silverware are given proper recognition, owners of silverware they designed have unique pieces.

Although Robert Wallace had taken as his partner William Simpson and the name became R. Wallace & Co. in 1855, the name was changed again when Wallace became sole owner in the late 1870s. It was now R. Wallace & Sons Manufacturing Co. Other variations of the name followed but Wallace was always predominant in the title. Wallace bought the Watson Silver Co. in 1955, later acquired Tuttle and all current advertising continues to feature the most popular Watson and Tuttle patterns under the Wallace umbrella. In 1956 the company name became WALLACE SILVERSMITHS.

Although the name endures, after long years as a privately held company, Wallace has met the fate of most of the silver companies in this country. In 1959 it was taken over by Hamilton of Lancaster, Pennsylvania (Hamilton Watches) and in 1971 became a division of H.M.W. Industries and a subsidiary of KATY INDUSTRIES of Elgin, Illinois. In 1986, KATY, a large holding company, sold both Hamilton and Wallace to SYRATECH whose headquarters are in Massachusetts but who moved the Wallace acquisition to its plant in Syracuse, New York. Syratech, which now owns Wallace, not only makes silver flatware and holloware but novelties, bric-a-brac, hobby kits, furniture, house hold glass, fiberglass, plastic, gifts and novelties.

Where once silversmiths concentrated only on the production of fine silver and pondered long and hard on whether to expand into other forms of silver, flatware manufacture has become just one of many operations of large conglomorates.

Since 1975, Wallace has produced what it calls STERLING II which accurately reflects the new interest in stainless as an easy care, long-lived adjunct to dining. The Sterling II patterns, OLYMPUS, COVENTRY FORGE, GRAND VENETIAN, PLYMOUTH COLONY and SCARBOROUGH are very well done and it would take an expert eye to look past the fine hollow sterling silver handles and detect the spoon bowls, fork tines and knife blades made of stainless. Using stainless in these parts of the flatware is cost effective and has the new required "carefree convenience" while still giving a feeling of elegance because of the sterling handles. It is a new concept and its future is still undecided.

What Wallace called its REMEMBRANCE GROUP of sterling silver flatware consisted of the following patterns: ROYAL ROSE, VIOLET, FELICIANA, WALTZ OF SPRING, LA REINE, MICHELLE, ROYAL SATIN, SILVER SWIRL, DEBUTANTE, LUCERNE, LAREMIE, DAWN MIST, WASHINGTON, EVENING MIST, COLONIAL FIDDLE, MY LOVE, NORMANDIE, AND FEATHER EDGE. Feliciana issued in 1969, was the last pattern made in this series.

WALLACE is a formidable name in American silver. Its patterns are monuments to the craft and its history is one which all admirers of the American business scene can track as a classic example of how a one man enterprise grew and changed. Once Wallace was a typical small operation with the name of the owner prominently displayed and the owner himself or perhaps one or more of his sons somewhere on the premises. The name has endured and only time will tell if it will survive another century. The company has always been known for its fine design work and some really magnificent patterns. Its GRAND BAROQUE leads many lists at retail outlets as the most desired pattern in all American Silver, its ROSEPOINT is also almost always up there in the top ten, and although such lists vary from region to region Wallace patterns continue to excite interest long after they were first introduced.

Older Wallace silverware has not yet achieved its full potential as a collectible but interest is growing. Many of the early patterns are the plain, simple line flatware which was nevertheless heavy, excellent quality silver and boasted fine workmanship and if found today, manages to blend in very well with our table settings. This, after all, is the true test of taste and quality - has the product endured? With Wallace, the answer is a resounding yes.

After more than 100 years St. Leon is still exciting, Viola quietly beautiful, Sappho massive and impressive, Irian complex and provocative and Lucerne, a fine example of a fairly mundane design. All in all Wallace has done truly examplary work and the newer patterns conform to the influence of the past and are so exquisite that many of them will probably not be duplicated for originality and style. ROMANCE OF THE SEA is already on the wish list, and the others bode to become investment quality silver.

Robert Wallace was not driven in the way some of the other early makers were, but he did love silver, he was industrious and talented and he was very fortunate in his sons, particularly the far seeing Frank. Where Syratech intends to take Wallace depends on intangibles; no matter, the WALLACE legacy is secure.

WALLACE PRICES

Pattern	Date of Issue	Dinner fork	Dessert knife	Dessert fork	Tea-spoon
Aegean Weave	1970	$50	$42	$56	$34

Aegean Weave

Pattern	Date of Issue	Dinner fork	Dessert knife	Dessert fork	Tea-spoon
Golden Aegean Weave	1971	65	50	75	40

Golden Aegean Weave

America	1915	28	23	30	22

America

Pattern	Date of Issue	Dinner fork	Dessert knife	Dessert fork	Tea-spoon
Antique	1926	$27	$23	$28	$23

Antique

Atalanta	1895	32	26	32	23

Atalanta

Berain	1907	48	38	50	30

Berain

Beauvais	1914	28	26	30	26

Beauvais

195

Pattern	Date of Issue	Dinner fork	Dessert knife	Dessert fork	Tea-spoon
Bessie	1894	$42	$32	$45	$28

Bessie

Pattern	Date of Issue	Dinner fork	Dessert knife	Dessert fork	Tea-spoon
Blenheim	1911	27	23	28	22

Blenheim

Cabot	1917	30	25	32	24

Cabot

Cairo	1908	30	24	32	24

Cairo

Campania	1914	30	25	35	25

Campania and San Juan are the same pattern. On Campania the handle tip is bent backward, on San Juan it is bent forward.

Campania

Caribbean	1984	58	40	65	35

Caribbean

Carmel	1912	40	30	48	30

Carmel

Pattern	Date of Issue	Dinner fork	Dessert knife	Dessert fork	Tea-spoon
Carnation	1909	$50	$40	$55	$30

Carnation

Carthage	1917	30	25	32	23

Carthage

Columbia	1915	28	23	28	21

Columbia

Concord	1926	28	24	28	21

Concord

Corinthian	1911	32	28	35	25

Corinthian

Custis	1911	27	23	28	22

Custis

Dauphine	1916	45	32	48	30

Dauphine

Dawn Mist	1963	30	25	35	24

Dawn Mist

WALLACE

Pattern	Date of Issue	Dinner fork	Dessert knife	Dessert fork	Tea-spoon
Dawn Star	1958	$28	$24	$28	$22

Dawn Star

Pattern	Date of Issue	Dinner fork	Dessert knife	Dessert fork	Tea-spoon
Debutante Designed by Stuart A. Young	1954	32	26	35	23

Debutante

Pattern	Date of Issue	Dinner fork	Dessert knife	Dessert fork	Tea-spoon
Discovery designed by Ernest F. Thomason and William Toth	1957	26	23	28	21

Discovery

Pattern	Date of Issue	Dinner fork	Dessert knife	Dessert fork	Tea-spoon
Eton	1903	45	32	45	30

Eton

Pattern	Date of Issue	Dinner fork	Dessert knife	Dessert fork	Tea-spoon
Evening Mist	1963	30	25	32	24

Evening Mist

Pattern	Date of Issue	Dinner fork	Dessert knife	Dessert fork	Tea-spoon
Faneuil	1925	28	24	38	21

Faneuil

Pattern	Date of Issue	Dinner fork	Dessert knife	Dessert fork	Tea-spoon
Feliciana	1969	40	30	45	28

Feliciana

Pattern	Date of Issue	Dinner fork	Dessert knife	Dessert fork	Tea-spoon
Figured Shell	c.1878	38	30	40	26

Figured Shell

Pattern	Date of Issue	Dinner fork	Dessert knife	Dessert fork	Tea-spoon
Figured Tipped	c.1880	$38	$30	$40	$28

Figured Tipped

Pattern	Date of Issue	Dinner fork	Dessert knife	Dessert fork	Tea-spoon
French Regency	1986	55	40	60	38

French Regency

Pattern	Date of Issue	Dinner fork	Dessert knife	Dessert fork	Tea-spoon
Georgian Colonial Designed by William S. Warren	1932	25	21	27	23

Georgian Colonial

Pattern	Date of Issue	Dinner fork	Dessert knife	Dessert fork	Tea-spoon
Grand Baroque designed by William S. Warren	1941	75	60	85	48

Grand Baroque

Pattern	Date of Issue	Dinner fork	Dessert knife	Dessert fork	Tea-spoon
Grand Colonial designed by William S. Warren	1942	60	48	70	40

Grand Colonial

Pattern	Date of Issue	Dinner fork	Dessert knife	Dessert fork	Tea-spoon
Grand Victorian	1973	60	50	65	35

Grand Victorian

Pattern	Date of Issue	Dinner fork	Dessert knife	Dessert fork	Tea-spoon
Hamilton	1911	26	22	28	21

Hamilton

Pattern	Date of Issue	Dinner fork	Dessert knife	Dessert fork	Tea-spoon
Hampton	c.1900	30	25	30	23

Hampton

WALLACE

Pattern	Date of Issue	Dinner fork	Dessert knife	Dessert fork	Tea-spoon
Irian	1902	$65	$50	$70	$45

Irian

Pattern	Date of Issue	Dinner fork	Dessert knife	Dessert fork	Tea-spoon
Irving	1900	40	30	42	28

Irving

Pattern	Date of Issue	Dinner fork	Dessert knife	Dessert fork	Tea-spoon
Ivanhoe	1893	38	30	38	27

Ivanhoe

Pattern	Date of Issue	Dinner fork	Dessert knife	Dessert fork	Tea-spoon
Juliet	1924	28	23	28	21

Juliet

Pattern	Date of Issue	Dinner fork	Dessert knife	Dessert fork	Tea-spoon
King Christian	1940	38	30	40	28

King Christian

Pattern	Date of Issue	Dinner fork	Dessert knife	Dessert fork	Tea-spoon
Kings	1903	48	38	50	32

Kings

Pattern	Date of Issue	Dinner fork	Dessert knife	Dessert fork	Tea-spoon
LaModerne	1926	28	24	30	23

La Moderne

Pattern	Date of Issue	Dinner fork	Dessert knife	Dessert fork	Tea-spoon
La Reine	1921	48	35	50	32

La Reine

Pattern	Date of Issue	Dinner fork	Dessert knife	Dessert fork	Tea-spoon
La Viola	1912	$38	$30	$40	$30

La Viola

Pattern	Date of Issue	Dinner fork	Dessert knife	Dessert fork	Tea-spoon
Larkspur	1937	27	24	28	22

Larkspur

Pattern	Date of Issue	Dinner fork	Dessert knife	Dessert fork	Tea-spoon
Louvre	1893	55	35	58	32

Louvre

Pattern	Date of Issue	Dinner fork	Dessert knife	Dessert fork	Tea-spoon
Lucerne	1896	65	45	70	35

Lucerne

Pattern	Date of Issue	Dinner fork	Dessert knife	Dessert fork	Tea-spoon
Madison	1913	27	22	28	22

Madison

Pattern	Date of Issue	Dinner fork	Dessert knife	Dessert fork	Tea-spoon
Marie	1895	27	22	28	22

Marie

Pattern	Date of Issue	Dinner fork	Dessert knife	Dessert fork	Tea-spoon
Melanie	1959	42	32	45	30

Designed by Amedie J. Germain

Melanie

Pattern	Date of Issue	Dinner fork	Dessert knife	Dessert fork	Tea-spoon
Melody	1929	30	25	32	24

Melody

WALLACE

Pattern	Date of Issue	Dinner fork	Dessert knife	Dessert fork	Tea-spoon
Michele	1968	$28	$23	$28	$20

Michele

| Monterey | 1922 | 25 | 20 | 28 | 19 |

Monterey

| Mozart | 1938 | 35 | 28 | 38 | 26 |

Mozart

| My Love | 1958 | 38 | 35 | 42 | 30 |

My Love

| Nile | 1908 | 28 | 24 | 30 | 24 |

Nile

| Normandie | 1933 | 32 | 26 | 35 | 24 |

Normandie

| Number 4 | 1896 | 32 | 28 | 35 | 28 |

Number 4

| Number 45 | 1910 | 28 | 24 | 28 | 23 |

Number 45

| Number 80 | 1909 | | | | 45 |

probably not a full line

Number 80

Pattern	Date of Issue	Dinner fork	Dessert knife	Dessert fork	Tea-spoon
Number 300	1907	$35	$27	$37	$25

Number 300

| Old Lyme | 1926 | 28 | 24 | 30 | 24 |

Old Lyme

| Orange Blossom | 1923 | 30 | 25 | 32 | 25 |

Designed by Henrick Hillbom

Orange Blossom

| Orchid Elegance | 1956 | 55 | 40 | 58 | 38 |

Orchid Elegance

| Penrose | 1962 | 28 | 24 | 30 | 23 |

Penrose

| Peony | 1906 | 48 | 35 | 50 | 32 |

Peony

| Pilgrim | 1915 | 28 | 23 | 28 | 20 |

Pilgrim

| Pompeii | 1916 | 27 | 23 | 28 | 22 |

Pompeii

199

Pattern	Date of Issue	Dinner fork	Dessert knife	Dessert fork	Tea-spoon
Princess Anne	1926	$30	$25	$30	$25

Princess Anne

Pattern	Date of Issue	Dinner fork	Dessert knife	Dessert fork	Tea-spoon
Princess Mary and Princess Mary, hammered	1922 / 1922	28 / 28	24 / 24	28 / 28	23 / 25

Pattern	Date of Issue	Dinner fork	Dessert knife	Dessert fork	Tea-spoon
Princess Pat	1914	28	22	28	22

Princess Pat

Pattern	Date of Issue	Dinner fork	Dessert knife	Dessert fork	Tea-spoon
Priscilla	1909	27	22	28	20

Priscilla

Pattern	Date of Issue	Dinner fork	Dessert knife	Dessert fork	Tea-spoon
Puritan	c.1910	27	23	28	20

Puritan

Pattern	Date of Issue	Dinner fork	Dessert knife	Dessert fork	Tea-spoon
Puritan, hammered	c.1910	27	23	28	20

Puritan, hammered

Pattern	Date of Issue	Dinner fork	Dessert knife	Dessert fork	Tea-spoon
Putnam	1912	28	24	28	20

Putnam

Pattern	Date of Issue	Dinner fork	Dessert knife	Dessert fork	Tea-spoon
Reflection	1920	25	22	25	20

Reflection

Pattern	Date of Issue	Dinner fork	Dessert knife	Dessert fork	Tea-spoon
Rembrandt	1938	35	26	40	30

Rembrandt

Pattern	Date of Issue	Dinner fork	Dessert knife	Dessert fork	Tea-spoon
Renaissance	1925	$28	$24	$28	$24

Renaissance

Pattern	Date of Issue	Dinner fork	Dessert knife	Dessert fork	Tea-spoon
Rheims	1919	30	25	32	24

Rheims

Pattern	Date of Issue	Dinner fork	Dessert knife	Dessert fork	Tea-spoon
Rhythm Designed by William S. Warren	1929	32	28	35	26

Rhythm

Pattern	Date of Issue	Dinner fork	Dessert knife	Dessert fork	Tea-spoon
Romance of the Sea designed by William S. Warren	1950	60	50	65	35

Romance of the Sea

Pattern	Date of Issue	Dinner fork	Dessert knife	Dessert fork	Tea-spoon
Rose	1898	38	30	38	27

Rose

Pattern	Date of Issue	Dinner fork	Dessert knife	Dessert fork	Tea-spoon
Rosepoint designd by William S. Warren	1934	60	50	65	38

Rosepoint

Pattern	Date of Issue	Dinner fork	Dessert knife	Dessert fork	Tea-spoon
Royal Rose	1962	48	38	50	30

Royal Rose

Pattern	Date of Issue	Dinner fork	Dessert knife	Dessert fork	Tea-spoon
Royal Satin	1965	28	24	30	25

Royal Satin

Pattern	Date of Issue	Dinner fork	Dessert knife	Dessert fork	Tea-spoon
St. George	c.1878	45	35	45	32

St. George

Pattern	Date of Issue	Dinner fork	Dessert knife	Dessert fork	Tea-spoon
St. Leon	1875	$65	$50	$68	$40

St. Leon

Pattern	Date of Issue	Dinner fork	Dessert knife	Dessert fork	Tea-spoon
Salem	1926	28	23	28	23

Salem

San Juan	1914	30	25	35	25

San Juan

Sappho	1895	65	50	68	40

Sappho

Saxon	1910	30	25	32	24

Saxon

Saybrook	1926	27	23	27	20

Saybrook

Shenandoah	1966	30	25	30	25

Shenandoah

Silver Swirl designed by William S. Warren	1955	50	40	50	32

Silver Swirl

Sir Christopher designed by William S. Warren	1936	$75	$50	$80	$40

Sir Christopher

Soliloquy	1963	35	30	35	25

Soliloquy

Somerset	1913	28	24	28	22

Somerset

Spanish Lace	1964	40	32	42	30

Spanish Lace

Standish	1917	28	24	28	22

Standish

Still Mood	1963	35	30	35	25

Still Mood

Stradivari designed by William S. Warren	1937	55	40	60	38

Stradivari

Tipped	1890	32	28	35	25

Tipped

WALLACE

Pattern	Date of Issue	Dinner fork	Dessert knife	Dessert fork	Tea-spoon
Versailles	1914	$28	$24	$28	$24

Versailles

Pattern	Date of Issue	Dinner fork	Dessert knife	Dessert fork	Tea-spoon
Violet	1904	42	43	45	30

Violet

Pattern	Date of Issue	Dinner fork	Dessert knife	Dessert fork	Tea-spoon
Waltz of Spring designed by William S. Warren	1952	65	48	70	38

Waltz of Spring

Pattern	Date of Issue	Dinner fork	Dessert knife	Dessert fork	Tea-spoon
Warwick	1914	28	24	28	23

Warwick

Pattern	Date of Issue	Dinner fork	Dessert knife	Dessert fork	Tea-spoon
Washington	1911	28	26	30	26

Washington

Pattern	Date of Issue	Dinner fork	Dessert knife	Dessert fork	Tea-spoon
Waverly	1890	$38	$30	$38	$27

Waverly

Pattern	Date of Issue	Dinner fork	Dessert knife	Dessert fork	Tea-spoon
Windsor Originally a Watson pattern	1890	25	22	27	22

Windsor

Pattern	Date of Issue	Dinner fork	Dessert knife	Dessert fork	Tea-spoon
Wishing Star designed by William S. Warren	1954	32	27	35	27

Wishing Star

Pattern	Date of Issue	Dinner fork	Dessert knife	Dessert fork	Tea-spoon
Wolcott (Walcott)	1910	27	23	28	23

Wolcott

THE WATSON COMPANY
Attleboro, Massachusetts

TRADE   STERLING   MARK

In silver circles Watson has become a reasonably familiar name only since 1955 when WALLACE SILVERSMITHS bought it and began to publicize some of its patterns. This is ironic because Watson is actually an outgrowth of a partnership founded in Attleboro in 1874. Among the partners were Clarence Watson and Fred Newell. The two took over the company in 1894 and as Watson-Newell proceeded to do a lively business. They came to sterling flatware late; their first patterns were issued about 1900. The Watson name continued well into the 1950's, however, still advertising new patterns.

Watson was a well known company in its time but in 1955 it almost disappeared with its acquisition by Wallace. With Wallace it ran the corporate gamut, first by Hamilton, H.M.W. Industries, Katy, and finally and currently Syratech of Syracuse, New York. Its well known patterns are few and those mainly because Wallace has focused advertising on them but there are many others out there waiting to be added to collections.

Here is a wide open market for collectors. The silver is more available than one would suppose and as the company advertised during the 1920's and 30's, upscale retailers should buy Watson, ''Buy Craftsmanship''; and touted ''the perfection of the Watson finish and the finesse of artisans and artists.'' In 1992 this is still good advice.

WATSON PRICES

Pattern	Date of Issue	Dinner fork	Dessert knife	Dessert fork	Tea-spoon
Bunker Hill	1908	$28	$23	$28	$23

Bunker Hill

Carrollton	1914	40	30	42	28

Carrollton

Chippendale	1918	32	26	35	26

Chippendale

Colonial	1917	30	25	30	26

Colonial

Colonial, engraved	1917	32	26	32	27

Colonial, engraved

Pattern	Date of Issue	Dinner fork	Dessert knife	Dessert fork	Tea-spoon
Colonial Antique	1923	$32	$26	$32	$28

Colonial Antique

Colonial Fiddle	1925	38	32	40	30

Colonial Fiddle

Commonwealth	1908	27	23	28	23

Commonwealth

Commonwealth, engraved	1908	28	24	30	24

Commonwealth, engraved

Dorian Rose	1934	40	32	45	30

Dorian Rose

Pattern	Date of Issue	Dinner fork	Dessert knife	Dessert fork	Tea- spoon
Dorian	1934	$38	$32	$45	$32

Dorian

Pattern	Date of Issue	Dinner fork	Dessert knife	Dessert fork	Tea- spoon
Etiquette	1923	25	22	25	20

Etiquette

Pattern	Date of Issue	Dinner fork	Dessert knife	Dessert fork	Tea- spoon
Foxhall Designed by William T. Brown	1942	40	30	42	30

Foxhall

Pattern	Date of Issue	Dinner fork	Dessert knife	Dessert fork	Tea- spoon
George II Designed by Percy R. Ball	1936	38	30	40	30

George II

Pattern	Date of Issue	Dinner fork	Dessert knife	Dessert fork	Tea- spoon
Governor Dummer	1925	30	26	32	24

Governor Dummer

Pattern	Date of Issue	Dinner fork	Dessert knife	Dessert fork	Tea- spoon
John Adams	1911	28	23	28	23

John Adams

Pattern	Date of Issue	Dinner fork	Dessert knife	Dessert fork	Tea- spoon
John Alden	1911	28	24	28	23

John Alden

Pattern	Date of Issue	Dinner fork	Dessert knife	Dessert fork	Tea- spoon
Juliana	1937	42	35	45	30

Juliana

Pattern	Date of Issue	Dinner fork	Dessert knife	Dessert fork	Tea- spoon
Kenmore	c.1926	$28	$25	$30	$25

Kenmore

Pattern	Date of Issue	Dinner fork	Dessert knife	Dessert fork	Tea- spoon
King George	1920	50	38	55	32

King George

Pattern	Date of Issue	Dinner fork	Dessert knife	Dessert fork	Tea- spoon
King Phillip	1904	30	25	30	25

King Phillip

Pattern	Date of Issue	Dinner fork	Dessert knife	Dessert fork	Tea- spoon
Laremie	1936	35	30	35	26

Laremie

Pattern	Date of Issue	Dinner fork	Dessert knife	Dessert fork	Tea- spoon
Laremie, engraved a variation of George II	1936	48	35	50	35

Laremie, engraved

Pattern	Date of Issue	Dinner fork	Dessert knife	Dessert fork	Tea- spoon
Laurel	1917	26	22	26	20

Laurel

Pattern	Date of Issue	Dinner fork	Dessert knife	Dessert fork	Tea- spoon
Liberty	1917	30	28	35	25

Liberty

Pattern	Date of Issue	Dinner fork	Dessert knife	Dessert fork	Tea-spoon
Lily	1902	$85	$60	$95	$45

Lily

Pattern	Date of Issue	Dinner fork	Dessert knife	Dessert fork	Tea-spoon
Lotus	1935	30	28	32	25

Lotus

Magnolia	1908	50	40	55	32

Magnolia

Marlborough	1918	30	25	35	24

Marlborough

Martha Hilton	1914	38	30	38	28

Martha Hilton

Martha Washington	1912	32	27	32	25

Martha Washington

Mayflower	1914	27	24	28	24

Mayflower

Meadow Rose	1907	40	35	48	32

Meadow Rose

Pattern	Date of Issue	Dinner fork	Dessert knife	Dessert fork	Tea-spoon
Mt. Vernon	1907	$38	$32	$45	$26

Mt. Vernon

Navarre	1908	28	25	32	25

Navarre

Old Colony	1921	32	25	35	25

Old Colony

Old Colony, engraved	1921	35	27	38	27

Old Colony, engraved

Orchid	1903	65	40	65	38

Orchid

Orleans	1915	38	30	35	27

Orleans

Priscilla Alden	1923	25	22	26	23

Priscilla Alden

Plymouth	1920	28	24	28	22

Plymouth

205

WATSON

Pattern	Date of Issue	Dinner fork	Dessert knife	Dessert fork	Tea-spoon
Putnam	1920	$60	$40	$65	$40

Putnam

Pattern	Date of Issue	Dinner fork	Dessert knife	Dessert fork	Tea-spoon
Queen Louise	1912	35	30	38	28

Queen Louise

Rochambeau	1919	35	30	38	28

Rochambeau

Sterling Rose	1935	38	32	42	27

Sterling Rose

The Lady Wellesley	1921	40	30	45	30

The Lady Wellesley

Tuscany	1930	27	24	28	22

Tuscany

Victoria	c.1930	40	35	42	30

Victoria

Virginia	1911	36	28	36	26

Virginia

Pattern	Date of Issue	Dinner fork	Dessert knife	Dessert fork	Tea-spoon
Watteau		$42	$32	$45	$28

Wedding Rose	1900	50	40	56	35

Wedding Rose

Wentworth	1913	32	28	35	25

Wentworth

Windsor	1920	27	23	30	23

Windsor

Windsor Manor	1936	38	32	40	30

Windsor Manor

Windsor Rose	1940	40	34	45	32

Windsor Rose

FRANK M. WHITING & CO.
North Attleboro, Massachusetts

Frank M. Whiting and Company is "that other Whiting". Much less well known than Whiting Manufacturing Co., of Providence, Rhode Island, Frank Whiting is nonetheless becoming a force in collectible silver. Recently at an auction, after some marked Frank Whiting silver had been bought, and I remarked on its beauty, the buyer said in some surprise "Oh, you know about Frank Whiting?" - A well kept secret probably not for long.

The early patterns such as Orleans, Esther, Tyrolean, Athene, Floral, Palm, Josephine, Gladstone, Roderic, Marquis, among a few others are reflective of their time in a fairly understated, elegant way. The Pearl pattern is a particularly simple but beautiful interpretation of the early American style. The patterns of this company, when it was truly Frank Whiting, are not so numerous as to ever make the collecting of them easy, but they do surface from time to time. I recently saw five place settings of one pattern—and it was worth the effort. The silver itself is of good weight - the company said it made its flatware in either medium or heavy. The design work is somewhat more imaginative than that of some companies working at the same time.

The time frame was, for the most part, Victorian although the exact date when Frank Whiting left the shelter of his father's firm, Whiting Mfg. Co., to branch out on his own is not known. Sometime certainly in the mid to late 1870s, he and two partners began a business in North Attleboro, MA, and it seems clear that by 1878 or 1879, he owned the company outright. There were several name changes in a minor way, by the late 1870s it was F.M. Whiting & Co. Later about 1890, it became F.M. Whiting. When Frank Whiting himself died and family members continued the business, an old newspaper calls his wife "heroic".

Not many patterns were issued during this period and by 1939 the company was in the process of being sold to Ellmore Silver Co. of Meriden, Connecticut. For collecting purposes, the silver made before this date will have more value.

FRANK WHITING PRICES

Pattern	Date of Issue	Dinner fork	Dessert knife	Dessert fork	Tea-spoon		Pattern	Date of Issue	Dinner fork	Dessert knife	Dessert fork	Tea-spoon
Antique	c.1885	$32	$25	$30	$23		Bow Knot	1890	$30	$25	$35	$25

Antique

Bow Knot

Antique B	1894	32	25	30	23		Crystal	c.1896	25	20	25	18

Antique B

Crystal

Athene	1888	42	32	48	30		Damascus	1894	40	32	45	30

Athene

Damascus

							Esther	1890	48	38	48	30
Autumn	1888	28	24	28	23							

Autumn

Esther

							Duncan Phyfe	1930	32	30	35	25

Duncan Phyfe

Pattern	Date of Issue	Dinner fork	Dessert knife	Dessert fork	Tea-spoon
Floral (Lily)	c.1902	$65	$48	$68	$35

Floral (Lily)

Pattern	Date of Issue	Dinner fork	Dessert knife	Dessert fork	Tea-spoon
Florence (Victoria)	c.1900	42	32	48	30

Florence (Victorian)

Genoa	1893	45	30	45	35

Genoa

George III	1891	38	28	35	26

George III

Georgian Shell	1948	36	25	36	27

Georgian Shell

Gladstone	c.1893	50	40	55	35

Gladstone

Gothic	1893	32	30	38	28

Gothic

Hagie	1885	30	25	34	24

Hagie

Pattern	Date of Issue	Dinner fork	Dessert knife	Dessert fork	Tea-spoon
Helena	c.1900	$36	$32	$38	$30

Helena	c.1894	30	26	35	24

Helena

Helena 1st	1892	32	26	32	24

Helena 1st

Josephine	c.1890	50	35	50	30

Josephine

Lily, engraved	1885	30	25	30	25

Lily, engraved

Marlborough	c.1895	35	28	35	24

Marlborough

Marquis	1889	60	42	65	35

Marquis

Narcissus	1886	45	35	48	30

Narcissus

FRANK M. WHITING

Pattern	Date of Issue	Dinner fork	Dessert knife	Dessert fork	Tea-spoon
Neaplitan	c.1895	$38	$30	$38	$30

Neapolitan

Pattern	Date of Issue	Dinner fork	Dessert knife	Dessert fork	Tea-spoon
Orleans	1892	40	35	42	32

Orleans

Palm	1887	48	37	50	32

Palm

Pearl	1888	35	28	32	25

Pearl

Plain Tip	c.1883	35	28	35	26

Plain Tip

Princess Ingrid	1945	38	30	42	27

Princess Ingrid

Puritan	c.1894	32	28	32	25

Puritan

Roderic	1893	$65	$40	$68	$32

Roderic

Rose, engraved	1885	35	30	32	25

Rose, engraved

Rose of Sharon	1954	40	32	42	30

Rose of Sharon

Shell	1890	35	30	40	26

Shell

Talisman Rose	1948	30	25	30	25

Talisman Rose

Troubadour	1945	40	32	45	26

Troubadour

Tyrolean	c.1900	50	35	50	30

Tyrolean

WHITING MANUFACTURING COMPANY
North Attleboro, Massachusetts

It seems a great loss that the firm founded by Alfred T. Tift and William Whiting in 1840 is forever buried in the designation WHITING DIVISION OF GORHAM, although that company did not buy Whiting until 1924. From then on this company which produced highly stylized, imaginative silver has been lost in anonymity. Some very sophisticated collectors own combs, hatpins and other small silver items made by this early company, for Whiting as almost all firms operating in the Attleboro area relied on such fancies as the backbone of their business. Whiting also made lovely holloware which is now expensive and desirable.

It was a busy, lively company which might explain the reason for the company's involvement in so much litigation. For some reason, although other companies were also involved in silver feuds which led to court action, Whiting seems to have been embroiled in an unusual number of suits for patent infringement. In 1920 a rather protracted court battle ensued when Whiting sued Alvin over a specific design patent infringement. Whiting won. Alvin appealed. So closely were designs copied with little variation in those days that most companies were producing much that looked the same but very few bothered to take the matter to court. The pattern involved in the Whiting-Alvin suit was Jenny Lind and line for line it seems the same pattern. Such was life in the fast silver lane.

Gorham at first merely acquired a financial interest when Whiting was operated by the Silversmiths Company, a holding company, but Gorham bought the Silversmiths Company in 1924 and with it its subsidiary Whiting. It was not the first contact of Gorham and Whiting however, in 1877 when the silver industry was in a tremendous slump Whiting approached Gorham about a possible buy-out but the matter petered out without resolution. When Gorham acquired Silversmiths and consequently Whiting, it moved the company to Providence, Rhode Island. Until this move in 1924, Whiting had operated as an independent silver company under the umbrella holding company.

Whiting was a very prestigious early silver company. It made some exquisite church silver now treasured and considered 'museum quality', they were very active in competing for the trophy market and many of their urns, vases and cups awarded for various competitions as well as commemoratives are housed in museums, some rest in sporting clubhouses and headquarters of organizations. This was a successful part of their operations and an important part of the silver business generally. A silver trophy was given on every suitable occasion. Whiting also did beautiful silver deposit work on cut glass. Whiting was active and eclectic in its work and much of it survives to be enjoyed. Much of it is overblown in the Victorian way and while some things are merely old hat, Whiting somehow managed to make things that seem old fashioned but with an endearing flair. It is precisely this quality which drives silver collectors today.

In 1874, in one competition for the creation of a vase to be given as a tribute to the poet William Cullen Bryant, Tiffany won, and the result rests in the Metropolitan Museum of Art in New York, but drawings exists for the Whiting entry which in fact seems more elegant and graceful.

Americans, who still seem awed by foreign titles, were quite receptive to the offerings of Whiting flatware patterns which like those of other companies of the time boasted names such as Prince Albert, Louis XV, Old King, King Edward, Duke of York; even Madame Pompadour made the list. Of course it must have been a prodigious chore to bestow distinctive names to patterns which were produced in such numbers. Whiting though seems particularly to have forgotten no royal house then in existence. This is a plus for collectors, it makes pattern names easier to remember and it gives a sense of history to the flatware.

What is to be said of a company such as Whiting which saw the progression of America from the days of the first silver factories to the mechanization of the craft and its own acquisition by a much larger company and for all practical purposes its inevitable disappearance. Whiting Manufacturing was fathered by a talented man from a talented family, made the early typical patterns, and was lucky in its choice of Charles Osborne as head designer. To him we owe the beautiful LILY pattern of 1902.

The silver flatware of this company is still monumentally underpriced and when prices begin to reflect true value, both actual and historic, it will probably be too late to begin a collection. This company really represents the pot of silver at the end of the rainbow.

Such patterns as Violet, Colonial, "one of the company's all time favorites", Lily, Lily of the Valley, Louis XV, the list is long and impressive. Magnificent catalogs were issued in the early days (which are things of beauty in themselves) picturing the favored patterns with all attendant pieces. Pampadour, King Edward, Duke of York, merited this kind of special treatment.

Studying the patterns of Whiting gives one a comfortable feeling. Most of the patterns reflect a time of opulence to which we have difficulty relating, at the same time the patterns are so well done, elaborate in such a tasteful manner than we cannot help but be charmed.

Pattern	Date of Issue	Dinner fork	Dessert knife	Dessert fork	Tea-spoon
Adam	1907	$30	$25	$30	$25

Adam

Pattern	Date of Issue	Dinner fork	Dessert knife	Dessert fork	Tea-spoon
Armor	1871	$35	$27	$35	$25

Armor

Alhambra	1870	48	35	50	32

Alhambra

Athenian	c.1890	30	24	30	24

Athenian

Antique Chased	c.1880	38	30	40	28

Antique Chased

Bead	c.1885	28	23	32	22

Bead

Antique Lily	1882	32	28	35	25

Antique Lily

Berry A	c.1880	48	35	48	30

Berry A

Berry B					

Berry B

Antique M 2	c.1880	32	26	35	25

Antique M 2

Burlington	1914	40	30	45	28

Burlington

Antique Rosette	c.1885	30	25	32	25

Antique Rosette

Cinderella	1925	35	30	38	27

Cinderella

Antique Tip	c.1885	30	25	32	25

Antique Tip

Colonial	1907	30	25	30	25

Colonial

Arabesque	1880-c.1885	45	30	45	30

Arabesque

Colonial, engraved	1908	32	26	35	26

Colonial, engraved

211

Pattern	Date of Issue	Dinner fork	Dessert knife	Dessert fork	Tea-spoon
Colonial B., engraved	c.1908	$38	$30	$40	$27

Colonial B., engraved

Pattern	Date of Issue	Dinner fork	Dessert knife	Dessert fork	Tea-spoon
Cox	c.1850 1855	30	28	35	24

Cox

Diamond	1875	48	35	50	32

Diamond

Dorothy Vernon	1909	42	30	45	30

Dorothy Vernon

Dresden	1896	48	36	50	35

Dresden

Duchess	1906	32	26	34	24

Duchess

Duke of York	1900	42	43	48	32

Duke of York

Eastlake	c.1885	28	20	28	20

Eastlake

Egyptian	c.1870	$40	$30	$45	$30

Egyptian

Empire	1892	38	32	40	30

Empire

Fairfield	1912	26	22	28	18

Fairfield

Fancy Tip	c.1878	38	30	42	26

Fancy Tip

Fiddle	c.1860	35	28	40	28

Fiddle

French Thread	c.1850	30	25	35	25

French Thread

Fruit	c.1876	45	36	50	32

Fruit

WHITING

Pattern	Date of Issue	Dinner fork	Dessert knife	Dessert fork	Tea-spoon
Gem Leaf	c.1870	$32	$26	$38	$25

Gem Leaf

Gibney (named after the designer)	c.1850	32	28	35	23

Gibney

Grape	c.1850 1855	40	30	45	28

Grape

Grecian	c.1865	35	26	35	24

Grecian

Heraldic	1880	48	35	45	30

Heraldic

Home	c.1870	28	24	28	23

Home

Honeysuckle	c.1870	45	32	48	30

Honeysuckle

Pattern	Date of Issue	Dinner fork	Dessert knife	Dessert fork	
Hyperion	1888	$50	$40	$55	$32

Hyperion

Imperial Queen	1895	55	48	60	39

Imperial Queen

Indian	c.1875	30	26	32	23

Indian

Italian	c.1875	30	25	40	25

Italian

Italian J	c.1875	35	28	42	26

Italian J

Italian K	c.1875	38	30	45	28

Italian K

Ivy	c.1874	40	30	45	27

Ivy

Pattern	Date of Issue	Dinner fork	Dessert knife	Dessert fork	Tea-spoon
Japanese	c.1875 1880	$70	$50	$80	$40

Japanese

	Date of Issue	Dinner fork	Dessert knife	Dessert fork	Tea-spoon
Jenny Lind	1920	32	26	34	24

Jenny Lind

	Date of Issue	Dinner fork	Dessert knife	Dessert fork	Tea-spoon
Keystone	c.1875	45	36	50	32

Keystone

	Date of Issue	Dinner fork	Dessert knife	Dessert fork	Tea-spoon
King Albert later advertised as a Gorham Pattern	1919	28	24	30	22

King Albert

	Date of Issue	Dinner fork	Dessert knife	Dessert fork	Tea-spoon
King Edward	1901	60	45	65	35

King Edward

	Date of Issue	Dinner fork	Dessert knife	Dessert fork	Tea-spoon
Lady Baltimore	1910	28	24	28	21

Lady Baltimore

	Date of Issue	Dinner fork	Dessert knife	Dessert fork	Tea-spoon
Laureate	c.1880	35	28	38	26

Laureate

Pattern	Date of Issue	Dinner fork	Dessert knife	Dessert fork	Tea-spoon
LeCordon	c.1850	$30	$25	$32	$23

LeCordon

	Date of Issue	Dinner fork	Dessert knife	Dessert fork	Tea-spoon
Lily 1902		95	60	100	45

Lily 1902

	Date of Issue	Dinner fork	Dessert knife	Dessert fork	Tea-spoon
Lily of the Valley	1885	95	65	125	50

Lily of the Valley

	Date of Issue	Dinner fork	Dessert knife	Dessert fork	Tea-spoon
Livingston A, engraved	1915	25	20	25	19

Livingston A

	Date of Issue	Dinner fork	Dessert knife	Dessert fork	Tea-spoon
Livingston B, chased	1915	27	22	28	23

Livingston B

	Date of Issue	Dinner fork	Dessert knife	Dessert fork	Tea-spoon
Louis XV	1891	40	35	45	30

Louis XV

	Date of Issue	Dinner fork	Dessert knife	Dessert fork	Tea-spoon
Madam Jumel later advertising spelled Madam with an "e"	1908	32	26	35	25

Madam Jumel

214

WHITING

Pattern	Date of Issue	Dinner fork	Dessert knife	Dessert fork	Tea-spoon
Madam Morris later advertising spelled Madam with an ''e''	1909	$30	$25	$32	$25

Madam Morris

Pattern	Date of Issue	Dinner fork	Dessert knife	Dessert fork	Tea-spoon
Madam Morris, engraved later advertising spelled Madam with an ''e''	1910	32	27	35	27

Madam Morris, engraved

Pattern	Date of Issue	Dinner fork	Dessert knife	Dessert fork	Tea-spoon
Mandarin	1917	35	27	35	26

Mandarin

Pattern	Date of Issue	Dinner fork	Dessert knife	Dessert fork	Tea-spoon
Mask	c.1880	32	28	35	24

Mask

Pattern	Date of Issue	Dinner fork	Dessert knife	Dessert fork	Tea-spoon
Newport	1917	28	24	30	22

Newport

Pattern	Date of Issue	Dinner fork	Dessert knife	Dessert fork	Tea-spoon
Old Bead	c.1880	30	25	32	23

Old Bead

Pattern	Date of Issue	Dinner fork	Dessert knife	Dessert fork	Tea-spoon
Old English	c.1880	28	24	30	22

Old English

Pattern	Date of Issue	Dinner fork	Dessert knife	Dessert fork	Tea-spoon
Old Empire	c.1870 1880	$30	$25	$32	$22

Old Empire

Pattern	Date of Issue	Dinner fork	Dessert knife	Dessert fork	Tea-spoon
Old King	c.1885	40	32	45	20

Old King

Pattern	Date of Issue	Dinner fork	Dessert knife	Dessert fork	Tea-spoon
Oriana	1916	26	23	26	20

Oriana

Pattern	Date of Issue	Dinner fork	Dessert knife	Dessert fork	Tea-spoon
Oval Thread	c.1850	28	24	28	22

Oval Thread

Pattern	Date of Issue	Dinner fork	Dessert knife	Dessert fork	Tea-spoon
Oval Twist	c.1900	35	30	35	25

Oval Twist

Pattern	Date of Issue	Dinner fork	Dessert knife	Dessert fork	Tea-spoon
Persian	c.1880 1885	38	32	40	28

Persian

Pattern	Date of Issue	Dinner fork	Dessert knife	Dessert fork	Tea-spoon
Plain Thread	c.1870	30	25	35	25

Plain Thread

Pattern	Date of Issue	Dinner fork	Dessert knife	Dessert fork	Tea-spoon
Plain Tip (tipped)	c.1865	$30	$25	$35	$25

Plain Tip

Pattern	Date of Issue	Dinner fork	Dessert knife	Dessert fork	Tea-spoon
Pompadour	c.1888-1890	65	50	70	35

Pompadour

Pattern	Date of Issue	Dinner fork	Dessert knife	Dessert fork	Tea-spoon
Pompeian	1913	30	25	32	24

Pompeian

Pattern	Date of Issue	Dinner fork	Dessert knife	Dessert fork	Tea-spoon
Portland	1913	25	22	25	22

Portland

Pattern	Date of Issue	Dinner fork	Dessert knife	Dessert fork	Tea-spoon
Prince Albert	c.1855	38	32	40	26

Prince Albert

Pattern	Date of Issue	Dinner fork	Dessert knife	Dessert fork	Tea-spoon
Radiant	1895	60	40	65	35

Radiant

Pattern	Date of Issue	Dinner fork	Dessert knife	Dessert fork	Tea-spoon
Rosette	c.1875	$35	$28	$38	$24

Rosette

Pattern	Date of Issue	Dinner fork	Dessert knife	Dessert fork	Tea-spoon
St. Martin's	1916	26	22	26	22

St. Martin's

Pattern	Date of Issue	Dinner fork	Dessert knife	Dessert fork	Tea-spoon
St. Martin's, engraved	1916	28	23	28	23

St. Martin's, engraved

Pattern	Date of Issue	Dinner fork	Dessert knife	Dessert fork	Tea-spoon
Stratford	1911	32	28	35	24

Stratford

Pattern	Date of Issue	Dinner fork	Dessert knife	Dessert fork	Tea-spoon
Stuart	1911	30	26	35	25

Stuart

Pattern	Date of Issue	Dinner fork	Dessert knife	Dessert fork	Tea-spoon
Tuscan	c.1865-1870	30	25	32	22

Tuscan

WHITING

Pattern	Date of Issue	Dinner fork	Dessert knife	Dessert fork	Tea-spoon
Villa	c.1895	$25	$20	$25	$18
Violet	1903	65	40	65	38
Wedgwood	1911	32	26	35	25

Villa

Violet

Wedgwood

WHITING

STERLING SILVER DOZEN WORK

TEA SPOONS
Small
Trade
Medium
Heavy
Extra Heavy

DESSERT SPOONS OR FORKS
Medium
Heavy
Extra Heavy

TABLE SPOONS OR FORKS
Medium
Heavy
Extra Heavy

SOUP SPOONS
Medium

CUTLERY
Tea Knife
Dessert Knives
Breakfast Knives,
Medium or Dinner Knives,

THE MANDARIN
Meat Carving Knife, with guard
Meat Carving Fork, with guard
Game Carving Knife, with guard
Carving Steel with guard
Steak Knife, large with guard
Steak Fork, large with guard
Steak Steel, with guard
Steak Knife & Fork, small
Bird Knife and Fork
Bread Knife, H.H.
Child's Knife, H.H.
Cheese Server
Fried Egg Server, H.H.
Fruit Knife, H.H.
Ice Cream Slicer, H.H.
Orange Knife, H.H.

Pie Server, H.H.
Cake Server, H.H.
Duck Shears
Roast Holder, small
Roast Holder, med.

DOZENS
Berry Forks
Bouillon Spoons
Butter Spreaders, sm.
Butter Spreaders, lg.
Chocolate Spoons
Coffee Spoons
Egg Spoons
Fish Fork, Ind'l, small
Fish Fork, Ind'l, large
Grape Fruit Spoons
Ice Cream Forks
Ice Cream Spoons
Iced Tea Spoons, 7½''
Nut Picks
Orange Spoons
Oyster Forks
Parfait Spoons
Pastry Forks, Ind., sm.

Pastry Forks, Ind., lg.
Salad Forks, Ind., sm.
Salad Forks, Ind., lg.
Salt Spoons, Ind.
Sherbet Spoons

PAIRS
Fish Knife, sm.
Fish Fork, sm.
Fish Knife, lg.
Fish Fork, lg.
Lettuce Spoon
Lettuce Fork
Salad Spoon, sm.
Salad Fork, sm.
Salad Spoon & Fork (Olive Wood)

SINGLE PIECES
Asparagus Server, sm.
Baby Fork, Stub.
Baby Knife, Stub
Baby Spoon, B.H., sm.
Baby Spoon, Stub
Baby Spoon, B.H., lg.
Beef Fork
Berry Spoon

Bonbon Spoon
Bonbon Tongs, lg.
Butter Knife, lg., B.H.
Butter Knife, sm., B.H.
Butter Pick, No. 1
Butter Pick, No. 2
Cake Knife
Cheese Scoop, sm.
Cheese Scoop, lg.
Child's Fork
Child's Spoon
Chocolate Muddlers
Cold Meat Fork, small
Cold Meat Fork, med.
Cold Meat Fork, lg.
Confection Spoon
Cream Ladle
Crumb Scraper, sm.
Cucumber Server
Dish Gravy Spoon
Entree Server
Food Pusher
Fried Egg Server
Fried Oyster Server
Gravy Ladle
Horse Radish Spoon
Ice Cream Server Ice
Cream Slicer, sm.
Ice Tongs
Jelly Server
Jelly Spoon
Layer Cake Server

Lemon Fork
Lemonade Spoon
Lettuce Fork
Lettuce Spoon
Macaroni Server
Mayonnaise Ladle
Mustard Spoon
Nut Spoon
Olive Fork, long
Olive Fork, short
Olive Spoon, long
Olive Spoon, short
Oyster Ladle
Pap Spoon
Pea Spoon
Pickle Fork
Pie Knife
Preserve Spoon
Punch Ladle
Salt Spoon
Sandwich Tongs
Saratoga Chip Server
Sardine Server
Sardine Tongs
Soup Ladle
Sugar Sifter
Sugar Spoon
Sugar Tongs, small
Sugar Tongs, large
Tomato Server
Vegetable Fork
Vegetable Spoon
Waffle Server

1907
THE MADAM JUMEL
STERLING SILVER

DOZENS
Berry Forks
Bouillon Spoons
Butter Spreaders, sm.
Butter Spreaders, lg.
Chocolate Spoons
Coffee Spoons
Egg Spoons
Fish Forks, Ind., sm.
Fish Forks, Ind., lg.
Fish Knives, Ind.
Grape Fruit Spoons
Ice Cream Forks
Ice Cream Spoons
Iced Tea Spoons, 7½''
Nut Picks
Orange Spoons
Oyster Forks
Parfait Spoons
Pastry Forks, Ind., sm.
Pastry Forks, Ind., lg.
Salad Forks, Ind.
Salt Spoons
Sherbet Spoons

PAIRS
Fish Knife, sm.
Fish Fork, sm.
Fish Knife, lg.
Fish Fork, lg.
Lettuce Spoon
Lettuce Fork
Salad Spoon, sm.
Salad Fork, sm.
Salad Spoon, lg.

Salad Fork, lg.
Salad Spoon and Fork (Olive Wood)

SINGLE PIECES
Almond Scoop
Asparagus Server, sm.
Asparagus Tongs
Baby Fork, Stub
Baby Knife, Stub
Baby Spoon, Bent Handle, sm.
Baby Spoon, Bent Handle
Baby Spoon, Stub
Beef Fork
Berry Spoon
Bonbon Spoon
Bonbon Tongs
Bouillon Ladle
Butter Knife, flat
Butter Knife, lg., B.H.
Butter Knife, sm., B.H.
Butter Pick, No. 1
Butter Pick, No. 2
Caddy Scoop
Cake Knife
Cheese Knife
Cheese Fork
Cheese Knife, L.S.H.
Cheese Scoop, sm.

SINGLE PIECES
Cheese Scoop, lg.
Child's Fork
Child's Spoon
Chocolate Muddler
Cold Meat Fork, sm

Cold Meat Fork, med.
Cold Meat Fork, lg.
Confection Spoon
Cracker Spoon
Cream Ladle
Crumb Scraper, sm.
Cucumber Server
Dish Gravy Spoon
Entree Server
Food Pusher
Fried Egg Server
Fried Oyster Server
Gravy Ladle
Horse Radish Spoon
Ice Cream Server
Ice Cream Slicer, sm.
Ice Spoon
Ice Tongs
Jelly Server
Jelly Server, lg.
Jelly Spoon
Layer Cake Server
Lemon Fork
Lemonade Spoon
Lettuce Fork
Lettuce Spoon
Macaroni Server
Mayonnaise Ladle
Mixer
Mustard Spoon
Nut Spoon
Olive Fork, long
Olive Spoon, long
Olive Spoon, short
Oyster Ladle
Pap Spoon
Pea Spoon
Pickle Fork
Pie Knife

Preserve Spoon
Punch Ladle
Salt Spoon
Saratoga Chip Server
Sardine Server
Sardine Tongs
Soup Ladle
Sugar Spoon
Sugar Sifter
Sugar Tongs, sm.
Sugar Tongs, lg.
Toast Fork
Toddy Spoon
Tomato Server
Vegetable Fork
Vegetable Spoon
Waffle Server

STERLING SILVER DOZEN WORK

TEA SPOONS
Small
Trade
Medium
Heavy
Extra Heavy

DESSERT SPOONS OR FORKS
Medium
Heavy
Extra Heavy

TABLE SPOONS OR FORKS
Medium
Heavy
Extra Heavy

SOUP SPOONS
Medium
Extra Heavy

CUTLERY
Tea Knife
Dessert Knives
Breakfast Knives,
Medium or Dinner Knives,
Meat Carving Knife, stainless
Meat Carving Fork, stainless
Game Carving Knife, stainless
Game Carving Fork, stainless

Carving Steel
Steak Knife, large stainless, with guard
Steak Fork, large stainless, with guard
Steak Steel, with guard
Steak Knife & Fork, small stainless
Bird Knife and Fork, stainless
Bread Knife, H.H.
Child's Knife, H.H.
Cheese Server
Fried Egg Server, H.H.
Fruit Knife, H.H.
Ice Cream Slicer, H.H.
Orange Knife, H.H.
Pie Server, H.H.
Cake Server, H.H.
Duck Shears
Roast Holder, small
Roast Holder, med.

LIST OF ARTICLES MADE
Plain or Engraved

Five O'clock	Tea Spoons	Dessert Spoons	Table Spoons
Tea Spoons	Dessert Forks	Table Forks	Soup Spoons

CUTLERY

Tea Knives	Dessert Knives	Medium Knives

CARVING PIECES

Meat Knife	Game Knife	Steel, Large	Beefsteak Fork
Meat Fork	Game Fork	Beefsteak Knife	Steel, Small

CARVING SETS

Meat Carvers	Beefsteak Carvers	Game Carvers
Meat and Game Carvers	Meat, Game, Steak Carvers	

ODD CUTLERY

Roast Holders	Bread Knife	Poultry Shears

DOZENS

Asparagus Tongs	Fish Forks	Ice Cream Forks	Oyster Forks
Berry Forks	Fish Knives	Ice Cream Spoons	Parfait Spoons
Bouillon Spoons	Fruit Knives	Iced Tea Spoons	Pie Forks
Butter Spreaders	Fruit Forks	Nut Picks	Salad Forks
Chocolate Spoons	Grape Fruit	Orange Knives	Salt Spoons
Coffee Spoons	Spoons	Orange Spoons	Sherbet Spoons
Egg Spoons			Terrapin Forks

PAIRS

Fish Knives	Lettuce Spoons	Salad Spoons
Fish Forks	Lettuce Forks	Salad Forks

SINGLE PIECES

Almond Scoop	Child's Spoon	Ice Spoon	Pea Spoon
Asparagus Server	(Tea)	Ice Tongs	Pickle Fork
Asparagus Tongs	Chocolate Mud-	Jelly Knife	Pie Servers
Baby Fork, Stub	dler	Jelly Spoon	Preserve Spoon
Baby Spoons, Bent	Cold Meat Forks	Layer Cake	Punch Ladle
Handle	Confection Spoon	Server	Salt Spoon
Baby Spoon, Stub	Cracker Spoon	Lemon Fork	Sandwich Tongs
Beef Fork	Cream Ladle	Lemonade Spoon	Saratoga Chip
Berry Spoon	Crumb Scraper	Lettuce Spoon	Server
Bon Bon Scoop	Cucumber Server	Lettuce Fork	Sardine Server
Bon Bon Tongs	Dish Gravy Spoon	Macaroni Server	Sardine Tongs
Bouillon Ladle	Entree Server	Mayonnaise	Soup Ladle
Butter Knives	Food Pusher	Ladle	Sugar Spoon
Butter Pick	Fried Egg Server	Mixer	Sugar Sifter
Cake Knife	Fried Oyster	Mustard Spoon	Sugar Tongs
Cheese Fork	Server	Nut Cracker	Toast Fork
Cheese Knife	Gravy Ladle	Nut Spoon	Toddy Spoon
Cheese Scoops	Horse Radish	Olive Spoons	Tomato Server
Child's Knife	Spoon	Olive Forks	Vegetable Fork
Child's Fork	Ice Cream Server	Oyster Ladle	Vegetable Spoon
	Ice Cream Slicers	Pap Spoon	Waffle Server

THE
LADY BALTIMORE
PATTERN
Sterling Silver Tableware

" At your Dealers "

LIST OF ARTICLES MADE

Five O'clock	Tea Spoons	Dessert Spoons	Table Spoons
Tea Spoons	Dessert Forks	Table Forks	Soup Spoons

CUTLERY

Tea Knives	Dessert Knives	Medium Knives

CARVING PIECES

Meat Knife	Game Knife	Steel, Large	Beefsteak Fork
Meat Fork	Game Fork	Beefsteak Knife	Steel, Small

CARVING SETS

Meat Carvers	Beefsteak Carvers	Game Carvers
Meat and Game Carvers	Meat, Game, Steak Carvers	

ODD CUTLERY

Roast Holders	Bread Knives	Poultry Shears

DOZENS

Berry Forks	Fish Forks	Ice Cream Forks	Orange Spoons
Bouillon Spoons	Fish Knives	Ice Cream Spoons	Oyster Forks
Butter Spreaders	Fruit Knives	Iced Tea Spoons	Pie Forks
Chocolate Spoons	Grape Fruit	Nut Picks	Salad Forks
Coffee Spoons	Spoons	Orange Knives	Salt Spoons
Egg Spoons			Sherbet Spoons

PAIRS

Fish Knives	Lettuce Spoons	Salad Spoons
Fish Forks	Lettuce Forks	Salad Forks

SINGLE PIECES

Asparagus Server	Chocolate Mud-	Ice Tongs	Pea Spoon
Baby Knife, Stub	dler	Jelly Knife	Pickle Fork
Baby Fork, Stub	Cold Meat Forks	Jelly Spoon	Pie Server
Baby Spoon, Bent	Confection Spoon	Layer Cake	Preserve Spoon
Handle	Cream Ladle	Server	Punch Ladle
Baby Spoon, Stub	Crumb Scraper	Lemon Fork	Salt Spoon
Beef Fork	Cucumber Server	Lemonade Spoon	Sandwich Tongs
Berry Spoon	Dish Gravy Spoon	Lettuce Spoon	Saratoga Chip
Bon Bon Scoop	Entree Server	Lettuce Fork	Server
Bon Bon Tongs	Food Pusher	Macaroni Server	Sardine Server
Butter Knife	Fried Egg Server	Mayonnaise	Sardine Tongs
Butter Pick	Fried Oyster	Ladle	Soup Ladle
Cake Knife	Server	Mustard Spoon	Sugar Sifter
Cheese Knife	Gravy Ladle	Nut Cracker	Sugar Spoon
Cheese Scoop	Horse Radish	Nut Spoon	Sugar Tongs
Child's Knife	Spoon	Olive Spoons	Tomato Server
Child's Fork	Ice Cream Server	Olive Forks	Vegetable Fork
Child's Spoon	Ice Cream Slicer	Oyster Ladle	Vegetable Spoon
(Tea)	Ice Spoon	Pap Spoon	Waffle Server

The
KING ALBERT
Pattern

TRADE W MARK.

STERLING

WHITING MFG. CO.
Salesroom and Factory, BRIDGEPORT, CONN.
SALESROOMS

15 Maiden Lane   140 Geary Street
New York City   San Francisco, Cal.

LIST OF ARTICLES MADE IN
KING ALBERT PATTERN

Five O'clock Tea Spoons	Soup Spoons
Tea Spoons	Table Spoons
Dessert Spoons	Dessert Forks

Table Forks

CUTLERY

Tea Knives	Medium Knives
Dessert Knives	Breakfast Knives

CARVING PIECES

Meat Knife	Game Fork	Steel, Large
Meat Fork	Beefsteak Knife	Steel, Small
Game Knife	Beefsteak Fork	Roast Holder

DOZENS

Berry Forks	Fruit Knives	Oyster Forks
Bouillon Spoons	Grape Fruit Spoons	Parfait Spoons
Butter Spreaders	Ice Cream Forks	Pie Forks
Chocolate Spoons	Ice Cream Spoons	Ramekin Forks
Coffee Spoons	Iced Tea Spoons	Salad Forks
Egg Spoons	Nut Picks	Salt Spoons
Fish Forks	Orange Knives	Sherbet Spoons
Fish Knives	Orange Spoons	Terrapin Forks

PAIRS

Fish Knives and Forks	Salad Spoons and Forks
Lettuce Spoons and Forks	Serving Spoons and Forks

SINGLE PIECES

Asparagus Server	Confection Spoon	Mayonnaise Ladle
Baby Fork, Stub	Cream Ladle	Mustard Spoon
Baby Knife	Croquette Server	Nut Spoon
Baby Spoon, Bent	Crumb Scraper	Olive Fork
Handle	Cucumber Server	Olive Spoon
Baby Spoon, Stub	Dish Gravy Spoon	Oyster Ladle
Beef Fork	Entree Server	Pap Spoon
Berry Spoon	Food Pusher	Pea Spoon
Bon Bon Scoop	Fried Egg Server	Pickle Fork
Bon Bon Tongs	Gravy Ladle	Pie Server
Bread Knife	Horse Radish Spoon	Preserve Spoon
Butter Knives	Ice Cream Server	Salt Spoon
Butter Pick	Ice Cream Slicer	Sandwich Tongs
Cake Knife	Ice Spoon	Sardine Server
Cheese Knife	Ice Tongs	Soup Ladle
Cheese Scoop	Jelly Knife	Sugar Sifter
Child's Knife	Jelly Spoon	Sugar Spoon
Child's Fork	Layer Cake Server	Sugar Tongs
Child's Spoon (Tea)	Lemon Fork	Tomato Server
Cold Meat Fork	Lemonade Spoon	Waffle Server
	Lettuce Fork	
	Lettuce Spoon	

WILCOX & EVERTSEN
New York, New York

Wilcox and Evertsen are not exactly household names, although to lovers of silver Wilcox is a familiar one. The Robert Wilcox of this company, however, was not related to Horace Wilcox of Meriden fame. But there were similarities. This Robert Wilcox was also one of that fascinating fraternity - the traveling salesman. For about 10 years beginning in 1880 he worked very successfully at selling for Rogers, Smith and Company. By the end of the decade he felt he could succeed on his own and so he formed a partnership with one Samuel Rowan.

Together they opened a factory in New York but the partnership was short-lived. By 1892 Wilcox had a new partner and the firm a new name - Wilcox and Evertsen. Wilcox and Henry C. Evertsen were doing fairly well and by 1896 had become part of Meriden Britannia Co. and moved to Meriden, Connecticut.

It was not until this move to Meriden that sterling silver flatware was first made under the Wilcox and Evertsen mark. In 1898 International Silver Company was formed and Wilcox and Evertsen became part of this new silverware giant. The entire operation was moved to Wallingford, Connecticut and since the Wilcox Evertsen firm was already renowned for its sterling holloware the decision was taken to begin making an equally prestigious line of sterling flatware. The first patterns were issued soon after the move to Wallingford - Revere and Litchfield. When the great depression of 1929 hit, the silver industry was naturally affected, none worse than companies such as Wilcox and Evertsen. Further consolidations took place and the silverware of this company seems to have been phased out.

The silverware this company made so well is not easy to find but worth searching for. Canny collectors always look for things currently out of fashion. In this case it is not the silverware itself (which is good quality) but the company name. The trademark itself is unique and interesting and some of the patterns deserve recognition.

The LORRAINE pattern would be a worthy addition to an Arts and Crafts silver collection. The pierced work on DRESDEN is quite fine. CLEOTA is an exceptional grape pattern little known among collectors of this type silver.

As truly American silver becomes scarce companies such as this will prove to be an untapped national resource.

Most of the patterns issued under the WILCOX & EVERTSEN trademark were simply absorbed into the International Silver Co. inventory. The following patterns were originally issued with the Wilcox & Evertson trademark but since International came to feel that, since made under the aegis of International, they were in fact International patterns, they are, for the most part, listed under the International Silver Co. in this book. These patterns are: Acanthus 1917, Alexandria 1915, Avalon 1900, Beverly 1910, Chesterfield 1910, Cloeta 1904, Deerfield 1913, 1818 (1930), Florence 1903, Fontaine 1924, Irene 1902, John Winthrop 1911, Kensington 1912, LaRochelle 1909, Litchfield 1898, Lorraine, hammered 1917, Marcell 1907, Napoleon 1910, Nathan 1912, Old Hampshire 1916, Pansy 1909, Pantheon 1920, Pine Tree 1927 and Revere 1898.

The following patterns (pictured here) were made by WILCOX and Evertsen and are not listed with International:

WILCOX & EVERTSON PRICES

Pattern	Date of Issue	Dinner fork	Dessert knife	Dessert fork	Tea-spoon
Durham	c.1912	$30	$25	$30	$21

Durham

Pattern	Date of Issue	Dinner fork	Dessert knife	Dessert fork	Tea-spoon
Essex	1915	25	20	25	19

Essex

Pattern	Date of Issue	Dinner fork	Dessert knife	Dessert fork	Tea-spoon
Norfolk	1915	24	29	25	18

Norfolk

Pattern	Date of Issue	Dinner fork	Dessert knife	Dessert fork	Tea-spoon
Queen Bess	1911	$32	$28	$35	$23

Queen Bess

Pattern	Date of Issue	Dinner fork	Dessert knife	Dessert fork	Tea-spoon
Scarsdale	1915	24	20	25	19

Scarsdale